D0196781

A Guide to

MAKING IT

in Real Estate

JAMES R. CARTER

A SUCCESS GUIDE for real estate lenders, real estate agents and those who would like to learn about the professions.

If you purchased this book without a cover, it is likely to be stolen property. In such case, neither the author nor the publisher has received any payment.

This book is presented solely for educational and entertainment purposes. The author and publisher are not offering it as legal or other professional advice. While best efforts have been used in preparing this book, the author and publisher make no representations or warranties of any kind and assume no liabilities of any kind with respect to the accuracy or completeness of the contents and specifically disclaim any implied warranties of merchantability or fitness of use for a particular purpose. Neither the author nor the publisher shall be held liable or responsible to any person or entity with respect to any loss or incidental or consequential damages caused, or alleged to have been caused, directly or indirectly, by the information or programs contained herein. No warranty may be created or extended by sales representatives or written sales materials. The advice and strategies contained herein may not be suitable for your situation. You should seek the advice or services of a competent real estate or legal professional in connection with the activities described herein. Any stories or characters and entities described herein are fictional. Any likeness to actual persons, either living or dead, is strictly coincidental.

No part of this book may reproduced, stored in a retrieval system, or transmitted by any means, electronic, mechanical, photocopy, recording, or otherwise, without the written permission from the copyright holder.

Copyright © 2015 James R. Carter
All rights reserved.

www.jamesraycarter.com

A Guide to MAKING IT in Real Estate is available on Kindle, Amazon, Createspace, iTunes, Audible and more. The author narrated the audio version of this book.

ISBN-10: 1508820295
ISBN-13: 9781508820291

Library of Congress Control Number: 2015908872
CreateSpace Independent Publishing Platform
North Charleston, South Carolina

MANUFACTURED IN THE UNITED STATES OF AMERICA

First Edition

Contents

Introduction

————•————

VERY FEW ENTREPRENEURIAL INDUSTRIES OFFER the realistic opportunity to go from zero to $20,000, $50,000, $100,000, or even $500,000 of revenue in the first year. Real estate is one of those rare industries. This book was written for the benefit of lenders and real estate agents, all of whom mostly operate 1) without a nine-to-five paycheck and 2) as self-employed small-business owners.

If we do a supersized simplification of the real estate business, the players go as follows: management, vendors, and producers (lenders and real estate agents). Over a twenty-year period, I was a real estate lender (first) and real estate agent (second), and the two professions are an overlapping mirror image of the same movie. Therefore, I will speak to both with one voice.

The real estate profession offers freedom, flexibility, self-employment, and unlimited income potential; there is, however, considerable discipline and hard work that goes along with that song and dance. So, allow me to show you some of the disciplines around winning.

To Your Success,

James R. Carter

Role Models

———◆———

IN MY REAL ESTATE BUSINESS, I largely applied lessons learned from the following people and reference them often in this book. Therefore, it is a pleasure to introduce them to you now.

Loretta Carter: This is my mom. She was a teacher, principal, and assistant superintendent of schools. She has mentored countless students, parents, and faculty and is a beloved and admired member of the education establishment. She and my wife are the most amazing women that I know. She is retired in California.

Dr. Bob Carter: This is my dad. He grew up as the neighborhood tough guy in the Hollywood area of Los Angeles in the 1950s. He played football in college and was drafted by the San Francisco 49ers in 1960. He went into teaching shortly thereafter and worked his way into administration, where he became superintendent of schools in two different states. He is retired in Ohio.

Coach John Reardon: This is my high school football coach. He was a marine, Golden Gloves boxer, and college football player and then became a teacher and coach. He is the winningest high school football coach in the history of Ventura County, California. His unyielding principles and toughness made a positive formative impact on me and thousands of other young men. He is retired in California.

Coach Claude Gilbert: This is my college football coach. I played for Coach Gilbert for three years at San Jose State. During that time, we went 20-4 my junior and senior years combined, the winningest back-to-back years in the history of Spartan football. Coach Gilbert had a career that spanned roughly forty years, and he won ninety-nine games as a college head coach. He is retired in California.

Getting Started

A Guide to Making It in Real Estate

1
Cornerstones of the Business

———◆———

The whole is more than the sum of its parts.
ARISTOTLE

IN REAL ESTATE, WE NEED to find deals, do deals, manage money, and keep our head straight; marketing, operations, finance, and attitude. These are the four foundational cornerstones of the real estate business. Four—but one plus one plus one plus one equals a number bigger than four. *The whole is more than the sum of its parts.* We need to be strong in all four areas to be strong in this business.

"Jim, what about branding, cold calling, contracts, legal, inspections, accounting, lead follow-up, the secondary market, technology, staff, payroll, education, and on and on?" If we are talking about a large multinational manufacturing firm, we may need to break it down. When I worked for that type of firm out of college, the organizational chart looked like a road map from Mars. Supply chain management, manufacturing, customer service, internal accounting, research, active product development, real estate, external marketing, and about a dozen more categories. We are providing a service in real estate, keep it simple. We find deals, we do deals, we manage some money, and we work at keeping our head straight. *Marketing, operations, finance, and attitude.*

When you are a producer in this business, *you are responsible for everything.* The vast majority of the industry is paid as an independent contractor. If you happen to be paid as a W-2 employee, however, don't fool yourself into thinking that you don't need to worry about marketing, operations, finance, and attitude. Don't make the mistake of thinking that your company will take care of pieces of that for you. As lenders and real estate agents, we are 100 percent responsible for our revenue line and therefore our own success. We need to be the owner of marketing, operations, finance, and attitude. Yes, we may ask (hire) our company to take care of this piece or that piece, but we are still the CEO of own our small business and therefore must be responsible for all four categories. Lots of people will be around to help, but we are the responsible party at the end of the day.

Keep it simple. Why is it important to keep it simple when you are a lender or real estate agent or commercial professional? We are called "real estate agent" or "lender" or "commercial professional"; but who do you think is the CEO of your small business? Who do you think is vice president of marketing or vice president of operations or vice president of finance; and who do you think is the director of attitude? We wear a lot of hats in this business. The majority of the industry does not have a full-time assistant. Therefore, at minimum, we wear six hats: CEO, VP of marketing, VP of operations, VP of finance, director of attitude, and lead sales representative. Six! Do all six have to work for the business to work? You bet. Can we neglect any of these six? No way. So don't overcomplicate it. Six is enough. Keep it simple.

Marketing. Marketing includes all those areas that are associated with finding new business. We have specific strategies that correlate to specific target markets. For instance, we may be targeting past customers, friends that we have never done business with, people that we don't know in a geographical area, or attorneys that we work with. The list is nearly endless for possible target markets and strategies thereof.

Ultimately, our goal is to generate leads and produce new customers. All those activities fall within marketing. Don't confuse marketing with sales; sales is simply a piece of marketing.

Operations. The customer hired us to do a job; we will deliver through our operations efforts. These are active transactions that you are currently working to complete. Your marketing efforts are responsible for generating new business, and your operations efforts will be responsible for getting the job completed.

Finance. There are four areas of finance: 1) the financial skills necessary to provide a good service for our customers; 2) the financial skills to manage a small business; 3) the financial skills to run our personal life; and 4) the financial skills to save and invest. Number one and number two are the primary focus of my efforts in this book.

Attitude. This may be the hardest area of all; we need to keep our head straight. Attitude has an overlapping impact on the other three categories of marketing, operations, and finance. What is my attitude about marketing, what is my attitude about operations, and what is my attitude about finance? Attitude is the one that is often neglected; this is also the one that will send your business to the moon many times over.

Everything we do in this business of real estate can be (if you allow it to be) placed in one of those buckets. What about legal? Put it in operations. What about bookkeeping? Put it in finance. What about lead follow-up? Put it in marketing. What about business coaching? Put it in attitude. What about the appraisal? Put it in operations. What about budgeting? Put it in finance. What about contracts? Put it in operations. What about staying fired up and motivated? Put it in attitude. Keep it simple. We find new deals, we manage current deals, we manage money, and we work to keep our head straight.

Marketing, operations, finance, and attitude. All these areas will need to work in harmony for your business to thrive. You can make $1 million per year for ten years straight, and if you have the wrong attitude and can't manage money, you'll be broke by year number eleven. You can provide the world's best service, but if you can't find new deals (marketing), forget it. You can be the world's best money manager, but if you can't find deals or do deals, you'll have no money to manage. You can find deals, do deals, and manage money well, but if you don't have the right attitude, you'll be inconsistent and never reach your full potential.

Don't be intimated by this. You can be successful in this industry by simply recognizing that the industry is more than just doing deals, doing deals, doing deals. It doesn't take a lot to be strong in all four categories. As a starting point, simply recognize the four categories exist, and then focus some time on each weekly; you'll grow strong over time. It's no different than an athlete focusing on 1) nutrition, 2) fitness, 3) skill development, and 4) attitude. Except for us in real estate, it's marketing, operations, finance, and attitude.

The real estate business can be incredibility profitable and at the same time incredibly confusing (because of the many hats that we wear). Keep it simple: we find deals, we do deals, we manage some money, and we work to keep our head straight: *marketing, operations, finance, and attitude.*

Go get 'em!

2
The First Step

The beginning is the most important part of the work.

PLATO

THIS MIGHT BE A GOOD time to have a somewhat boring, but short-short conversation about terminology.

Real Estate Lending. Here are some loose terms that could define a person that is originating loans secured by a piece of real estate: loan agent, loan officer, mortgage broker, broker, mortgage lender, mortgage loan originator, agent, originator, producer, lender and more. Further, now that the giant brokerage houses have jumped into the game of real estate lending, the above list could be expanded to include wealth managers, vice president of investments, and many more. Don't stumble over the terminology here. The bottom line: this is a human being that is originating a loan that is secured by real property. In the interest of keeping it simple, I have mostly referred to this person as either a *lender or a producer*.

Real Estate Sales. Here are just some of the terms that could loosely describe someone involved in real estate sales/brokerage: real estate agent, broker, broker associate, real estate broker, selling agent, listing agent, buyer's agent, seller's agent, procuring agent, property agent, producer, vice president and more. You may have noticed that

I excluded the term, REALTOR®. The term is a trademark of the National Association of Realtors and should be used only to describe membership thereof. Again, in the interest of keeping it simple, for people involved in real estate sales, I will be referring to this group as either a *real estate agent or a producer.*

I'm glad that's over! Let's move-on to some things that will help you move down the road.

Here are some possible categories of real estate to consider: residential brokerage; residential lending; commercial lending; warehouse sales; warehouse leasing; office sales; office leasing; retail sales; retail leasing; manufacturing sales; manufacturing leasing; small unit apartment sales; medium unit apartment sales; large unit apartment sales; institutional apartment sales; small, medium, and large hotels and motels; farmland sales and leasing; gas station sales and leasing; storage facilities; churches; residential care facilities; medical buildings; hospitals; and garage/parking leasing and sales.

This list covers most of the large categories, but there are more. Here is an example of a piece of real estate that does not fit neatly into the above. Let's assume that an abandoned rail station in a downtown metropolitan area needs to be sold. The property has complicated ownership rights going back over one hundred years, given the installation date of the American railway system. Undoubtedly there will be environmental issues to consider relevant to the ground, water, and possibly air. And, just to complicate things further, let's assume the property was omitted (by accident) some years past from the general plan when the city moved that area to high-density housing. This is an example of *specialty real estate:* those projects and areas of real estate that are niche.

It may be prudent to note at this time that whenever a piece of real estate is traded, there is usually a real estate broker and mortgage broker involved in the deal. The property could be a $60,000 condominium in a suburb of Cincinnati or a $300 million office building in downtown San Francisco. In either case, real estate brokers and lenders are on hand to help facilitate the transaction and ultimately earn a fee upon the successful completion thereof.

Now, where to start? No one gave me this advice when I started out, and the following is probably some of the most valuable coaching I could have received, so I am a slightly passionate about sharing this information with you now. *Do your homework!* Spend a minimum of six months researching the categories and the industry at large. Read, read, read. Then talk, talk, talk—to everyone. You need to understand the intricacies of the categories before you can take that next step and decide on a category.

Okay, let me be more specific. The reading part is easy to figure out: books, Internet, whatever you can get your hands on. The talking part, however, is the magic. *Reach out to professionals in all the different categories.* For instance, I have a family friend that is literally one of the top apartment brokers in California. How many times has a person new to the industry reached out to him to chat? I asked him, and the answer was almost never. Why not? "Well, he is so busy and won't have time for me." Really? I will bet $100 that if you called him right this second, you could reach either him or his secretary and get on his calendar for lunch or coffee.

Don't assume, *big* mistake. Some people actually have a passion for helping other people. Some people like talking about the industry or their own personal challenges and successes in those industries. There was a period of time when I was one of the larger producing lenders in Silicon Valley; same thing when I switched to residential brokerage. My phone number was not a secret; I didn't have it hidden away in a vault so no one could get hold of me. I can literally count on my right hand how many times a young person new to the industry has reached out just to have coffee and learn about the industry. And those rare times that it did happen, I was literally tripping over myself to rearrange my schedule so that I could meet him or her. Hey, I enjoyed it.

Call the producers. We are all human and need to eat, so ask them to lunch or coffee. If they would rather meet in their office, then fine. Work within their schedule, but I suggest early morning or later in the afternoon. Busy people get busy as the day moves along, and you want to avoid them cancelling at the last minute. I call these *meet and greets*. Just explain that you are considering a career in real estate and trying to understand the different categories. Be honest. Phrase it however you feel comfortable. Everyone has time in his or her day and loves a break from the day-to-day grind. Do it!

Reach out to the producers, but *don't forget the support staff.* They will have a different perspective and see the business through their own lens. You'll be surprised how much you learn from the support staff. Remember, they are the ones dealing with the fifty or so agents in that office on a daily basis. They can more accurately paint the picture of the average producer. They are also the ones handling checks/income in most cases. You can talk with a producer and then talk with a support staff member (in the same office), and they will paint, in most cases, different and possibly even opposing pictures of the same industry. Have those conversations. You need to understand the good, bad, and ugly of each category.

Meet and greets with the managers should be a piece of cake; they will most likely turn the table and attempt to recruit you. Great, fine, no problem. Ask them questions, very probing and serious questions. You will naturally need to dance around a little when talking with the producers and support staff, for obvious reasons, but not the managers. This is your career (and your life at the moment), so come loaded with questions. *Nothing should be off limits when talking with managers.* When I started in real estate, I met with a few mortgage companies. I arrived at my first meeting one hour early and made a list of questions, twenty-eight in total. I used those twenty-eight questions in the remainder of my meetings. I suggest doing these meetings at managers' offices. Try to take it all in: the lobby, front desk staff, the décor, maintenance of the office, how the agents treat each other, how the agents treat the support staff and vice versa, and, of course, those intangibles such as feel, rhythm, energy, synergy, etc.

We have all heard the terms *B to B* and *B to C*. Those terms are defined as doing business from business (B) to business (B); and business (B) to consumer (C). The real estate industry has B to B and B to C, and in some categories of real estate we have both. Why is that important to understand? Good question. *What kind of customers do you want to work with?* Do you want to work with mom-and-pop consumers dealing with their own personal business affairs? Or do you want to work with professional businesspeople that are typically employees of a company working nine to five? One of those options is a personal business transaction; the other is business—only business. If you want to work with consumers dealing with their personal business affairs, then residential lending or brokerage could be something to consider. If you say, "I only want to work with customers that are professional businesspeople acting on behalf of their company," then you may want to consider being a tenant representative for a national chain or a corporate leasing expert representing a few technology companies. Have you thought of that? I hadn't early in my career. The customer dynamics literally never crossed my mind when I was starting out in real estate. The only way to understand those intricacies is to get out and talk with people face to face. Meet and greet—a lot.

Don't let any of the categories intimidate you. We don't know it until we know it. Do something enough and you'll learn it. I have an uncle in Southern California that had a successful career in industrial buildings. This was loosely defined for him as warehouse and manufacturing, both sales and leasing. For whatever reason, when he started in real estate in his late thirties, he focused on this area with a partner. He started slow, but he learned and became one of the power players in Orange County for a couple of decades. Whatever category of real estate you choose, don't worry, you'll learn it.

Research for six months; that's twenty-six weeks. Do one meet and greet daily for six months; that's 130. Can you imagine how strong you will be if you *actually* do the full 130? No one will be able to fool you; you will be muscle strong and razor sharp. Fully informed. You will know who's on first and what's on second. You will be bigger, stronger, and faster. You will understand every position in the field and the responsibilities thereof. You will know compensation details in each category and at each level of production in each category. You will have a better understanding of whether you should be a lone wolf or part of a team.

It will be brutal to switch categories at a later date. Take the time and do it right.

Go get 'em!

3
Choosing a Manager

———◆———

*People are like dirt. They can either nourish you
and help you grow as a person, or they can stunt
your growth and make you wilt and die.*

PLATO

CHOOSE YOUR MANAGER WELL. THIS decision will have a positive or negative impact on the first few years of your real estate career. My managers were all fantastic. I learned something from all of them and truly enjoyed them as people. I learned *process* from my first manager. I learned to *relax* from my second manager. I learned to *utilize adrenaline* from my third manager. I learned to *slow it down* from my fourth manager. And I learned the *depth of customer service* from my fifth manager.

Remember, the job of a manager is to help us to produce. He or she must ensure his or her agents are hitting the mark, putting up the numbers, and doing deals. The manager's performance is based on numbers. Numbers don't lie, and the manager's salary, bonus, and job stability are directly correlated to his or her ability to recruit, train, and retain good agents. Your success is his or her success. There is no difference. You build up a database of two hundred. He or she builds up an office of one hundred agents. You are hoping you can generate enough business from your two hundred. He or she is hoping to meet or exceed company exceptions with the one hundred.

As a point of understanding, the manager is an employee; you are not an employee. As such, he or she has a real live boss hanging over his or her head. This is why some agents are reluctant to transition into management. It's hard to go from no boss to boss. When you go from agent to manager, you move from Free-as-a-Bird Jill to monthly performance quotas. It's great for some people, but it doesn't work for others. It's a tough job. Respect it as such. Put high value on what the manager has to do on a daily basis. But don't forget, there is a difference: managers are mostly employees and agents are mostly not employees.

You work for them or they work for you? This is an age-old discussion. We need them and they need us; that's the bottom line. Does the manager really manage of us (the agents) in a manner that is consistent with a manager/employee relationship at Google? Of course not. Many of us are attracted to this industry of real estate because it offers freedom, flexibility, limitless income, and no boss. Having a boss would fly in the face of all that. So no, we are not managed the same way that an employee at Google is managed. It's a mutually dependent relationship. Accept it as such. We are equals—agent and manager, agent and company. We need each other to prosper in this competitive industry.

The manager must be your biggest fan! Period.

When selecting a manager, don't jump. Take your time. Talk with lots of people. Before you commit, ask to attend the office or sales meeting, or both. Most offices have a weekly or monthly meeting to discuss sales and miscellaneous items. Ask if you can attend as a fly on the wall. Just sit and observe, feel it out, you'll know. Do the agents engage or roll their eyes? Does the manager go through the motions or truly have an instinct for wanting to help other people (the agents)? Do the agents like each other or just barely tolerate each other. If the agents don't like each other, watch out. Run. That's *all* leadership. That's on the manager. Culture and office dynamics always begin and end with leadership, in this case the manager. Take your time. Talk with lots of people.

Choose well because you are married to your manager. Yes, you can always switch offices, but switching is time consuming and expense. So, you are married. You will spend more time with your manager than your family in many if not most cases. Make sure you like him or her, make sure you respect him or her, and make sure that you can ultimately make money with him or her. Managing is an instinct as well as a trained skill. Look for someone who *truly* likes to help people succeed.

At the end of a day, you are looking for a coach. That is the best definition of what the manager is to the agent.

Go get 'em!

4

Do a Lot of Business Quickly

*Things may come to those who wait, but only
the things left by those who hustle.*
PRESIDENT ABRAHAM LINCOLN

YES, IT TAKES TIME TO build something worthwhile. Then why am
I encouraging you to rush it and do a lot of business quickly?
Because if you don't, it's possible that the demands of life will force
you out of this business before you have a chance to *Make It*.

Make a decision to push it for 180 days. I will work ten-hour days
six days per week for 180 days. You might struggle with the pace for
a few weeks, but you'll grow stronger and get comfortable after about
a month. And it might be noteworthy to mention that I am assuming
here that you want to go big and push for big numbers. It's perfectly
fine if you want to go small or medium; the below plan, however, is
only if you want to go big—and do a lot quickly.

Continuing on, "Jim, ten-hour days, six days per week sounds like a
lot of work." Yes, it is. Your goal is big, so your effort has to be big. Your
goal is big, so your commitment has to be big. You have to be all in.
Name me another business other than real estate that you can go from
ground zero to twenty-five thousand, one hundred thousand, two hundred thousand, three hundred thousand, four hundred thousand, or

even five hundred thousand in one year. Maybe you could dream one up, but the opportunity is sensational in this industry nonetheless. So recognize it and get fired up about it.

Ask your manager to coach you/mentor you for 180 days. It's not his or her job to earn money for you. That is your responsibility. So, when you meet with your manager at these weekly coaching sessions, come loaded with questions. Don't cry to him or her; be a pro and review the goals for that week, plans for the following week, and things that you need help with. Yes, a good manager will know how to push, support, coach, and help you grow. But don't count on them to do that, however. Don't place your future in someone else's hands. Take responsibility for your own income and life. Simply use your manager as an additional resource. Use his or her experience and know-how. You run those meetings, not him or her. Ask questions. Take control. "Fortune befriends the bold"—*Emily Dickinson.*

Attend every staff meeting, round table, lunch club meeting, free seminar, and social function that your company has to offer. Be part of the conversation; become part of the fabric, if you will. Don't miss anything. By doing this you will digest the rhythm of your office (e.g., who's on first, what's on second, and who is doing third). Understand the relationships in that office, listen to people, and ask questions about the industry. You'll be able to turn this information into dollars down the road. I'm not going to tell you how; you figure it out.

Eat. Most of us need to eat breakfast, lunch, and dinner, and I think have a coffee from time to time. Take one day off weekly if you need to, but have lunch five days weekly with either someone in your office or a friend. Cheap is good. My personal business attorney is one of the best in Northern California. We get lunch every six months. Here are our last three lunch locations: Armadillo Willy's, In-N-Out Burger, and Ike's Sandwich Shop—average cost per person is $10. For lunch, keep it simple and cheap. Lunch or coffee five days per week with a friend or someone in your office is doable. You'll build momentum. Take fifteen minutes to prep some questions. Get him or her talking. Have something to offer in terms of information. Learn something new and share it. Make it natural, because it should be natural.

Be visible and work long hours. Your manager and colleagues in your office will become believers if you show up day in, day out. Don't forget, they see people come in and out of this business daily with big dreams and ambitions, in and out, in and out, in and out. You can earn their respect only with your work ethic and eventually your production. Until you start doing business, it will need to be your work ethic. Work day in, day out. It's quite possible that your manager and colleagues will respect this type of work ethic and reach out to you in some tangible fashion. "Hey, Jim, I see how determined you are to make this happen. I have a big deal I'm working on now, and I'll pay you $1,000 to run around and you can learn some things. Sound okay?" Sure. Or your manager says, "Hey, Jim, you are working hard, I see that. There is a lead that came in yesterday, and I am going to give it to you. You work it, but since you are green, I am going to have Lisa keep an eye on you, and you two split the commission. Sound okay?" Sure. You never know what type of doors may open by you simply being there and working hard.

Work through referrals. A referral is a lead that comes from someone that you know—period. "Well, Jim, I have never done a deal, so how am I going to get referrals?" I'll say it again. A referral is a lead that comes from someone that you know—period.

"Hi, Steve, this is Jim" (I have never done business with Steve, but he is a friend from my previous job). After a little bit of chatter, "Steve, is there possibly anyone you know that needs assistance? Yes, great.

Can you make that intro for me? Yes, great." Now I am talking with Adam through Steve. Adam and I talk. He is ready to sell his property in six months. Great. "Hey, Adam, I'll send those comps tomorrow over e-mail. Also, just by chance, is there possibly anyone else you know that needs assistance? Yes, great. Would you mind making that intro for me? Yes, great, thank you, Adam." Now I am talking to Susan through Adam. Now I have two warm referral leads to follow up with, Susan and Adam. I go back to Steve and say thank you very much and send him a $5 Starbucks card or write him a note. Steve is rich, but when is the last time someone gave him something tangible as a thank you? Now I have three "friendlies" in my hip pocket, two of whom are going to do business in the next six months.

Let me give you another example. I am at an open house and meet Glen and Stacey for the first time. We have a little chitter-chatter and then right then and there or later through e-mail or by phone, "Hey, Glen and Stacey, is there possibly anyone else that needs assistance? Yes, great." Now I am talking with Carlos through Glen and Stacey. Which lead is more likely to close? Carlos or Glen and Stacey? Carlos. You got it! Why? Because Carlos is a warm referral lead and Glen and Stacey are a cold lead. "Hey, Jim, that's not fair, you didn't you *really* know Stacey and Glen." Yes, I did, I knew them for five minutes. *Remember, a referral is a lead that comes from someone you know—period.* It's a fine distinction and you'll probably want to work Carlos like crazy and completely drop Glen and Stacey. One generates income and the other does not. One is a warm lead and one is a cold lead. One will successfully drive your life and business, and the other one will drive you out of the business.

I am telling you right here and right now, that is how I was able to do so much business so quickly both in loans and then when I switched to real estate brokerage. It's one of those *Key to the Kingdom* type of concepts. If you can figure out another way to go from ground zero to the moon in one year, then that is fine. But the above is my recommendation nonetheless.

And finally, don't get paralyzed by what to say or how to say it. Just be yourself, focus on the process as outlined above, modify it as you wish, understand where you are trying to go with the process, and be yourself. Don't be a robot, people hate that. Be yourself and get after it.

Go get 'em!

5

Find Something You Enjoy

Pleasure in the job puts perfection in the work.

ARISTOTLE

I NATURALLY GRAVITATE TO FORMER athletes, military, and law enforce-ment type personalities. So one year into my real estate career, I stumbled onto the VA (Veterans Affairs) loan programs. A colleague in my office was working this market, so I asked to spend a day with him to learn the product. I was hooked; super, top-quality, great peo-ple, and I loved the customer: current and former military, awesome. Not a lot of people were working this niche market, so I was able to advance quickly. For the most part, lenders were trying to do this busi-ness over the phone and by mail. I decided to meet face to face with the customers, most of the time at their homes. It was not a bother or inconvenience to me because I truly enjoyed the customers, and because I enjoyed it and was willing to meet face to face, I believe the customer was the benefactor of that additional layer of service.

Think about something that makes you tick, something possibly exciting or possibly meaningful to you. Maybe your dad or granddad owned a small retail commercial building and you have fond memo-ries of that, so maybe retail commercial. Maybe your aunt worked the residential sector and did a great job with presale tune-ups, and you have fond memories of that, so maybe residential with a value-added component. Maybe the bank didn't treat your brother or sister well in your opinion, so you want to be a strong advocate for people and help them through the maze of complicated lending requirements, so maybe financing is for you. Maybe you love-love-love your own neighborhood, so maybe the residential neighborhood specialist for you. Maybe the idea of working with corporate America is intriguing to you, so possibly corporate leasing.

When I transitioned from lending to brokerage, honestly, I was happy and thankful to take whatever came my way. But after a few years, I concentrated my efforts to a single geographical area that I knew well and enjoyed. Now let's be honest; that's not to say I was not willing to take something outside the strike zone, but at least I knew the boundaries of the strike zone. Concentrate to graduate! By identifying the strike zone, a few things happened: 1) I actually did indeed get business from the strike zone, 2) the service I was providing improved, and 3) my enjoyment of what I was doing improved.

Everyone wins when you enjoy all or at least parts of what you are doing.

Go get 'em!

6

Go to Work

———◆———

Life grants nothing to us mortals without hard work.

HORACE

"**N**O ONE HAS EVER WORKED hard enough to stay with the Russians. Gentlemen, we are going to work hard enough." That was certainly my favorite scene from the movie *Miracle*. Coach Reardon would tell us, "While you are resting, your opponent is working." As a high school athlete, that did it for me. I got it. Clear as a bell. And for some reason, it motivated me on those days when I didn't want to do it. The thought of someone else getting a little stronger while I sat watching reruns of *Happy Days*, eating Twinkies, infuriated me.

Listen, the world is competitive. You take the loan or listing or buyer—or someone else will. Yes, do it with grace and honor, but take it nonetheless. When I transitioned from lending to real estate brokerage, I made a conscious decision that I wanted to work in the office with some of Silicon Valley's premier real estate agents. I figured if I could get a couple of them in my sights daily, it would motivate me. I asked several agents three months in, what is your secret sauce? No secret, they said as paraphrased. *"I/we just work a little harder than the average bear."* It's true; the top group was usually the first ones to work in the morning and typically the last ones to leave in the evening.

Sophocles said, "Without labor nothing prospers."

There is a lot to think about in real estate: phone, car, computer, advertising, selling, accounting, preparing paperwork, legal, operations, networking, loan programs, inventory, and on and on. Sometimes, the list is so long that it is paralyzing. Work! How about just work? Talk to customers and work. Smooth out the bumps later—work. Throw yourself into action. When I made the transition from loans to real estate, I told my manager, "I will put the hours in to be successful" (he didn't really believe me). "It's your job, Mr. Manager, to ensure I'm involved in the right activities." He was good with that, and we did a ton of business that year (he became a believer).

My dad is a retired superintendent of schools. When the district was negotiating on important pieces of business, he would get home at one to two o'clock in the morning and I would hear him leaving again at roughly five in the morning. Day in, day out, for sometimes one to two weeks at a time. How hard do we work as real estate agents and lenders? Do we work eight hours daily; do we work four, do we work sixteen? Just a question. Work. Keep your knees high. Work. Work. Work.

Work has a tendency to equalize the playing field—the business playing field. It can transcend intelligence, God-given beauty and talent, education, and the right family background. It's a competitive weapon—deploy it!

Go get 'em!

7

Make $1 Million Year One

———✦———

Chaos is inherent in all compounded
things; strive on with diligence.

BUDDHA

A FTER ABOUT A YEAR WORKING as real estate agent, management asked me to teach a class called "How to Make One Million Year One." Here was the outline of that class:

Declare—failure was not going to be an option. What drove me that first year? Fear of failing. I ran loans in parallel with real estate for roughly three years, just in case. It wasn't like I was going to go broke if I didn't make it as a real estate agent. But still, I was fully exposed. My friends knew I was making the move, the community, my family, my wife's friends, and most of my network. I was terrified with the thought of not being successful. I simply said to myself, "I will dominate and make it happen." That was it—nothing special.

"We are not interested in the possibilities of defeat. They do not exist"—*Queen Victoria.*

Do—whatever it takes. I have always been a hard worker, I wasn't worried about this. But I also knew that sometimes things are not the way they seem at times. Once I started, it was indeed quite different

23

than I thought. I really didn't know what I was going to do, but I knew I was going to do, do, do, and do more than anyone else. If the earliest guy or girl arrived at worked at 7:00 a.m., then I would be there at 6:45 a.m., that kind of attitude.

Manager—I put a lot of pressure on my office manager. Coming from lending, I was already comfortable around a real estate transaction, but I was concerned about wasting time. I would throw ten to fifteen hours into a day, no problem, but I wanted that time to be productive. So I put pressure on my manager to ensure he kept me straight on productive activities. It was a bumpy but productive first year. If you are planning on doing a lot of business that first year, you will need a strong manager to back you up and, in some cases, clean up behind you.

Bumpy—I knew that it wasn't going to be smooth. I think it's nearly impossible to start from zero and go to the moon in one year and have it be smooth. I would smooth it out later. I was willing to accept the chaotic, bumpy nature of the building process and the occasional brain damage therefrom. I knew it upfront. For me, this was an important mind-set because I really had no idea what I was doing that first year, and there are naturally lots of bumpy days. Lots of business creates anxiety and challenge. Again, Buddha said, "Chaos is inherent in all compounded things; strive on with diligence."

And then—we were just barely able to touch on some various other topics regarding marketing, operations, finance, and attitude—if we had time.

Frankly, the class was only one hour, and I presented for roughly thirty to forty minutes, and there were always a ton of questions that kept us beyond the one-hour mark. So really, it was an easy and fun class to teach. My goal was for each student to procure just one idea from that class that he or she could implement. I think I walked away with more ideas than the students.

If you plan to do a lot that first year, I suggest revisiting this chapter several times, because you are going to need a lot of encouragement once you get going and into "the battle" of it all. Big numbers in a short period of time can produce big growing pains. I would rather deal with growing pains, however, than no money.

Go get 'em!

8
A Giant Year

The will to win, the desire to succeed, the urge to
reach your full potential...these are the keys that
will unlock the door to personal excellence.

CONFUCIUS

S O YOU ARE A VETERAN and want to put up some big numbers this year. Or maybe you are new to real estate and want to crush it year one. Can we literally twinkle our nose and make that happen? Yes. *But be prepared to work like a dog.* There are years we can do it and there are years we can't. I recognize management may not like to hear that, but it's true. It's called *life.* The volume of work necessary to crush it is gargantuan. I know firsthand. There were years when I was not willing to commit that level of push for one reason or another. Here is the good news: if you can muster up the energy and commitment level to crush it this year, you can throttle back slightly the next (if you want). Again, that's not a very popular thing to say in some circles. But trust me, I have done it; it's called *the fruits of our labor.* Go at a level ten for a year, go at an eight the next, and then go back to a ten. When you build a strong business, you can do that; you can build it up and then "coast" for a year. Should we do that? No. But can we do that? Yes.

Important note: Make sure your level ten is truly a level ten. *Get a coach if you have to.* Sometimes we think we are at a level ten and we are at a four. When I am coaching my fourteen-year-old youngsters in football, I say, "Now do it again, but give me your *very best effort*." They do a little better, but it's still not the best product their body and mind can produce. It's simply the best they can do at the moment. It's okay, we continue the process. That's why a coach is helpful at times.

With that coaching tip duly noted, let's assume that you decide that this year is going to be your Super Bowl year.

Step 1: Get your home life sorted out. You figure it out. But make sure you have buy-in from your partner, spouse, family, etc. If you are single, make sure your tight group of friends knows what you are about to do. Who knows, they might even help you by sending deals. Reminder, in real estate we work September through August as it relates to originations. Everything you originate past September 1 will close that following calendar year. Some would say October 1, but I'm not a big risk taker, so I say September 1; so, all-out pedal to the medal from September 1 to August 31. Got it! Make you're your friends, family, and loved ones know that time line.

Step 2: Be tough about Step 1. "Jim, what?" You will be off track before you even start if you are not tough on Step 1. My wife was a superstar champ at this; she was always 100 percent on board for whatever I wanted to do. But here is an example of someone not so supportive. The phone call comes in on Thursday morning. "Can you cut out from work at noon today so we can take a three-and-a-half-day trip to the coast?" No, remember about the Super Bowl year? "I know, but it's just this one time. Come on, let's do it. If you love me, you'll do it. It will be fun—you only live once." Aw, okay (like a big goofy sucker we give in). "Well, Jim, what about balance in your life?" Yeah, what about it? You really think you can have a giant year and be good at everything? Think again. If you are not willing to pay the price, then don't go for the big numbers. It's not a requirement of the job to go big. You can go medium or small; either option is perfectly fine. This advice is only if you are willing to pay the price and go big.

I can't tell you how many real estate careers I have seen derailed by either a) not obtaining adequate buy-in from family or b) the real estate professional not holding the family accountable to the commitment, or both. The family will pay the price, so the family will reap the rewards. Conversely, the family will suffer the economic consequences if the family is not on board and disciplined to the effort. I worked the hardest in my life those years I overlapped from lending to brokerage. My wife was 100 percent on board. She understood that it was important to me to be successful and that the economic success of our family hung in the balance. She was awesome.

And what is Step 3, you might ask? It doesn't matter, because if you are willing to do the work and your family will support you, you'll figure out how to have a giant year. Use that helmet that sits on your shoulders and go to work. And if you are still not sure what to do, the ideas in this book should keep you busy for the next two hundred years or so.

Go get 'em!

"Every action has its pleasure and its price"—*Socrates.*

9

Personality Traits of a Real Estate Producer

———◆———

They might not need me; but they might. I'll
let my head be just in sight; a smile as small as
mine might be precisely their necessity.
Emily Dickinson

WILL MY PERSONALITY EVEN WORK in this industry? When I started writing this book, this was a topic that my wife was interested in knowing about. That quote above by Emily Dickinson says it all in my view and is one of my favorites in this book.

I'm not outgoing, can I be successful? My people skills are so-so, can I be successful? I'm more of the analytical type, can I be successful? I'm long on charisma but short on patience, can I be successful? I'm rather abrupt at times, can I be successful? I'm a bit of a wallflower but very sweet to everyone, am I tough enough to be successful? By nature, I'm suspicious of almost everything and everyone and it comes across as negative, can I be successful? I'm rather overbearing, can I be successful? I'm completely unorganized but very friendly, can I be successful? I'm an artsy type, can I be successful? I'm all business and a little stiff, can I be successful? I am the submissive type, can I be successful? I'm the overly emphatic, caring type, can I be successful?

I'm shy beyond reason, can I be successful? I'm sweet, sweet, sweet and maybe borderline weak, can I be successful?

Here is a sampling of several lender colleagues I worked with: One guy was completely unorganized, short on details, long on promises, big personality, but at the end of a day, he delivered the goods. One lady was stiff, rigid, you would probably call her unfriendly, all business, but successful. A forty-something-year-old guy that was suit and tie only, everything by the book, successful. Another guy that would literally wear shorts to appointments, California casual personality, "hey dude," successful. A quiet-as-a-mouse single mom, very sweet, successful. A brand-new-out-of-college, reserved young lady, doing well. A sixty-something-year-old man on a second career, modest, approachable, quiet, doing well. A midtwenty-something guy, short on confidence, medium intelligence, reserved, doing well. A midforty-something lady, overbearing, doing well. All colors of the rainbow can work. Be you.

A few years into my brokerage career, I was having lunch with a close friend who works in technology. I was carelessly commenting/complaining (with envy) to my friend how this one agents was doing a truckload of business (more than me), life-of-the-party type personality. He said to me, "Jim, don't sweat it. Be you. Many people will like that type of personality, but an equal number will run from it." He was being a friend, of course, but good, solid advice nonetheless. Be you.

Here is a small sampling of some successful real estate agent colleagues: Late thirty-something female, cold, by the book, successful. Early thirty-something single female, sweet, sweet, total pushover, successful. Midfifty-something first-time-working female, nervous but overbearing, inexperienced, doing well. Midfifty-something male, cocky, abrupt, successful. Fresh-out-of-college twenty-something male, bright, didn't have a clue, but smooth, doing well. Early fifty-something female, arrogant, abrupt, successful. Late forty-something male, quiet, reserved, generous, experienced, giant amounts of business. It takes all kinds. Be you.

Okay! I'm going to make up a story and take this to an extreme (hopefully a funny extreme) so you really buy in to what I'm saying. We all know "jerky" type people. It's rare, I know, but yes, jerky type people do exist in the world. Please meet one of them; his name is Homer. Homer is a real estate agent person and is one of those jerky types of people. Jerky people know other jerky people. Let's politely refer to the jerky people as JPs moving forward. You can always tell when one of Homer's JP customers enters the lobby of the office because JPs attract other JPs and we can all smell a JP from a mile away. I believe we all have a built-in "JP" radar (everyone but the JP), where we know immediately when someone that qualifies as such enters the room. It's a scent that the aforementioned JP emits to the world. Well, that radar is at full tilt when Homer (the JP) has one of his JP clients enter the office. Hey, what can you expect? Like attracts like. JPs attract JPs. *But in this business even a JP can build a clientele—of other JPs, of course.* Different strokes for different folks. Be you. If you are sweet and nice, over time your clientele will be sweet and nice.

The good news is that 99.9 percent of all real estate professionals do not qualify in the exclusive JP group—they are instead just good, solid, hardworking folks. So whatever your personality may be, you can attract clientele. If you work hard and give it enough time, you'll be able to attract a clientele that suits your personality. Be you.

By "being you" and completely "owning you," you will be differentiating yourself from the pack. What else do you have to offer this crowded industry other than the unique way in which you do things? Nothing. You are not going to create some one-of-a-kind loan that everyone needs or some special way to show a property. Let's be honest, there are a lot of people very capable of getting the job done in this industry. Be you and only you. *This is your competitive weapon; this is your number one marketing advantages.* Dilute you, try to be someone that you are not, and you will dilute that one thing that makes you stand apart from the competition. You are truly one of a kind. Own that fact. Love that fact.

Are there people/personalities that just flat out cannot be successful in this industry? Yes, of course. If you are lazy and if you lie a lot and are not willing to put in the years that it takes, then you will not be successful. But if you work hard, can go the distance relevant to the number of years it takes to become successful, and can handle yourself with an element of honor, then you will *Make It* in this business.

Go get 'em!

10

See the Future

The soul never thinks without a picture.

ARISTOTLE

I WAS EXPOSED TO MENTAL preparation at a relatively young age in high school. One of our volunteer football coaches was interested in visualization, setting goals, seeing success before it happens, etc. Before the Friday night game, roughly sixty high school kids would lie down on their backs, quiet as mice, and envision themselves making a successful play, a great block, a great tackle, a great kick, a great run. With our eyes closed in a semitrance state, the coach would walk us through the game in progressive fashion. In the final analysis, I'm not certain if the coaching staff thought this was a productive exercise, but for me, I loved it.

This was my first institutional exposure to visualization. I believe to some extent we all dream, and from time to time see ourselves on the podium. But this was different. This was a structured attempt to produce an exact outcome—an outcome that was due to happen that same day. Visualize your reach block on fifty-eight sweep against an odd front when your opponent is in a three technique in a two-point stance. Now visualize your first three steps to gain control of your opponent. Now drive that man ten yards downfield until you send him ass over tea kettle. I was hooked. I could literally feel how good that block felt upon completion. When my mom and dad were not around (for sure), I could spend up to an hour lying in my bed visualizing the upcoming game. I'm laughing thinking about the conversation that must have taken place with our marine Golden Gloves boxer truly tough guy head coach.

"Coach Reardon, I would like to help the boys with visualization," says the assistant coach.

"What the heck is visualization? And I can tell you right now, I don't like it," says Coach Reardon.

"It helps the boys see into the future and experience success before they actually do it," says the assistant.

"Hocus pocus, they just need to play their tails off—period—and they better. And by the way, I can see into their future right now, and if they don't play well, then Monday's practice is not looking pretty for their future," says Coach Reardon.

"I agree (smart to agree), but can we try it anyway?" says the assistant.

"Yes, but it better not take very long, and it better work," says Coach Reardon.

That made-up conversation might not have been too far off the mark. P.S. I got Coach Reardon's permission to include that funny exchange. There are naturally many different levels of seeing into the future. When I was doing loans, I would take a few minutes each night and envision taking three loan applications that next day. On the brokerage side, I would constantly spend time daily thinking about an effortless, fluid conversation that took place on a listing appointment, no selling, no pushing, just be there for the customer, educating the customer—and I would envision us enjoying each other's company and wanting to do business together at the conclusion of our meeting.

Several years into my real estate brokerage career, a friend referred me to a client who wanted to buy a luxury home. I said great and thank you. I went to meet with the client, and he quickly told me his story. Bank number one turned him down; bank number two turned him down; and several others did as well. This was a supersuccessful guy with lots of responsibility. His income, however, was extremely complicated—extremely. It almost looked like he made no money. I told him, before I can commit to doing anything, I need to see your financial picture top to bottom; don't hold anything back, please. He agreed and I took a look. After a quick review, I could see a way to get this done, but it wasn't going to be easy. I called my friend at bank number three and told him the story. He said no way! I said yes. He said no way. I said, you wimp! He was a former professional athlete and slightly younger than me, so I knew how to get under his skin and get those competitive juices flowing. I told him, we will do it together, side by side, me and you until the end. We are going to *envision the ball hitting the back of the net*; he was a soccer player, so I had to make it easy for him. We are not done until the ball is in the back of the net—got it? He groaned. So off we went to get this done.

Now, I normally would not have taken on this type of project, particularly given the fact that the financing was not in place, but there were some valid reasons in this case to dig in:, 1) The guy who referred him was superimportant to me/my business, and that referring individual knew how successful the client was and would have never understood why I couldn't help him. 2) I really liked the client personally, just my kind of guy, and I knew he needed some-one to fight for him, and trust me, it was indeed a fight. 3) I had a background in lending and I was confident that we could navigate our way through this and succeed. 4) I had a solid lender in my hip pocket that I knew wouldn't run and hide at the first sign of trouble, and trouble there was. And, finally, 5) it was a great challenge and a great price point.

So, I worked on showing them some homes, and my lender at bank number three started on the loan. Rejection number one! Remember, *ball in back of net, see future.* Start again. Rejection number two. Remember about the ball in the back of the net, lender friend. "This is crazy, Jim, no way this is going to happen." Finally, not an ap-proval, but "I'm really confused on this file but I don't want to reject it," says the underwriter.

Aw, an opening. Here is our chance. "Jim, they basically said no."

"No, they said, 'I'm confused, explain it to me, give me more in-formation, make it simple for me to understand.' " We naturally had to explain it in writing. I think I prepared no less than ten different spreadsheets (for the underwriter) that week—I knew this was the mo-ment of truth.

"Okay, I'm still confused, but I will send to this my manager to review," says the underwriter. All the while we are looking for a house and my lender keeps pulling away to work on easier deals (I didn't blame him and did anticipate this happening).

"No, no, no, get back here. Remember about the ball in the net—visualize the future, you wimp. What, you are going to quit and run like a chicken? Ball in net."

"Okay, I hate you, Jim, you're an ass." This is the way it went for two months until such time as a senior, senior, senior executive at bank number three did a final approval on the deal. As I recall, it went up the ladder no less than five levels and several different departments. Ball in net, superhappy customer, lots of great referrals, *the future realized.*

See the future—then do the work. See the future in a minute, in a day, in a week, in a month, or possibly a longer-term goal of one, two, or five years. For example, you may have a three-year goal of doing thirty deals yearly as a real estate agent. Great! Good goal. Now, you can come back to today and plan out the work necessary to get there and the landmarks along the way. Or, you may have a five-year goal to open up your own mortgage brokerage company with a banking operation attached. Good goal. That's a very specific vision and will require specific landmarks that need to be met along the way. See the future, then do the work to get you there.

Are there times when the future is cloudy or we can't quite see it at all? Of course. But those are the times to lean on mentors, advisors, and people we respect. The truth is that the primary reason I switched from lending to brokerage was that I couldn't envision how to make that next big jump in loan production (revenue), and I needed a new challenge. In lending, I had successfully reached close to the top of the mountain in terms of production and income and felt stuck. I couldn't envision how to make more money or do more deals. *I had a limiting vision of the future.* The irony is that I very much enjoyed doing loans but ultimately decided that the top 1 percent of real estate agents made more money than the top 1 percent of lenders. That's largely why I switched. Right or wrong, that's why I switched. In retrospect, I could have kept going in loans for sure, grown the revenue line, and continued to build. But again, my vision of the future was limited at that moment and I didn't successfully reach out to my mentors for advice; a good lesson about leaning on mentors. I have no regrets about switching; I will tell you, however, that switching product lines is very challenging, and I do not recommend it.

See the future, and then go to work.

Go get 'em!

11

Serial Dater

———◆———

Drive thy business or it will drive you.
BENJAMIN FRANKLIN

THE FOLLOWING EXAMPLE IS FOR a residential real estate agent, but the concept could be applied to lending or commercial. So you arrive back in the office after showing your clients five more houses. This is the second time you have been out this week with them and the seventh time overall. Given preparation and showing hours, you have spent roughly forty man-hours with these clients so far. But that's okay, because you have a "really good relationship with them" and just clicked when they came through your open house a couple of months ago. You connected—it was marital/client bliss.

The next day, you decide to join the office round table meeting, where everyone discusses current needs. "Hey, I have this listing come up," or "Hey, I have a buyer that is looking for the following." That kind of thing. Your colleague Susan stands up. "I have buyers who are hot to trot, married couple with two boys under the age of ten, and they are looking for anything in the Spartan District between four hundred thousand and five hundred thousand, preferably with four bedrooms. Please let me know if you have anything coming," says Susan.

"Hmmm," says you. Wow, that sounds oddly similar to my clients, but it can't be the same because my clients are looking in only the Trojan District, not the Spartan District. But you are still curious. After the meeting, you visit Susan in her office. "Hi, Susan, just by chance, tell me a little more about your clients, I have a client that I have been showing property to that sounds eerily similar," says you. Ut oh! And then it all comes out. The buyers are using Susan for the Spartan District and you for the Trojan District. Someone just wasted forty hours of his or her life.

Let's break it down.

The quality of the lead. Where did the lead come from? An open house. When you work with anything but a referral lead, you are taking a huge risk. Time is our primary asset in this business. Some people take a hundred hours to complete a deal and some people take twenty. Wasted time is the worst, however. You have nothing to show for it but a few bumps and bruises. It's a hollow feeling when we waste time; I know, I made all those mistakes early on. Your business should be built on referrals. Even if you have never done a deal, your business should be built on referrals. When I started from day one in the loan business, one of my tightest friends in the world went out of his way to help me. I hadn't even closed a deal and had several leads just from him. In addition, my mom sent me several as well within that first month. When we start, we don't need many of those types of people; we only need one to three. Second, it's your job to contact everyone you can think of and see if they know anyone that needs assistance. You contact your friend, he or she makes the intro for you to the clients, you follow up with the clients, and within a few weeks they are solid referral clients. They are very unlikely to double date you, serial dater. Why? Because you and the clients have the same friend, so they have their reputation at stake at this point. Who ever said that a referral has to come from a person that you have done business with? A referral comes from someone that you know, period.

Assuming. Did we assume that the buyer clients in the above example were only going to be working with us? I do recognize that most clients have the common sense to know that working with two different selling agents is disingenuous at best. But the world is a big place. People do business lots of different ways around the world. Did we ever ask the question, "Are you working with any other agents?"

"Well, Jim, the relationship was going so well and I didn't want to rock the boat."

Well, then, that is your fault for not asking. It's quite possible that the clients didn't even know they were doing anything "wrong." We could have saved forty hours of our life by simply asking the question. Usually, someone that is in the position to purchase a $400,000 home is not necessarily in the habit of lying on a day-to-day basis. The clients probably would have told us the truth if we had simply asked the question. Forty hours of our life saved.

A commitment in writing. In many subcategories of real estate, the buyer must make a commitment in writing to the agent/broker; some form of a procuring agent agreement depending on the state and country. I'll be honest; I have never done this but do recognize and appreciate how important this can be in many markets and instances. This is one of those items that you will need to discuss with your manager.

An oral commitment. Do this for sure. First, ask the question. Make sure that you can look your clients in the eye, and they you, and you have a commitment that you, and you only, are assigned to complete the task at hand. I know some colleagues go into this long dissertation about how important it is to their livelihood that you don't double date and cheat on them. My belief is that if I have to give that speech, those people are not clients that I want to work with. I will commit blood, sweat, tears, and loyalty until the task is complete, but I expect the same in return. Experience will be your teacher on this. You will be able to "size people up" in a nanosecond over time. And if in doubt, pass on the project. Just pass.

Are there instances in which you would consider continuing the relationship? Sure, switching gears to commercial for a moment. For example, if you are a commercial broker working in a tight market, let's say in New York or San Francisco, and the client is on a 1031 exchange, then you may want to consider working with him or her. In this case, let's assume that demand is exceeding supply; there are more buyers than sellers. So, you will need to work and dig like crazy to find a seller that wants to sell. And most likely in this case, the buyer will be completely honest with you and let you know that he or she is in contact with lots of brokers because of the time crunch that he or she is under (given the 1031 exchange). The good news is that you have a willing, able, ready, and motivated buyer that for sure is going to buy something in the next few months. And who knows, you may be able find a seller that wants to sell and represent both parties in the making.

You drive your business—period! You are in control—period! If you are not feeling comfortable for whatever reason, pass on the project. It's not worth it. You have a responsibility to yourself and your family to be discerning.

Go get 'em!

12

The Transition

———◆———

Delay is preferable to error.

THOMAS JEFFERSON

*P*ICK ONE PRODUCT AND RIDE that mule until you or it dies. The guys and girls doing big business in real estate, really large numbers, traditionally picked one product and did that their entire career. For instance, I have a friend that chose large institutional apartment buildings doing large numbers. I have another friend that specializes as a tenant representative doing big volume, many friends that specialize in residential brokerage doing good numbers, and still more doing a large volume in lending.

The transition. The transition from lender to real estate agent! As I started doing a lot of business that first year as a real estate agent, I could practically hear the chatter through the Sheetrock. "Well, Carter is doing so much business because he came in with a giant database from lending, and he is converting his lending clients to brokerage clients." It is true that I had a strong customer base from lending; the part that is not true, however, is that I was able to successfully convert them from lending clients to brokerage clients. It simply didn't happen like that. In fact, I was *never* able to successfully convert my lending clients to brokerage clients. Yes, there were a few here and there, but nothing that would even remotely move the needle.

In their mind, I was a lender, and as much I tried to tell them that I was a real estate agent now (well, I hedged my bet for a while; I really told them I was both a lender and a real estate agent, which confused them even further), they continued to think of me as a lender.

"Jim, you're a real estate lender."

"But no, I'm a real estate agent."

"Sorry, Jim, you're a lender to me."

They didn't say that, but I knew. What they did say was, "Jim, I trust you as a person based on our business relationship. I am happy to refer you to my friend Susan, who is about to list her home." What they didn't say but they showed me through their actions was, "Jim, it is just not going to work for you to be my real estate agent, I simply can't make that transition." So Jim, go list Susan's home—but not mine. But wait a minute, Mr. and Mrs. Customer, in my business plan called *Transition from Lender to Real Estate Agent*, I was counting on you to hire me as your agent. See right here where it says *Revenue*? That's you. I frankly never would have guessed my customers wouldn't want to go with my plan. After all, real estate lending, real estate brokerage, they both have to do with real estate, don't they? What's the problem? My lending customers didn't see it that way. I had successfully convinced them over several years that I'm lender, I'm a lender, I'm a lender; I'm the money man. It didn't work.

Basics of branding. Starbucks can't just one day wake up and say, "I know you think of me as coffee, but now I'm a nursery selling plants. I promise I am—give me a chance and I'll show you my pretty daffodils." Or Burger King says, "I know you think of me as the Whopper, but I'm now going to offer you a whopper of a deal in hair care products. Forget that burger thing and welcome to my hair colorings." Or

Home Depot saying, "Forget about all those home improvement products I used to sell. I now want you to buy these bats and balls and yo-yos. I'm a sporting goods store now—promise I'll do a good job." Or Target saying, "Forget about those low-cost items you bought from me. Now I'm an athletic gym, come ride my StairMaster." Or, something more closely aligned, the title company says, "Forget about all that stuff about title and escrow. I was just kidding. I'm now a lender. See my handsome interest rates?" Yeah, yeah, I know; those are outrageous examples, but you get the point. Real estate lending, real estate brokerage, what's the problem? I'm a lender, now I'm a real estate agent, now you see me, now you don't. Well, really, I'm wearing the costume of a real estate agent by day, but I'm lending by night until this new real estate agent thing works out. It didn't work, too big of a branding change for my customers.

Full circle. The point of this story is to reemphasize the need to make the right selection on product lines from the beginning. I hope I have successfully convinced you that switching later on is tricky, tricky, tricky business. When you pick a product and then start on the journey of promoting that product, you are beginning the hardwire process for your customer. Jim = lender. Jim = lender. Jim = lender. It becomes hardwired over time. Think of it as a road you are building, linking your customer to you. At first that road is bumpy and dusty and barely recognizable; then throw in a little sand and gravel for texture; and then add some form boards and more gravel for structure; and voila, before you know it, that road has evolved into rock-hard cement over the years. Your customer didn't do that; you did that. Residential Real Estate Agent = Joe. Tenant rep = Carol. Commercial lender = Steven. That kind of thing.

This story wouldn't be complete without at least addressing what I did with my lending clients. First, I kept selling them loans for several years (I could do that because I had a broker's license). Quietly, discreetly, and off the radar, if you will, so as to not dilute my new messaging of I'm an agent, I'm an agent, I'm an agent. Hey, I'm not dumb; I wanted to make sure that this real estate agent thing was going to work before I abandoned my golden goose. Second, if my lending clients were not going to let me list or sell their home, then I would simply ask them to help me by referring me to their friends who *would* allow me to list and sell their homes. Their friends didn't think of me as a lender; instead, they knew me as a real estate agent. Once I accepted that fact and made that distinction, the floodgates opened.

Carefully select the right product when you start. Reference the section "Getting Started" in this book, the chapter titled "The First Step."

Go get 'em!

13

Limitless Income

You must pay the price if you wish to secure the blessing.
PRESIDENT ANDREW JACKSON

THIS WILL BE A FUN topic.

I was making a steady but nominal wage at my technology company. My wife worked at and owned a small one-room dance school that was barely profitable at the moment. We had one child and another on the way and a sizable mortgage payment. By this time, I had been studying my friends in real estate and was confident I could do it. I was ready to do it, but wow, is that a gut check when you actually resign from a steady paycheck at a good company. I wrote the following letter to myself about six months before I resigned:

Dear James:

I am pleased to offer you the position of mortgage broker at our company. We expect you to be our number one producer within sixty days. As such, your compensation will be $200,000 yearly. We know you are a rising star and believe in you. You're a champion.

Sincerely,
Your New Company

I was giving myself an enormous pay raise; hey, I thought I was worth it! I read that letter thousands of times before I started. As I arrived on the job day one, I was sky high, even though I hadn't made a dollar; I had literally convinced myself that I took a new job paying $200,000 yearly. I could feel that feeling. It was real as real can be. I read that piece of paper, and the more I read it, the more convinced I became. I envisioned this imaginary person believing in me, someone that had my back and was willing to do that for me. There was no way was I going to let that person (whoever that was) down. No way. Can you imagine someone believing in you, in me, to that extent? Imagine if that were true. I don't know about you, but I would literally run through the wall for that person.

Belief. Now, most of us in realty don't have that person in our life that says, "Go get 'em, I believe in you, and by the way, here is $50,000." We can all create that, however. We usually play at the level at which we are expected to play. I think our opinion of ourselves matters. What do you think you are worth? "Well, Jim, I don't have that level of confidence in myself, and I'm not that kind of a 'fighter' personality." I understand. Try this: write the above letter (or modify it) to yourself, and then read it to yourself about a thousand to ten thousand times, and then check back with me and see if that helped. You may surprise yourself. Hey, if nothing else, you are not going to hurt yourself, that's for sure. It's better than moping around down in the mouth saying, "Forget it, I'm a bum, this will never work." That letter really helped me on some dark days when I started in lending, and then when I re-started again as a real estate agent.

Small income goals. We are all going to want different things out of this industry. My granddad was an executive at Warner Brothers for almost forty years. He would bring us to the studio regularly; it was nothing to him, just another day at the office. When he retired from Warner Brothers, he sat around and goofed around for about a year, and then he went into real estate with very small income goals. At first he did it just to get out of the house and meet some new people. He didn't make much money; he did a few deals here and there. After a couple of years of that, he accidently had built up a pretty good reputation. Before you know it he was doing twenty to thirty deals yearly. Frankly, that was never his plan, and it got a little too hectic for him at that pace, but that is how it developed nonetheless. He had small income goals for his real estate business, so when he reached roughly twenty-five deals yearly by accident, he throttled it back again to meet his lifestyle and goals.

Medium income goals. There is nothing wrong with having moderate income goals. That is the beauty of real estate. This industry allows for tremendous freedom and flexibility to paint the picture (your life) the way you want it painted. I know of a lady that was roughly fifty years of age, recently divorced, with two children still in the home. Naturally, her number one responsibility was her children, but at the same time, she needed to make some money on a consistent basis. She was fairly well known in the community so she decided to become a lender. She was quite thoughtful from the beginning. She knew she could generate some leads through her network, but she also knew that she didn't have the time to provide a good service given her family responsibilities. She decided to partner with an experienced veteran that had a seasoned team in place. She would find the lead and then turn it over to the operations team to complete the project. This was a good solution for both her and her customers. She made a nice, steady income from this recipe and was able to take care of her children without too many work demands.

Large income goals. This is probably going to be a person that is committing thirty-five to forty-five hours weekly to this industry. In addition, it's most likely someone that is the primary breadwinner in the home. This was me most of the time. You have to push at this level, stay on your game, and go. There can't be a lot of wasted motion if you have large income goals. You have to get up early, make your list, and work. *Large* can be defined only by you. You know what large means in your industry in your area. It will be different from town to town, region to region, and niche to niche. Be prepared to dig in at this level.

Giant income goals. Now, before you say, "Oh, that's me, mark me down, I'm a giant," be careful. There is a price to be paid at each level. Depending on what I was doing over the years, I would range from medium to giant. When I started in lending, I was a giant. When I restarted as a real estate agent, I was a giant, but all the times in between, I frankly ranged from medium to giant depending on other business interests at the time. During the times that I was involved in this or that on a personal or business level, I would simply throttle it back to a medium. My granddad gave me the best advice early on. "Jimmy, I know you are entrepreneurial by nature, and naturally you will want to be involved in this and that over the years, but don't forget your bread and butter. Keep your real estate moving at all times." There are large numbers of entrepreneurial types of personalities that are attracted to this industry. The challenge for us entrepreneurial types is to stay focused and channel all that juice into this one product, real estate.

Some of the Jolly Green Giants, just for fun. Yes, they exist. I'll rattle off a few examples: a commercial broker earning roughly $2.5 million yearly; an apartment broker making roughly $4.0 million yearly; a residential real estate agent in a beach town making roughly $3.0 million yearly; a retail strip mall broker making upward of $5.0 million yearly; a residential broker making roughly $3.5 million yearly. Again, you and only you can define *giant* for yourself.

Exciting and limitless. This industry is truly exciting in so many ways, but the income part is superexciting. You can make as much or as little as you want. You can dream about $200,000 yearly as you are making $30,000, knowing all the while that you can actually make the $200,000 if you really dig in and pay the price. Your income will be limited only by your own ingenuity and determination.

Go get 'em!

14

Dual Agency

———————

All virtue is summed up in dealing justly.

ARISTOTLE

I'M TAKING A BIT OF a risk covering this topic; but it's important to your success that you have a basic understanding of what we are about to talk about, particularly so if you are new to real estate. Your success is my goal—so here goes!

We are going to be talking about dual agency, double ending a deal, and rules of the game, all in the same breath. First, what does dual agency mean? It means representing both the buyer and the seller on a real estate transaction. In lending, there is only one principal, or customer, so dual agency does not apply within the same context.

Clarification: Jill is from ABC Real Estate, and Joey is from ABC Real Estate as well. Jill represents the buyer and Joey represents the seller. Is that dual agency? Yes, because they both work for the same company. Is that double ending a deal, in layman's terms? No, because Jill earned the selling fee and Joey earned the listing fee.

I am going to cover commercial in this chapter, just in case you are new to the business and considering commercial real estate. We'll deal with that first.

Commercial. If you see a commercial property coming to the market from a commercial office, you can almost be assured that several buyers have already evaluated it off market. What do I mean?

Rules of the game. In commercial, it is common practice to sell as much product as possible in house. Step 1: Find someone that wants to sell something. Step 2: Get a listing contract signed. Step 3: Call anyone and everyone that you know that may want to buy it. Step 4: If you don't personally have anyone to buy it, then sell it within your office to one of your office mates. Step 5: Your office mates call anyone and everyone that they may know to buy it. Step 6: If they can't find anyone, then put it on the open market.

It's common practice in commercial real estate to either double end a deal (by a single agent) or sell the deal in house involving two agents (dual agency). What does double end mean? There are usually two commissions on an average real estate transaction that are paid: one to the agent representing the seller (the listing fee) and one to the agent representing the buyer (the selling fee). If you double end a deal, you are paid both commissions. That is also called dual agency; you are becoming the agent for both the buyer and the seller. People that live in the world of commercial transactions understand and accept these rules of the game. And, by the way, please do not confuse the stating of the rule as an indictment or endorsement of the rule— it's just simply the rule, without judgment or prejudice.

Relationships are important in any industry, but your relationships become increasingly important in commercial. You list something; you don't have a buyer, you go to your office mate, Carol, and give her a shot at it. The next time Carol lists something, you hope she returns the favor.

There is a phrase in real estate called "list to last." It means you have to control a piece of the inventory to be viable long term in this business. You have to develop the skills necessary to *list property*. Listing is the starting point to generating income. If you only have a commercial buyer, you are running around like a chicken looking for a seller to mate with. If you have a seller (the listing), however, you will have more control of your own income. You will likely be paid on the listing side of the commission (I'm guessing 90 percent chance you will be paid), and you have a chance, at least, of earning the selling side as well (I'm guessing 20 to 40 percent chance). If you only have a buyer, you have 0 percent chance of being paid on the listing side and maybe, maybe, a 30 to 50 percent chance of being paid on the selling side (after two hundred hours of work). Listings are the golden goose—*list to last.*

One note before we jump to residential. Laws that govern real estate business practices may/will differ from city to city, county to county, state to state, country to country, and certainly commercial to residential. For instance, in California, the requirements for commercial agency representation have been modified as of 2015. Therefore, double check any and all laws that govern your industry in your region, and speak with your manager.

Residential. *Rules of the Game:* It is not as prevalent to double end a property in residential. Step 1: Get the listing signed. Step 2: Prepare the home for the market. Step 3: Put the home on the open market. I am obviously omitting many steps here, but that is the summary nonetheless from an agency perspective. There are many instances, of course, when a home is double ended and/or does not make it to the public market; the majority, however, make it to the open market.

Consumer protection: As a general statement, there are laws that govern residential that do not govern commercial. Why? Because commercial buyers and sellers are assumed to be "professionals"; they know what they are doing. In residential, however, the consumer is doing one, two, three, maybe four transactions in a lifetime. He or she is involved in a process that is not familiar to him or her. Therefore, the consumer in residential naturally needs more consumer protection.

Example of why most residential property makes it to the open market: I take a nice listing in my target market. I record it with the office. It will take about two to three weeks to get everything ready to go before it is time to put it on the Multiple Listing Service (MLS). About three days into the process, my colleague Julie knocks on my door. "Hi, Jim" with a big smile. "I heard you have a great listing on Cranberry Circle. Any chance they would look at an offer before it goes for sale? I have a buyer." Now think about that. In most states, did Julie's comment technically qualify as an offer? And do we have a responsibility to communicate all offers to the seller, written or verbal? I am asking that as a question. But you should consider it. So, I decide in this case, well, I better call my client. I tell client the story. The client says, "Gosh, Jim, if it's a great offer, why not?"

Ugly: The property is still a mess, the paperwork is not prepped, the seller is not fully educated, and the advertising is not ready. Nonetheless, I have Julie taking her clients over to see a product that is clearly only 35 percent ready to go. Do I (on the seller's behalf) have negotiating strength in that case? Not really, because we are dealing with only one *potential buyer* at the moment.

Nonetheless, Julie's client makes an offer. Seller accepts. The communications are off market at this point, but naturally all your colleagues (in your office) know about it. Two weeks into the process, Julie's client gets cold feet and backs out of the deal. What do you think when you hear that someone backed out of a deal? Exactly: What is wrong with that property? And do you think that people in one real estate office possibly talk with people in another real estate office? You guessed it again. So I am now launching (fresh to the open market on

MLS) a listing that is a dead-duck-doomed-from-the-beginning-tainted-dog listing. Yes, maybe I'm exaggerating to make a point. But do you think it's a good thing that the real estate community knows that Julie's clients already backed away from the house? You likely know the answer.

Here is another example of why double-ending is not as prevalent in residential.

Johnny (who is broke) just inherited his cousin's house. Johnny's buddy wants to buy the house. Johnny doesn't have a lot of experience dealing with real estate or money, but Johnny is pushing hard to have his buddy buy the house (for some reason). The agent is advising against it, and also advising that the property should go on the open market, but Johnny keeps pushing. Johnny is the boss, so that's what they ultimately do: sell to the buddy off market. Property is sold and closed for five hundred thousand. Everyone is happy. Johnny spends all the money within one year. Johnny starts thinking about the transaction and how broke he is. Johnny starts pointing fingers and retains legal counsel. Grounds for the complaint are that the property should have been put on the market.

And, by the way, in the above example, let's also assume that the buddy doesn't have an agent and Johnny doesn't want to pay the selling side commission because Johnny says that he found the buyer. So, the agent is compensated for the listing side only. Is that dual agency? Yes, because the agent was the only real estate professional that was part of that deal—even though the agent was not compensated to be representing both parties.

I could write another ten pages on examples of why double ending a deal is not as prevalent in residential. I am dealing with this topic so that you have a basic understanding of dual agency, double ending a deal, and the accepted rules of the game of residential and commercial. Further, I handled it in some level of detail, but as in all things, *don't let it intimidate you*. By having this knowledge, you are now better prepared for success than you were ten minutes ago.

Go get 'em!

15

Athletes in Real Estate

———◆———

Our greatest glory is not in never falling,
but rising every time we fall.
CONFUCIUS

A MONG OTHER LESSONS, ATHLETICS TEACHES to us to fall, fall again, and again, and be expected to rise every time we fall. This type of training and mental toughness transfers well into the real estate business.

I was talking with a mentor friend the year I was graduating from college. He owned a medium-size manufacturing company in Silicon Valley. Their distribution model was to hire in-house salespeople; they had a team of about twenty sales representatives. The owner said to me, "I try to hire primarily former athletes, men or woman, and they don't need to have played in college or the pros; high school is fine. In the interview, I try to understand the details of their athletic experience, what did they play, for how long, their coaching experiences, the lessons they learned, etc."

He was roughly sixty years old at the time and was one of those guys that loved to mentor people, and he loved talking with me. He didn't know it, but he was one my primary role models at that time of my life. He had a great family; he was easygoing, a business owner and entrepreneur; everything that I wanted. I had no idea what I wanted to do, but I knew crystal clear at that age that I wanted to be a small-business owner/entrepreneur. And, oh yeah, I didn't want to have a boss either!

"Jim, I have hired all kinds of people in sales over the years, but I migrated back to athletes. I run the business like a team, like a coach. I create the culture that you and I are familiar with in sports. You don't even need to tell former competitive athletes their quota; they'll bust right through it on their own when they see their colleagues trying to kick their butt. It's an instinct, Jim."

Former athletes do well in real estate. One of my go-to lender friends played professional soccer for four years and made it to the top of the mountain in lending in short order. The commercial real estate industry is littered with former professional athletes of all kinds. Residential, commercial, sales, leasing, lending—you name it and you will find all of it chock-full of former athletes.

Even if your athletic career was limited to high school, it's part of your blood. Think about it. From the age of roughly five, you were part of this system that we call "athletics." So if you played until your senior year in high school, you were engrossed in a way of being (and acting) for thirteen years. Call it brainwashing; I call it good preparation for life. Athletics teaches cooperation, competition with your own teammates, competition with an opponent, winning, losing, and, most importantly, *being knocked flat on your back and being expected to get up.* Robert Green Ingersoll said, "The greatest test of courage on earth is to bear defeat without losing heart."

Listen, in the sales meeting you can smile and clap and be supportive of the guy or girl getting the award—and thinking in your mind, "I will kick your butt next month, friend." It's called healthy and normal. It's called having the mettle to be prepared to succeed in real estate.

As an aside, where did all the athletes go? My college teammates and I joke about the fact that you can always find the athletes years later in one of three industries: construction, real estate, or sales (of some kind). These are all entrepreneurial industries where you eat what you catch; perfect for former athletes. So if you ever lost track of your old teammates, you might want to check in the real estate library!

Athletes, set your sights on the top dog—and your instincts will do the rest.

Go get 'em!

16

The Word *Producer*

I am not afraid of an army of lions led by a sheep—
I'm afraid of an army of sheep led by a lion.

ALEXANDER THE GREAT

WHEN YOU ARE A PRODUCER in this business, you need to understand a few things. You are the entrepreneur. You are at the top of the food chain. No one is going to think like you, act like you, or be like you. You are the small-business owner—the buck stops with you. You are the one that could make $200,000 this month and lose $30,000 the next. You have no paycheck and no safety net. Just that fact alone requires different thinking. It requires intentional action. You can't fake it or call it in or go through the motions when you are on a no-paycheck plan. You have to kick butt—and do it daily—and do it with intention.

Human nature is to want and need security. You have little to none as a producer. And whatever form of security you do have, you will have built with your own hands. Sound tough? It can be. But great things follow success in this business, financial and otherwise. Playing the role of producer in this business is not for the faint of heart or weak in the knees, however.

I wrote this book largely because no one has adequately addressed producers as producers, from the voice of a producer to the ears of a producer. If you are not a producer in this business, it's just different. It's not bad, it's not good, it's just different.

Look at real estate as an industry and then look at the players: management, administration, and vendors. And then there are *the producers,* those folks in lending and sales making rain and originating deals.

What do producers need to do to succeed (in addition to providing a good service to current customers)? We train ourselves to hunt and find and search and market and target and seek; it becomes a way of thinking. You become an expert marksman. You become a laser-guided missile able to cut through to the core of the apple. "Here is how we will find customers." Be a producer in this business and it will become largely who you are in business (over time). When I look at any business or investment today, my brain immediately jumps to marketing: "How do we get customers?" The thought of operations and finance are secondary. And it's not a ho-hum think-tank thought with cigar smoke over a two-week period. No. Your brain will jump there (to marketing) in a nanosecond—and it will also jump to a solution. It's the way a producer must "think" to be successful.

Truly understanding the role of producer. Normally when you move up the corporate ladder in America, you make more money. If you are a top producer in lending or sales and go from top producer to manager, that's not necessarily true. What? Yes, that's correct. I've considered managing this office or that office (in both lending and sales) many times over the years. In the final analysis, however, I couldn't afford it.

There are exceptions, of course, but real estate is one of those industries where (top) producers make more than the managers. *Risk and reward.* Herodotus says, "All men's gains are the fruit of venturing." In corporate America, both the manager and the salesperson are employees. In real estate, the manager is an employee (minimal risk and a paycheck) and the producer is an independent contractor (tons of risk and no paycheck). So therein lies the rub, the opportunity, and the dynamics. No one puts limits on the producer's income; the boss, however, has put limitations on the manager's income.

Now, before you cry for the manager, the manager can make a very good living. In fact, if the manager is running a high-performing office, he or she is doing very well, thank you very much. Let me give you some rough numbers so you understand the financial dynamics. Let's say the superstar top dog producer in the office is making $500,000; the average producer is making roughly $75,000; the manager in that case is probably making $150,000 to $250,000. These are rough estimates, so don't stumble over the exact numbers, but understand the concept nonetheless. Why? Because it speaks to the heart of the industry and more specifically to the role of the producer, which of course is my focus here.

Again, this book is intended to help the producer in the real estate industry (sales and lending); and as such, I'll leave you with this: you are at the top of the food chain, the lead dog, the hunter, the entrepreneur, the brave champion, the risk taker, the achiever, the doer, the courageous one, and the person that has taken control of your own life.

Go get 'em!

17

Seabiscuit

———◆———

If passion drives you, let reason hold the reins.

BENJAMIN FRANKLIN

SEABISCUIT WAS A SECOND-RATE HORSE until someone finally figured out how he was "wired." He had good breeding but was a little scrawny, ate a lot, and was purportedly lazy. He was written off by the age of three as a tier-two racehorse, at which time he was bought by Charles Howard for $8,000 in 1936. Howard paired Seabiscuit with a trainer named Tom Smith and a jockey named Red Pollard. Together, as a team, they figured out how Seabiscuit was wired. "Pull him back slightly on the final lap to make sure he can *see his competitor,* and then cut him loose." Seabiscuit became one the greatest racehorses of all time, including winning a landmark "match race" in a head-to-head battle with the great War Admiral in 1938.

Some of us are wired like that. We need to be around it, we need to see the competition. Some of us are motivated by seeing someone else trying to be bigger, stronger, and faster than us. I'm convinced a fair number of people that jump into real estate as producers are wired like Seabiscuit. Now before I get too far down the road and dig myself a giant hole, my wife reads all of these as I write them, and she jumped in with vigor on this one. "Wait, wait, wait, what about all those folks that are not competitive in that way?" she asks.

A lot of very successful real estate producers are not wired in that way, and that's okay, no problem. In fact, I'm probably only speaking to a minority group here. You don't have to be wired like that to be successful in this business. If you are not wired like Seabiscuit, I think you'll find something in this section helpful nonetheless. At the very least, maybe you could consider how you *are* wired. With all that said, the following is coaching for you Seabiscuit types.

As I was making the transition from lending to sales, I talked to my dad. He and my mom and my wife understand my temperament (wiring) the best. He said, "I know you, Jim. Get in with the best, and if you see someone else that is bigger, stronger, and faster than you, that will drive you. You will do everything in your power to compete and attempt to win. Use that competitive spirit to your advantage."

I don't think you can teach it or coach it. We are all a little different; it's simply who we are. It's fine either way. But if you are wired that way, *then use that to your advantage.* Get the top dog in your sights. See your competition. Get to that office. Work there. Force yourself to be around him or her. This is goofy and a little embarrassing, but on my way to work at my new job as a real estate agent, I would literally say to myself in the car about a thousand times, "I will kick your butt today, top dog" (whoever that happened to be that month). And then I'd walk into the office five minutes later, a mild-mannered, low-key, ho-hum guy. But in my mind, it was on! It motivated me. It energized me.

Seabiscuit!

Use office dynamics to your advantage. I will be forever grateful to senior management of the real estate company that I started with because they built that competitive culture. That didn't happen by accident, or by luck. They were strategic. They wanted the best for their people. They wanted their team to do well, support their families, invest, and have a good life. I truly believe they wanted that with all their heart. So they made the office a locker room, a boys' and girls' locker room. It was carnal competition at its best (in a healthy way). I frankly hadn't been around that type of environment since I completed my senior (college) year in football thirteen years prior. When I stepped in the office, wow, it was like the lights went on again. All the juices flowed. My competitive spirit went to a level ten in a nanosecond. This was no fake-it-jake-it office. You would find it very difficult to float in the corner—production was expected and somewhat required. The office had roughly one-hundred-plus agents, and I'm guessing that three or four of them were teetering on those seven-digit-income numbers. This was the real deal run by pro managers.

I would have rather had nettles poked through my eyes than sit through those first few sales meetings. I was still doing loans and not quite engaged yet, but I started attending the monthly sales meetings nonetheless (just to get warmed up). This person made $2K; that person made $15K; So-and-So made $91K; and on and on. Everyone that did a deal that month was recognized. And as the manager announced your name, they threw a Kudos bar your way. I literally started dreaming every night about that lousy Kudos getting thrown in my direction. My loan business was at full tilt, so I was not under any financial pressure—the Kudos bar, however, motivated me. Jack Standtall made $14K this month with the toss of the Kudos bar—and then as the Kudos landed in Jack's lap, everyone clapped once, in unison. My goal in life was to get that Kudos bar. Do whatever it took to get one, and if I could get them *all*, that would be preferable. I knew the motivational trick that was being played, it didn't matter, and it worked. I wanted the bar.

After about three months of attending these meetings, I had had enough. I could either stop attending the real estate sales meetings or start selling (which would certainly impact my loan production);

or maybe I could both. One thing is for sure, there was no way I was going to continue to attend those meetings without getting my Kudos bar. I went to the manager after attending three of those monthly meetings and told him, "Sorry, manager, I'm not coming to the sales meetings anymore until I do some business. The good news is that I plan to start doing some (sales) business." I didn't tell him about my (secret/weird) motivation to get the Kudos bar (recognition), he was just happy that I was ready to do something. So, I missed that next meeting, closed a deal, went back to meeting number five, and got my Kudos bar. Frankly, I never even ate the Kudos bars (I gave them away); I just wanted lots of them thrown my way in the meetings. I never missed getting a Kudos bar from that moment forward. It drove me up the wall.

Sometimes, you just have to be around it. *See the competition.*

When I started my career in lending, I recruited the top loan agent into my own office. True story. I'll explain.

I had been "casing" the business for about a year as I was wrapping up my paycheck job. Talking with friends, studying this and that, finding out who is doing what, when, where, how, why. I had bought a home a year prior and used one of the top dog lenders in Silicon Valley. He was also a friend of a friend; a referral. As I was winding it down those last three months (from my paycheck job), I started talking to this guy, telling him what I was doing. He was real curious about the company that I had chosen to work for (and the manager running the show). Turns out, he was actually thinking about making a move to another office at that time—good timing for him and me. In addition, my new office gave me a bonus if I recruited other producers, so I was naturally motivated in that way as well. He met the manager, liked him, and decided to join.

So, the way the timing worked out, he started at the new company before me. He kicked everyone's butt by a roughly two-or-three-to-one margin for a while. I started. It was the best thing that could have happened to me to have him there. I needed to be around someone that was producing at that level. The truth is, he is the nicest guy in the world; modest, capable, thorough, and people loved him. So there was certainly no carnal instinct to try and kick his butt (on production).

This is a quick and possibly risky digression, but may be helpful nonetheless. I believe that when we see someone that has his or her chest pushed out, walking around like a peacock, bragging about this and that, there is a tendency to want to kick his or her butt (not in a physical way). On the other hand, when someone has a smile on his or her face and is showing some element of vulnerability, the instinct is literally 100 percent the opposite. We want to protect that person. My friend (in lending) was the latter. Neither is good or bad; just a point.

I caught him (my lender friend) pretty fast, and we traded the one and two (and sometimes three) spots that entire first year. Without him in that office, I'm estimating my income would have been 20 to 35 percent less. Basically, his level of production became my level of production. His standard became my standard.

Starting out. If you are new to real estate and not 100 percent positive how you are wired, ask your mom or dad or someone you grew up with. I've asked my dad that question literally a dozen times over my working career, just as a double check. This is something to think about *before* you decide which office to work for.

All things remaining nearly as equal as equal gets, go to a low performing office and you will perform at that level; go where there are a bunch of average producers, that's what you will be over time; go to the office with the (male and female) lions, and your income (and family) will be the benefactor.

Go get 'em!

18

Quality Interaction

———◆———

Let the beauty of what you love be what you do.

RUMI

WHO DO YOU WANT TO be around on a day-to-day basis in real estate? Socrates taught Plato, Plato taught Aristotle, Aristotle taught Alexander the Great. Daily interactions are important and play a long-term role in our development and enjoyment of the business. Your customer: whom do you want to serve and interact with daily? "The worst wheel of the cart makes the most noise"—*Benjamin Franklin*.

I had already made the switch from lender to real estate agent. I was into that transition for a few years, and by that point I had completely turned off the nozzle on my loan business—no more loan income. My production as a real estate agent was actually strong, but I found myself in a rut, not liking big pieces of what I was doing.

I sat down with a friend of mine that had been selling property for twenty-five-plus years. He and I have similar backgrounds athletically, and I could always count on him to pull no punches. I told him my moan-and-groan story. Within five minutes, with laser-guided precision, he had an answer to my woes. He told me the quality of the interaction was starting to wear on me. What in the world does that mean, Mr. Mentor Friend? He said, "Jim, what if everyone you worked with 1) trusted your advice, 2) respected your experience, and 3) you enjoyed them on a personal level?" Naturally I said that would be great.

The problem. To make a long story shorter, I was doing sizable volume, but it was coming from all over the place: some warm, some cold, some this, some that, and some I just frankly never figured out where it was coming from. Then came the two-by-four over the head. "Jim, you don't have to do business with people that you don't like. In fact, if you don't like them, there is a high probability that they don't like you either." No punches pulled as promised, staying true to form.

Wow, Mr. Mentor, you are right. I do have a choice.

I literally went through my entire database that very next week and reviewed every single person in that database. I asked myself this question: "Do I like them and do I want to work with them?" I did this with my team, of course. Let me tell you why it's important to do this with your team. We would look at a name (customer), and I would say, for instance, keep him or her, and then someone else would say, no way. Hmm. Okay, let's hear what you are saying. "Jim, they were really nice to you, and I didn't want to tell you this, but behind the scenes they were hard on me." Okay, that's good that we are doing this together. Then off the list they go. We eliminated over three hundred names from our customer database in one week. Remember, I'm calling this a "customer database," but these were not all customers. But it didn't matter who they were; if the consensus was a no, then off the list they went, never to return again.

In parallel, I talked with another friend of mine that same week about this topic. He was about ten years older than me and owned a company with about a hundred employees. Hey, you gotta have a lot of people around you that you respect! He said, "Oh, for sure, Jim, you constantly have to be upgrading your equipment, upgrading your staff, and *upgrading your customer lists.*" Finally I had a term to correlate with what we were doing.

We were upgrading our customer list and the quality thereof.

We were making a conscious decision to include only those people we enjoyed working with (and for) and that were nice people, in our opinion. By doing so, we were improving the quality of the interaction on a daily basis. By improving the quality of the interaction with our customer, we were improving our enjoyment of the job. By improving our own enjoyment of the job, we were improving our customer service.

When we initially made the upgrade, business dipped a little. It didn't take long, however, before the fruits of our intentions and labor began to payoff. We roughly dropped a little/went flat for about eight months and then started growing again, but with customers of our choosing.

We all have to make our own business decisions on this topic. I understand, when you need business you need business. *I'm encouraging you, however, to be careful.* You may love this business; love the service you are providing; have your heart in all right places; but if your customer is beating you up every day, it's going to dilute your enjoyment of what you do.

Please be slightly selfish and certainly discerning on this topic. You will love this business if you love the people that you are working for and with.

Go get 'em!

19

Paycheck

To find yourself, think for yourself.

SOCRATES

THE ECONOMIC WORLD OPERATES ON a steady, consistent paycheck system. Someone gets a job; he or she receives a paycheck from his or her employer, roughly the same amount every month. Someone teaches at a high school for thirty-five years; he or she has earned a steady paycheck from the state until he or she dies. Someone retires from the military after twenty or thirty years, he or she has earned a paycheck for the rest of his or her life. This is the financial payment system of the world. The check rolls in every month right on schedule, without fail.

In real estate, if you get a job with an escrow or title company, you receive a biweekly or monthly paycheck. If you get a job as a manager at a loan or real estate company, you operate with a paycheck. If you get a job as an inspector for a large firm, you get a paycheck. As lenders and real estate agents, we operate without the luxury of a steady nine-to-five paycheck. That's what we signed up for, but there are some things we need to discuss to ensure success in this area.

The recognition of it. Recognize that you are starting a business and all that entails. Yes, the world knows you as lender or real estate agent or commercial professional. But you have all the same responsibilities of any small business owner. Some of the complexities are minimized, but the line items of your profit-and-loss statement are roughly all the same: revenue, advertising, payroll, licensing, facilities, technology, car, variable costs per deal, taxes, etc. Does that sound like a business? You are starting a business, and the service of your business happens to be real estate. When you think about what you are doing within that context, you are in a stronger position for success. You understand you are running a small business and therefore are required to "think" in a different way; marketing, operations, finance, and attitude. We find deals, we do deals, we manage some money, and we work to keep our head straight. We are running a small business. Recognize it.

The psychology of it. There will be lots of people around that are happy to extend a helping hand, but we are on our own to get it done. We are in control of our own revenue line. If you make $75,000 this month, that was you. If you make zero the next, then look in the mirror. If you earn $11,000 the next, you did that. We own the revenue line. There are no limits; we can make $100,000 monthly for six months. Great. We always point the finger to ourselves. We thank lots of people, but we never point that finger at anyone else. Yes, we are a team player. But we are also the CEO of our own small business and therefore are 100 percent responsible for our own revenue line. We take responsibility for everything. Know it. Own it. Get fired up about it.

The discipline of it. You can be a dreamer and a schemer and also exercise great discipline all at the same time. When you have a paycheck job, there is a certain amount of discipline that is associated with that job. There is an equal and even greater amount of discipline needed to operate successfully in real estate without a paycheck. Get to work late four days in a row, you just lost six hours of productivity.

There will be a time when you know what your time is worth. Let's say for now that your time is worth $100 per hour to your revenue line. You lost $600 for that week. Do that for a month and you lost $2,400. Well, I'm my own boss, I can do that. Yes, that's true. We wear a lot of hats. You are the boss, you are the worker, you are VP of marketing; you are all those things and more. So hold yourself accountable, Mr. or Mrs. Boss. Discipline.

The process of it. Trust the process: marketing, operations, finance, and attitude. If we get low on funds and low on deals, we went off course somewhere. We neglected one of the big four: it was marketing or operations or finance or attitude. Or, it might have been a combination thereof. It's a system! It's a process! It's a business! And frankly, it's a very simple business, not easy, but simple—clean. Don't make it complicated. We find deals, we do deals, we manage some money, and we work to keep our head straight. Trust the process. When you have a paycheck job, you can neglect some of the fundamentals for a little while and be fine. But when you own your own small business (as a producer in real estate) and neglect the fundamentals, you may get your tail handed to you. Trust the process and kick butt.

The transition of it. If you are coming out of college and real estate is your first job, you should have an easier time adjusting to this world of no paycheck. If you are transitioning into real estate from a corporate paycheck job, it may take a little longer to adjust. Its fine, it's normal, don't worry. But it might take a little longer. When the check rolls in monthly or weekly in a paycheck job, it starts to become who you are, how you think, and how you act. The same is true for small-business owners who are responsible for everything. It becomes who they are, how they think, and how they act. It will take some time. There may even be times when you want to run back to safety— "Forget this real estate thing. I need to go get a job, and I need to get one fast." That's called normal. Don't worry. It will pass over the years.

And don't forget that you became a producer in real estate partially because you wanted freedom, unlimited income, and no boss. Yes, it may take years. But it will pass.

It's an exciting process to be operating a small business in real estate as a lender or real estate agent or commercial professional. It will become who you are over time. It took me about five years to completely adjust. I define the word *completely* with the following: I would not consider taking a paycheck job. It may take you more time or less time; just understand that whatever you are feeling in the meantime is very normal.

Go get 'em!

20

Your First Deal

When you are asked if you can do a job, tell 'em, "Certainly
I can!" Then get busy and find out how to do it.
PRESIDENT THEODORE ROOSEVELT

IT'S AN IMPORTANT AND EXCITING time when you close your first deal.
Congratulations! You proved to yourself and everyone around you
that you can do it. Let's start at the beginning.

Hunting for that first one. Don't assume where it will come from.
My first deal in lending came from an advertising campaign that my
company was running. Those that wanted to participate could chip in
money for the campaign, and then we shared the leads. So I walked in
the door day one as a lender with a bunch of leads from referrals and
friends, but the one that actually closed first was from a cold source.

My first deal as a real estate agent came from a friend of a friend
of a loan client. I attempted to tell my lending clients that I was now
a real estate agent. They weren't buying it. What they were happy to
do, however, was float my name around to their friends. So I would
simply ask my friends, old customers, really anyone, "Do you know of
someone that might need assistance with real estate?" I kept asking
and asking and found my way to my first closed deal.

Don't assume where your deal going to come from. It's likely it will come from a warm source, such as a friend or family member. But keep your options open—it might surprise you. And there is no wrong answer here, so embrace any and all leads and the sourcing thereof. It's important to get that first one under your belt and out of the way.

Continue looking. When you think you've found your first lead, keep looking even harder. When you do something new, it's simply new—we don't know how to do it yet. So it might look like a lead, smell like a lead, walk like a lead, and talk like a lead—but it's really not a lead. Or it might be a lead, but not a lead that you want to pursue at the moment. But for the beginner, it looks like a lead. It's going to happen. When we start, we don't have the experience to know what a lead really is. It happened to me, it will happen to you, it happens to everyone. Over time we become wise and discerning about what a lead is. When you think you've found your first lead, that is the time to pour it on and find more. Keep going...

Schedule. When you are in the business a couple years and are hitting a stride, you will be spending some time daily on marketing, operations, finance, and attitude—the big four. But when you start, you have no deals and no money to manage, so your time should be spent on marketing and attitude. It will be a little rough to be spending all day every day on marketing and attitude, but make it fun and do it. It's very important to get that first one done and out of the way. That lopsided day of marketing and attitude will not last forever; once you hit your stride and start to add some pending deals and closed deals to your menu, you'll be able to shift your day to a more balance approach of marketing, operations, finance, and attitude. But for now, pour it on—and go hard and fast on marketing and attitude. Keep going...

Confidence. Keep saying to yourself, I can do it, I can do it, I can do it—about a million times per day. But the reality is that you are not really going to believe that until you actually do it. But in the meantime, say it anyway. It's one of the best things we can say to children. "You can do it, Sabrina" or "You can do it, Johnny." So why not be equally gracious to ourselves? Find that first lead. Even if it's a terrible lead and would never close in a thousand years, find that lead anyway. It will start to build your confidence. Then, find another, and another, and another. Before you know it, you'll have ten leads—eight crummy ones, one decent one, and one good one—but your confidence will be growing. Keep going. Find ten more. Now you have sixteen crummy ones, two decent, and two good. Keep going and your confidence continues to grow—find ten more. You still don't have a clue what a lead looks like or smells like, but you are on the move! Now you have three decent leads and three good ones. Keep going, don't look back…

You have momentum now. You still don't know what a lead is or is not—but you are finding stuff nonetheless. You are finding mostly junk leads, but you are on the move and building momentum. Slowly but surely you are learning to be discerning about what a lead is and what a lead is not—for you. You learned something. Three more marbles go into the confidence bucket. Keep going. Check with your manager if your three good leads and three decent leads are anything worth working on. Keep going. Find more. Make numbers your friend. Throw away the twenty-four crummy leads or file them away as "friendlies" to be worked at a later date. Your manager and colleagues are now becoming convinced that you mean business. Keep going. Find ten more. Now you've found forty leads. Most of them were a train wreck— but who cares? You did it. You were able to set a goal, hunt, and find. Way to go! You still haven't closed a deal but you are feeling (deep down inside), "Wow, I actually think I can do this." Keep going…

Work the deal. Now you have eight leads, and you also have the confidence that you know how to keep finding more. That's giant— don't underestimate that confidence that you just *earned*. But in the meantime, keep saying "I can do it, I can do it, I can do it." You and your manager determine that three of those leads are worth persuading. Don't do it alone. Don't be greedy on that first deal. I know you need the money (all of it). But don't do it. Talk with your manager and work the deal together with an experienced person. You ever notice how an expert in any field makes it look so easy? The expert knows how to drive the car without crashing. There are about a thousand possible obstacles in the road of a real estate transaction that could cause a crash. An expert knows where those bumps are and how to avoid them. Team up! Do the deal with an experienced veteran. Talk with your manager, and make the selection together. This is serious business (for your customer) you are dealing with; you are helping someone with a loan or piece of real estate. These are long-term commitments that the customer is making. Make sure you have a pro in tow to help you. Keep going...

Find more. Between you, the veteran, and your manager, determine how to handle the deal. You be the doer, but take the coaching and advice from the veteran and the manager; get the process moving. Now you have an element of operations to be installed into your business. Not a lot, because, after all, it's only one deal. But you can shift your day from marketing and attitude to marketing, operations, and attitude. Only a portion of the day should be spent on managing your one deal. I know it's exciting and I know that you want to do a good job on your one deal, but maintain some mental discipline. You decide how many hours to spend daily on your one deal (operations). I am going to help you by suggesting that you spend three hours daily on operations. Keep going, however. Spend the remaining five to seven hours daily on marketing and attitude. Find more leads. What if your single deal falls apart at the eleventh hour? How will you feel? Make numbers your friend and at the same time provide a good service to your single client. Three hours daily is more than enough time. Keep going...

Overcommunicate. Overcommunicate to your customer, to your manager, and to the veteran that is helping you. Have the discussion with your customer that it's a process and that you will be explaining all the steps as we move from point A to point Z. I know you won't necessarily know those steps, but that's why you have your manager and the veteran to help you. Make sure you know step fourteen. Talk it through with your manager and veteran, study it, digest it, and then explain it to your customer. You will learn it, do it, and then explain it (teach it). You will internalize it that way. Don't assume anything. Over communicate with your team, manager, veteran, customer, and maybe an internal processor. Tell your manager, veteran, and processor that you are eager to learn and will be a good student. Ask them to set you straight when they think you are heading off course. Make them truly feel comfortable. Be coachable. Find more as you are doing all this. Keep going...

Find more. Maybe you have two active deals at this point in different stages of the process. Deal number one is scheduled to close in four weeks, and deal number two is scheduled to close in six weeks. What if both deals fall apart? Not fun! Find more. Keep looking. You still haven't closed a deal, so keep up the push. You know how to find stuff now, so find more. You now have a more balanced day with marketing, operations, and attitude. You are managing some of your own seed money but don't have any commission money to manage at the moment. You have your team together to handle your deals, you know how to find more, so keep going. Find ten more, and then another ten, and then another. Now, maybe you are up two pending deals, three decent leads, and five really good leads. You are making progress. Congratulations. But you need to close your first one, and the longer time goes on, the more your confidence will crack. I can do it, I can do it, I can do it. You still haven't done it, but you are almost there now. Find more. Keep going...

Don't count the money. We all do it, but don't do it. Fight it. Push it out of your brain. Focus on the customer, focus on providing a good service, focus on finding more while you are providing a good service on that first deal. The money will come. Find more deals, manage your current deal(s)—marketing, operations, and attitude. You'll be thinking about the commission money hourly now, maybe every sixty seconds. Here it comes again—purge it. Here it comes—purge. It's not helping you and it's not healthy. Don't think about it. It will happen. Find more deals, manage your current deal(s). The money will come.

Congratulations! *You just closed your first deal.* You did IT by following a process. It might have felt like a rather haphazard, chaotic process—but it was a process nonetheless. You just earned $3,000 or $30,000 or $90,000. Whatever that number was—you did it! And you did it by focusing on the process and not the economics.

Say thank you. Demonstrate good manners and say thank you. There will be a lot of people who likely helped along the way: your family that was nervous for you; your customer; your manager that is now proud of you; the veteran colleague that helped you; the internal office team that cheered you onto victory; other colleagues in your office that you likely leaned on for advice; your vendors, such as your escrow team, inspectors, insurance people. Thank them all. They will remember how you handled yourself during this challenging part of your career.

You are now at full stride and ready to conquer the world.

Go get 'em!

Marketing

A Guide to Making It in Real Estate

21

Simple Marketing Plan

Life is really simple, but we insist on making it complicated.

CONFUCIUS

I'M BLENDING LESSONS (I LEARNED) from two real people into one imaginary person. There was a guy, we'll call him *Homer*, I knew in lending that would show up fifteen minutes early to all customer appointments. Homer was pleasant enough, but not exactly going to set the world on fire. Before I really got to know him, I would describe him as somewhat lazy, so-so intellect, average lender, work ethic of C-plus, and unorganized. Homer was no green pea to the industry, however. He had been doing this for about fifteen years and was never a top producer but certainly earned an average, consistent living.

Homer had literally no marketing plan; at least I thought there was no plan. One day Homer and I started talking about marketing and the business in general. He told me that he did indeed have a marketing plan. Really. He said, *"Showing up early to customer meetings is my marketing plan."* Okay, I'm listening, Homer. "Jim, I personally see the customer twice at the most, once when I first meet with them, and once when we complete the deal. I put my best foot forward during those two face-to-face meetings. Their perception of me is based on those two meetings, mostly. Yes, I need to produce a result. And yes, I need to get them a loan at the end of a day. But you I and both know that once the loan is originated and the deal points are resolved, the processing team does most of the work. I just let them do it."

Showing up early. "I get to where I need to be about fifteen minutes ahead of time, without fail. When I arrive at the meeting location, I get myself sorted out for a few minutes. Then, at almost exactly seven minutes before the agreed-upon meeting time, I enter the office. Let's assume we are meeting at the customer's office. The receptionist usually has me wait in the lobby or puts me in the conference room. Then, she rings my client. Receptionist says, 'Hi, Client, Mr. Homer from DowntheRiver Lending is here.' Wow, he is early. By being on time (and even a little early), am I not demonstrating, right from the get-go, that I am a reliable person?" *Win number one.*

The customer is late. "I sit quietly and wait for my client. I don't fidget or hammer at my phone or scramble for this or this. I just sit there and quietly wait, and wait, and wait. Nine times out of ten, the client walks into the meeting three to eight minutes late. Normally, this is considered on time, but given the fact that the client knows I was there five minutes early, he or she is now feeling a little guilty that I have been waiting for almost ten minutes. Because of that, he or she almost always apologizes for being late. I graciously let him or her off the hook and naturally tell him or her that it's no problem at all. I'm no psychologist, but there is something about someone apologizing before you start a business meeting. The apologizing party just seems to be more agreeable and pleasant than normal." *Win number two.*

Leading the meeting. "Because I am early and the customer is late, I can just *feel* that the customer is unusually receptive to me. I know I am beginning the meeting—leading the meeting." *Win number three.*

Blank sheet of paper. "Jim, you know me a little. I'm not that organized. I spent years trying to prepare all kinds of 'stuff' for meetings.

Half the time I was late to the meeting trying to prepare my stuff; some of the time my stuff was only half done; and the remainder of the time I forgot to bring my stuff altogether. Forget all that. The only thing I bring with me now is a blank pad of paper. A brand new white pad of paper, fresh with the top virgin sheet standing at attention. I sit there quietly waiting in the office with my blank pad of paper at the ready, pen in hand, prepared to write down the important information that the customer is going to tell me (as if this is the first time I have heard it). What does that say to the customer? Possibly that I am interested, that I am courteous, that I care what they have to say, that I am organized, that I am efficient. Maybe they think some of that, maybe none of that, and maybe they are thinking other things. Whatever they think, they know one thing for certain: they have my complete attention and I'm ready to go. They are the most important thing in my life at that moment." *Win number four.*

Another advantage of the pad of paper. "By bringing along just a single pad of paper, what else could that be saying to the customer? Could the customer be thinking, 'Wow, why doesn't this guy have anything with him? He is either really dumb (or possibly unprepared); or maybe, just maybe, so confident in his abilities that he is able to handle things off the top of his head.' Jim, I really don't know, all I can tell you is when I only bring myself and my pen and my paper (and my calculator too), I am 100 percent in the game and focused on my customer." *Win number five.*

"Let's go back a couple of steps," says Homer. "Okay, Homer, I'm with you," says Jim.

My appearance. "I don't overdo it, but I'm clean and my clothes are clean. I modify my dress so that I am dressing only slightly, ever so slightly, above their (the clients') level. Too much differential is bad. I want them to feel comfortable but at the same time know that I respect the meeting (and them) as a business meeting. If they are in flip-flops and I'm in a tie, I find that makes them (and me) feel uncomfortable. But if they are a level-seven dresser, then I show up as an eight. I have to guess a lot, so I always guess one point high. By conforming to their environment, I believe I am respecting their environment (and them) and putting them at ease. *Win number six.*

"Okay, Homer, now that makes sense to me why you are always dressed differently day to day," says Jim.

The conversation continues and Homer and I are getting hungry, so we continue the meeting at the five-star restaurant next door, Goal Line Taco Shop.

Let's review the scoreboard. "Jim, I haven't even said a word yet, and I have already scored six points with the customer. Yes, I did. I'm telling you, I did! Let's review them. The customer may think that I am reliable; I am meeting the customer when he or she is in an agreeable mood; the customer is open to me; the customer knows he or she is the most important thing in my life at that moment; the customer knows that he or she has my complete attention; the customer does not see any clutter on me or around me; he or she sees I am clean and professional and that I respected him or her by conforming to his or her environment and dress."

"Homer, I don't know if you *really* scored all those points," says Jim.

"Well, maybe not, but it's better than me racing in fifteen minutes, hair on fire, unorganized, with three armfuls of crap to show them, having to excuse myself ten minutes into the meeting because in the panic of it all I forgot to go to the bathroom, and then when I return from the bathroom, my zipper is down and toilet paper is stuck to both my mustache and the bottom of my shoe," says Homer.

"Okay, you might have a point," says Jim.

The meeting. "The meeting starts. Nothing fancy happens here. I simply take notes and ask questions. Jim, you and I both know I'm not smart enough or slick enough to know what to say or how to say things the right way most of the time, so I just take notes and ask some questions. If you have done a few dozen loans, there are only a handful of questions that happen anyway. What is the rate? What are the costs? What are the terms? How much paperwork do you want from me? Do I qualify? Can you get it done? And when can you get it done? There are really only a handful of pertinent things that need to be addressed. But you would think I am writing a novel. I would walk out of that room with a good solid five pages of chicken scratch. 'Wow, he is thorough!' *My winning streak continues.*

"Jim, don't fall asleep from those six tacos you just ate—we have a few more things to discuss," says Homer.

"Okay, I'm here (barely)," says Jim.

Marketing budget. "Jim, how much did you spend on marketing last year?" asks Homer.

"Hmm, roughly $100K," says Jim.

"Do you know how much I spent on marketing last year?"

"No, how much, Homer?"

"One hundred thirty-eight dollars, and most of that was spent on business cards that the office made me buy. I know $100K works for you, Jim, but $138 works for me. This year I have increased my budget to $150. Now, with a budget to $150 per year, I have to get the most out of my opportunities. My biggest opportunities are when I am face to face with my customers. That's why I am so thoughtful about those meetings, both before the transaction and after the transaction."

Marketing is about generating your next piece of business. "Jim, remember, marketing is about producing more business from referrals. Who wants people calling you off the streets? If they called you, then they also called ten other people. Forget that. Marketing is about generating more business from people you know, preferably from clients, but if that doesn't work, then anyone that you know could possibly send you a referral.

"When my clients refer me to one of their friends, are they not taking a risk? Of course they are. Anything could happen. There are a lot of moving parts to a real estate transaction. Things get squirrelly from time to time. Let's reverse it. When you send a referral, do you not think twice? Wow, I am 95 percent confident with my CPA and would love to refer him to my good friend Wayne, but wow, what if something weird happens? Is that going to affect my relationship with Wayne? It could. It's possible. That is why a referral is a *huge* compliment. The referring party has to be confident that the vendor will be a stand-up person when (not if) things get squirrely."

Homer gets to the point. "So, back to my story, Jim. I want my customers to refer me to their family and friends. So I show up early, I'm ready, I'm clean, I'm organized, I'm attentive. All this communicates professionalism, but more importantly, it communicates *they can count on me.* No, not to be perfect, just to be a stand-up person. If they can count on me, they will refer me. If they can't count on me, they will not refer me. Simple as that. Everything I do (namely those two face-to-face meetings) is designed around sending this subtle message of 'Mr. and Mrs. Customer, I am a stand-up person; you can count on me, *all the time.*' You can make a small fortune in this business if enough people can count on you. Jim, I could spend $200K yearly on advertising, but if they cannot count on me, they will not send me a single referral."

A simple marketing plan from a simple guy—thank you, Homer.

Go get 'em!

22

Competition

———◆———

This above all—to thine own self be true.

SHAKESPEARE

I LOVE THIS TOPIC OF competition—and it's not where you might be thinking we are heading. I am writing this chapter on a Wednesday, and on the previous Monday I spoke with a colleague on this very topic. She was frustrated over how competitive it has become to secure good listings.

The world is competitive. But for me, how many times have I really "convinced" someone to do business with me? They did business with me because they wanted to do business with me. They did business with you because they wanted to do business with you. And in the future, the same will apply.

How do people make a decision on a real estate professional? Is this person capable and do I like him or her? Well, there are lots of people that are capable. How in the world are we going to differentiate ourselves in an industry that is filled with capable people? Literally, day two in my real estate career, the top dog in the office said to me, "Your customers will eventually look like you do." I don't know if he meant physically look like I do, but certainly he meant they will share similar core values and talk, walk, and act like me (figuratively). Even though I was green as a pea at that point, I understood. *To thine own self be true.*

We are constantly chasing deals, getting frustrated. I believe the following statement with every bit of my being: *"largely, the deals we are losing we never had a chance to begin with."* I'm guessing and saying that 90 percent of the time, customers know who they want to do business with. They go through the process of talking to several people because they feel they need to go through the process of talking to several people. Period! They know. You know most of the time when you are hiring somebody to complete a task. You might talk to a few people, but you know; if this works out and that works out, I would like to use So-and-So. Based on my experience, roughly 90 percent of real estate customers *know* who they want to do business with. That leaves 10 percent of the market that truly has an open mind—brain damage! Are you kidding?

Now, back to my friend.

She is a great real estate agent, very capable and friendly; I would hire her to list my own house, which is the highest compliment I could pay anyone in real estate. She is going out on appointments that are the 10 percent. Guaranteed, I know her. Practically her whole day is filled with brain damage associated with attacking this 10 percent, contacting them, convincing them to give her a shot, preparing for the meeting, going to the meeting, and then dealing with the rejection of not getting the business. "Well, Jim, I'm a pro and I don't get my feelings hurt." Are you from another planet? This is hard on our psyche. I know. I used to do it—a lot!

"So, Jim, how do I grow my business if 90 percent of the people already know?" I said 10 percent don't know—and actually I believe it's more like 5 percent. I didn't say that you couldn't build your business from the 90 percent. "Hey, Steve, anyone you know that is going to be moving soon and needs some help?" Yes, great. "Any chance you could make that intro for me?" Yes, great. Now I'm talking with Amy through Steve. There is no guarantee that Amy is in the 10 percent. She might be a 90 percent type personality. You contact her, you stay in touch with her, you build a relationship with her, and you naturally end up doing business with her. Amy is now in the 90 Percent Club and knows who she wants—you. "So, Jim, you are saying do business with 100 percent referrals or close to it?" For heaven's sakes, yes! You will dig yourself a quick grave if you focus on the 10 percent. *That's how I did so much business in a short period of time when I started.* Okay, okay. Yes, I attacked the 10 percent as well. I went after everything. Hey, I was scared and was in attack mode early on, but I hardly got any of those deals. Maybe I got 5 to 20 percent of those deals—one in ten—brain damage. Did I say brain damage? Instead, the vast majority was coming from referrals from lots and lots of people. I generated referrals from people that I had never done business with. I was so excited, scared, and energetic about it, I guess they just figured I knew what I was doing—ha!

If you decide to market to the 10 percent, I can almost guarantee you that will you be spending 70 percent (plus) of the marketing time, and money, on that small little group. Remember the eighty-twenty rule. Why not dump it and focus that 70 percent of your time on people that you know—people that are giving you 90 percent of your business? "Well, Jim, I will run out of people and contacts." That's valid. Get creative. There is always something else you can do. Nothing is staying the same, everything is moving and changing. Figure out a way that you can stay in touch both individually and collectively with people, and grow that group. I am not saying hand out recipes. You are a pro, be a pro. Stay within the real estate industry. Find a way to add value to people's lives in an industry where they only need our services every five to ten years.

Attack the 90 percent.

Go get 'em!

23

Bread and Butter Play

———◆———

*If I were again beginning my studies, I would follow
the advice of Plato and start with mathematics.*

GALILEO

ILEFT A STEADY TECHNOLOGY job to enter the exciting world of real
estate. My family consisted of my beautiful wife, three-year-old
daughter, one on the way, and me. We had just bought a home a few
months before I resigned from my steady job, producing some sleep-
less nights for my father-in-law. I had technically resigned from my
job, so there was no severance package; the safety net had been fully
retracted. It was a bit of gut check—but I was ready.

I had been carefully watching several of my friends in lending and
brokerage for a couple of years. I was pretty confident I could do it,
and I knew (for sure) that I would work like a dog to make it happen.
But I needed a *bread and butter play* nonetheless, something tangible
that I could lean on, a competitive edge of sorts. I found it in the
HP12C. Yes, the calculator. Ho-hum, boring—hear me out.

Five months before I started full time, I started studying. How? You
know the user guide that comes with most calculators and electronics,
the one that we all throw away? That one. I literally studied it page by

page. I can tell you with all honesty, I truly became an expert before I ever did my first deal. The more I studied, the more I enjoyed it. My confidence was brimming. I was dealing with loans at the time, so I could analyze a real estate deal upside down, inside out, in a nanosecond. It didn't matter what question the customer asked me; I immediately brought the conversation back to the numbers. "Hey, Jim, what would happen if I pay double now, but then just pay the regular payment while my kids are in college, and then pay double again for five years—what would be the loan balance?" Bam, done. "Here's the answer, Mrs. Customer."

I know "floor time" is a thing of the past in most cases, but at that time we still did some floor time. I would pick up one deal every week or so just from floor time. I was almost excited to do it because I knew where I was going to take the conversation every single time. It was easy. The customer didn't have a chance. They could figure out within about a minute that I knew the math; I simply took the lead and led. They followed. Why not? Isn't that why they called to begin with? To talk with someone that knows what in the heck they are talking about? Of course. From time to time I would even have a colleague rush over to me in a panic as he or she put a client on hold and say something to the effect of, "Jim, take this call, I don't know what in the world they are asking me. Handle it and we'll split it if it happens."

I know that all sounds a little braggadocious. I am saying this to help. I believe it's our job to know the math both as a lender and real estate agent. We are dealing with numbers both on the financial and brokerage side of a real estate transaction. This is by far the largest personal business transaction that someone completes in a lifetime. Should we not be fully equipped to help them? Possess the skills to answer their questions. Trust me, you become an expert at the math, you will separate yourself from the pack.

When I switched from lending to brokerage, I used this skill to produce large amounts of business in a short period of times; Silicon Valley is littered with bright people; a master's degree is common place within many companies. The customer base knows when someone is trying to fake it. I have been asked countless times something to the effect of, "Jim, how in the world did you do so much business that first year as a real estate agent?" I worked hard. In addition, I made a conscious decision to use that skill as a competitive weapon. We would talk about all the things that you need to talk about as a real estate agent—paperwork, comps, construction, open houses, etc.—and then I would whip out my HP12C and shift the conversation to the math. I knew that very few people would be talking about the math and had the financial skills to adequately help the customer in this area. So I used that to my advantage and to the customer's advantage. I know real estate agents, successful real estate agents that have been in the business for over twenty years, that can't determine a mortgage payment. Okay, who am I to make an indictment on someone that is successful? I'm simply saying that I did a ton of business (both as a lender and real estate agent) from my ability to know that HP12C inside and out.

Think about it this way. Let's say a basic home requires ten tons of concrete to build the foundation (I have no idea, let's just play pretend and say it's ten tons). What if you made the foundation wider and deeper and used twenty tons of concrete? Would it possibly be stronger? More resilient to bad weather? Last longer? I can hear the structural engineer now—"Well, Jim, that is not exactly correct." But you know what I mean. My dad has reminded me countless times, "Build your base deep and wide so you can handle the occasional setback." Coach Reardon would say as paraphrased, "It all starts with the base. If the base is strong, then you are strong; base is broken, you are broken."

In my view, the math is the base—or, at the very least, it's one of the most important ingredients of the base. It's a foundational component of the job. If you are feeling something is off for one reason or another, you may want to assess your financial skills. The good news is that it is a skill—not a God-given talent. I completed my MBA before I started in the real estate business. There was relatively no correlation between my education and what I learned in that HP12C user guide. Anyone can learn. Just put in the work and separate yourself from the pack—and in doing so you will likely improve your personal production and the industry as a whole.

Go get 'em!

24

Broaden the Base

A valuable principle of life is not to be
too addicted to any one thing.

TERENCE

FIND TEN GREAT REAL ESTATE agents and "schmooze" them. That's roughly what I was told when I started in lending as a green pea. What if I can't find ten that want to do business with me? And what if it takes me two years to build those relationships? What do I do for income in the meantime? What if I can only find three? And what if one of them gets mad at me? What if all of them get mad at me?

So off I went, finding these ten golden-goose real estate agents. Someone gave me some tapes on how to do it, so I listened. Send this letter this day, call this day, drop by this day, and on and on. I remember it like yesterday. I stayed at work all night one night trying to load all these prospects into the computer, then do a mail merge (whatever that was), then print—it was a mess. This went on for three months, with no progress to speak of, no love from my real estate agent golden-goose prospects. I even had real estate agent friends; they knew I was in the lending business now, and no love from them either. Everyone said, "It will take time, all great things take time, blah blah." Now it's month number six, no results, and I had followed the instructions almost without exception. That was it; I'd had enough of Happy Sam's Real Estate Agent Marketing Program.

It's important to note that during that six-month period, I stumbled onto a lot of business through my friends, my network, floor time, and some luck. So it's not like I wasn't producing, but in my mind, I was only filling time until the real estate agent people started sending me carloads of business.

Okay, Jim, you need a new plan. I had a meeting with myself. I studied the industry again and decided that I gave up my steady-pay-check job for lots of reason, but two of them, and they were at the top of list, were *freedom* and *control*. I felt like a hostage to these soon-to-be (currently invisible) real estate agent people (don't forget, I was one of them later on). These ten phantom people were in control of my career, my income, and the success of my family. The more I thought about it, the less sense it made to me. So, I have to base my entire success in this industry around ten people? Hmmm. They (whoever *they* were, because they hadn't sent me a single deal so far) get to dictate my income, my business, my future? I don't think so.

I made a decision to never be too reliant on any one source of business again. *Look at the quote at the beginning of this chapter.* If something didn't work out, no big deal, the ship sails anyway. If Carol Standtall the real estate agent didn't send me a single deal that year, no problem. If my direct-mail piece didn't work out, it was just a hiccup. If my family didn't send me a single deal for eight months, I'd survive. If my display ad campaign didn't produce a lead, I was strong anyway. If my past customers didn't have any leads for me that year, I was still kicking butt. If my college friends didn't need help at the moment, I was growing anyway. If my speaking engagements produced nothing in the last year, I enjoyed it nonetheless. If floor time produced a big goose egg last month, I didn't even break a stride. Make numbers your friend. *Broaden the base.* Lots of sources of business are good. Never again! Never again was I going to be too reliant on any one person or grouping of people to drive the revenue line of my business.

Broaden the base. This one marketing concept can save your business in this business. Make numbers your friend. Multiple sources of leads are good. Think of it as a chair with ten legs in support. All 10 legs are naturally sources of business. Now envision all ten of those legs all having roughly equal strength. Now, remove three of the legs. The chair is still strong. But what if one leg is ten times stronger than all the others? And what if you remove that single strong leg? Would the chair survive? Maybe. The chair would be severely wounded—for sure.

When you are building a business, you are building it for strength, speed, and endurance. When you are launching a career in lending or brokerage, you are doing that exact same thing, except with fewer personnel. As an aside, if you have enough lead flow, you can hire people to help you with operations. So building a strong real estate business is largely about lead generation and, more specifically, *broad-based lead generation.* Be thoughtful about that. Small, medium, and large companies crash and burn yearly because of this lopsided deal-flow model. They lose one big customer, and they are crushed. Don't be that person; keep control over the business and broaden your base.

"Commerce with all nations, alliance with none, should be out motto"—*Thomas Jefferson.* Multiple sources of leads are good.

Go get 'em!

25

Set the Date

———◆———

Force has no place where there is need of skill.

HERODOTUS

IT WILL BE WORTH YOUR while to read this chapter twice. I am going to blend two concepts together in this section, incremental psychology and lead follow-up. This chapter will make you money. I will guarantee little—but I'm telling you, you can make money from this chapter. Let's go.

First, let me set up a real-world problem or opportunity so that I have your attention. You are competing head to head against a competitor. It's a dead heat. The customer is honestly torn—the score is 50 to 50. It could go either way. There is a $20,000 commission on the line, depending on who gets hired. The customer is stuck—you need to get him or her to move in your direction.

Okay, is that good? Change the economics to your economics if you prefer. Maybe your average deal is $5,000, maybe it's $100,000, so change it. Either way, that's a real-world problem/opportunity. Win two or three (or more) of those per year, and you change your performance for the year. *So let me teach you how to win.*

A customer is a customer and a lead is a lead. A customer has made a commitment; a lead has not made a commitment. So in this section we are dealing with a lead that we would like to convert to a customer.

When you are doing lead follow-up and trying to convert a lead to a customer, you need to maintain control and *set the date.* You must take 100 percent responsibility for the conversation. *Never leave it up to your prospect to take that next step.* If you do, you are dead.

Here is the right way to do it. "Okay, Sue, sounds good, I'll buzz you tomorrow to get you that information about title insurance." I set the date. "Okay, Steve, I'll drive that comp tomorrow and get back to you with feedback." I set the date. "Okay, Stan, great meeting you and Esther yesterday. I'll call you tomorrow with more information on that insurance question that you had." I set the date. *You tell them* the next step. You tell them what is going to happen next. You set the date with them. Never leave the conversation hanging.

Here is what not to do. "Thank you for your time yesterday, Steve, I'll be around if you have any more questions." No date. "It was great meeting you yesterday, Kim. I'm happy to give you more information if you need it." No date. "It was so good seeing you yesterday, Armando. I'm so excited, and please, please let me know what else I can do to earn your business." No date. "I really enjoyed spending time with you yesterday, Bill. Any more questions?" No date. Those are nice things to say. But those are also dead-end statements. Where do you go from there? Nowhere. You just lost control of the conversation.

When you do it right, *you are setting a date.* Just like a date when you were dating. No, maybe not exactly the same, but you are setting an expectation that you will be talking again soon, very soon. "I really enjoyed spending time with you yesterday, Bill. Any more questions?" No date. "Okay, Steve, I'll drive that comp tomorrow and get back to you with feedback." Steve and I have a date tomorrow.

It's a fine-line distinction, but it's the difference between winning and losing when you are in a neck-and-neck battle. I'll let you take a minute and digest that while we digress.

Incremental psychology. One of my business friends told me about this concept in the late 1990s. He actually just said it in passing one day: incremental psychology. Still to this day, I have done little reading on the subject, but I understood what it meant (for me) the second he said it. I asked him to back up, and we talked about it. "Jim, I literally use this concept daily in business." He was a senior executive at a publicly traded technology firm at the time. "Jim, once I learned this concept, I became a better businessperson." Donald Trump indicated in one of his books that he pays attention to "momentum" daily. Well, my friend pays attention to "incremental psychology" every day.

What do you think it means (to you)?

"Hi, Mrs. Jones, can I have a penny?" She seems like a nice lady, so Mrs. Jones gives her a penny. The next time she asked for a dime. Wow again, but it's only a dime after all. The next time it's a dollar, and the next it's ten. The commitment was small, and now it's bigger and growing. And you have just made four separate commitments. The level and frequency are growing. Now they are up to $100. Would Mrs. Jones have given the nice lady $100 if she had asked for that amount from the beginning? Maybe, but unlikely. But by the time they arrived at the $100 level, Mrs. Jones and the lady had a relationship, and Mrs. Jones had already made *multiple and progressively larger commitments* to the lady.

Back to lead follow-up and converting the lead to a customer. When you are in control (not in a controlling way) of the conversation, you are asking the customer (in a gentle, helpful way) to make multiple and progressively larger commitments to you. Simple. And for you supercreative types, you'll love it because you can utilize all those creative juices that are running around in your head 24/7 to keep the conversation moving.

You'll figure how to do it over time. But for now, I'll give you a tip to get you going. A real estate transaction is serious business; there is a lot money involved for the customer, and there are tons of moving parts. Listen, shhhhhhhhhhhh, listen. Plato says, "Wise men speak because they have something to say, fools because they have to say something." There will be some things that your prospect brings up that you won't be able to fully and adequately answer right on the spot. *That is your moment.* That is your moment to set the date. That is your opportunity to continue the conversation. It could be something supersmall or superbig; either way it's fine. Set the date. Trust me, your competitor is going to let it die by saying something to the effect of, "I am so glad we talked and I enjoyed meeting you. I'm here for you, I really want to work for you, and I think I can do an amazing job and help to produce a great result, so please let me know if you have any more questions." Dead end. While he or she just ended the conversation, you are continuing it.

Once you learn and believe in this concept, it's not even a fair fight anymore. You are playing with bigger, more powerful knowledge, know-how, and machinery. It's like a major leaguer playing with a high schooler now.

Here is a personal example. I was competing on a listing with another real estate agent. We were both referrals. It was a neck-and-neck battle. Both of us had already made listing presentations. I knew that staging and all the dynamics thereof were important to the prospect. So I called later that day (actually I called as I was driving back to the office) and suggested that I would be happy to send over a stager to take a look, no obligation, and they could hire the stager independent of hiring me. *This is key:* I told the clients that I would follow up after they met with the stager (set the date). They agreed and met with the stager (without me). I followed up to see how it went, as I said that I would do. They decided that they couldn't afford the stager and they would do it themselves. That's fine, I said, I would be happy to come over and give them an opinion on some staging ideas in that case; no obligation (set the date). They agreed. I went and did my thing. They still weren't ready to commit, but at that point they made two additional commitments to me (while at the same time I was helping them move the process forward). I met with them to give them my personal opinion on staging. While I was there I gently reminded them of how important good curb appeal can be to the end result. I also said that I would be happy to send my tune-up landscaper guy over to take a look, no obligation. They agreed. I said that I would get back to them with a time and date (set the date). I called them back, set a time, and gently said that I would be happy to attend to give them my personal opinion on curb appeal (set the date), no obligation, of course. They agreed. We all met at the property and had a good meeting. I said I would get back to them the next day with the landscaper's proposal (set the date). I called the next day, at which time they decided to hire me. *I was having this ongoing conversation with them while my competitor was waiting around for a decision.*

The action of lead follow-up is to set the date, and the concept (behind the action) is incremental psychology. Sometimes the customers will just be ready to go. Fine. Get the contract signed and move forward. Sometimes the customer is stuck and you need to get from point A to point Z in tiny baby steps. In those cases, ask the customer for *multiple and progressively larger commitments* along the way until such time as they are comfortable with hiring you!

You got this.

Go get 'em!

26

Strategy to Stay in Touch

Slow but steady wins the race.

AESOP

How do we *STAY IN touch* with clients that need our services only every ten years or so for real estate and possibly five years for loans? How do we do it without "bugging them"? Additionally, most of us live within the same community in which we work, so how do we generate leads and add value to people (customers) that we literally see at the grocery store daily—awkward at times. I think this is an area that many of us struggle with from time to time. Furthermore, let's be honest. When you get busy, do you really call your clients religiously to stay in touch? Are there times when you are not consistent on mailing something to them? Yeah, me too.

A little love/stay in touch will go a long way. In the mid-1990s I started giving to a nonprofit that did outreach to high school and college students. I met with the founder, loved what they were doing, and made this part of my monthly giving budget. Every month or two, they would send a newsletter and an envelope to send money. I was happy to be a donor; in fact, I looked forward to the newsletter. One year went by, then two years. No call, no e-mail, no stay in touch. Another five years went by; my feelings were a little hurt but I kept giving. No call, no handwritten note, and no e-mail. At that time, I became reacquainted with some college teammates and was intrigued with a nonprofit related to college athletics. The group made me feel wanted and needed, and I moved nearly my entire giving budget to that cause, and increased it. Honestly, if the high school-college group had done anything to show me just a little love, I would have doubled or tripled my budget years ago. Possibly a good stay-in-touch lesson.

Now, back to real estate. At my technology job out of college, we were on e-mail before anyone even knew what e-mail was. Depending on what kind of mood I happened to be in at the time, I would have my real estate database as low as 150 and as high as 1,300. I mailed, called, wrote notes, advertised, you name it (with the exception of door knocking). I did it all in an attempt to *stay in touch*. But regardless of the method of stay-in-touch marketing I did, I struggled with consistency and intimacy; actually intimacy more than consistency. Because, back to the high school group for a moment, they were very consistent but not intimate. So, one day, I pulled out my list and started e-mailing people.

"Hey, Ruth, was thinking about you guys, drove by your place the other day looking at a listing on Echo Drive—hope you guys are well. Jim."

"Hi, Mike, hope your dad is doing well. Always here if you have real estate questions. Jim."

"Hey, Steve, hope it all worked out on the landscaping. Always here if you have questions. Jim."

"Hey, Jack, did it work out with the contractor that I referred to you? Hope so. Let me know if you need anything. Jim."

"Hey, Melinda, did that property line issue get resolved? Please lean on me if you need me. Jim."

"Hey, Don, I know you said a couple of years until you are ready to move. Just to keep you posted, here is one that sold nearby. Here if you need me. Jim."

"Hey, Steven, glad your refi is complete. I'll contact you when rates drop again. Call if you need me. Please say hi to Lori for me. Jim."

"Hey, John, I'll let you know when it makes sense to consider moving from a 5/1 ARM to the thirty-year fixed. Call if you need me. Jim."

I had two rules on sending these e-mails: 1) it had to be personal to them only; 2) it had to be somehow, some way, related to real estate. When I started doing this, it was magic because I was having an ongoing conversation (through e-mail) with one hundred to two hundred people all at once. I did it in the morning when I was fresh and my creative juices were flowing. Be honest, be creative, be interesting, but be professional. Hey, who am I to say that passing out recipes and handing out pumpkins is a bad thing? It just never was right for me. And can you imagine my high school coach calling me to say hi as I'm passing out pumpkins?

"Hey, Jimmy, how are you doing?" says Coach.

"Great, Coach, I'm at work walking around handing out pumpkins," says me.

"Ohhhhh, thaaaaat's interesting, Jimmy. Is everything okay with you? By the way, what is this pumpkin thing? I thought you were a big-shot real estate guy," says Coach.

"Yeah, Coach, no, it's fine, it's just what we do. Hold on, I need to fill up my basket with more pumpkins, stand by," says me.

"Throw those pumpkins away and do something else to get business," says Coach.

"Okay (thank God)," says me.

Frankly, the unedited version was much funnier, but I decided to error on the side of caution! Pumpkins! Just not for me. That's fine if it works for someone else, not for me. We are in real estate. We are experts in one of the largest personal (or business) transactions that a person will complete in a lifetime. What does a pumpkin have to do with lending? What is the correlation between a recipe and title and escrow? It's fine, if that's what you want to do. Hey, this is America, home of the free-to-hand-out pumpkins. Cool. Just not for me. There are literally thousands of value-added topics that we could be talking about (*to stay in touch*) that are relevant to the real estate transaction. Get creative. Be a pro. Stay in your wheelhouse and out of the pumpkin patch.

Does the customer know we are staying in touch for a reason, that we have ulterior motives? Come on. This is business, of course. You can be sincere, do your job, stay in touch, and market all at the same time. Think about it this way: Have you ever been asked to attend a sporting event by a vendor, so you are the customer in this case? Do you think they invited you because they simply love you? Don't you think they would have rather brought their son or daughter or spouse or close friend? They want to show you some attention. They want to *stay in touch with you*. They want to stay in front of you. We are doing the same thing with an e-mail (or text, if you prefer). It's a personal interchange between two people, not some blanket boilerplate ad; it's intimate and specific to your craft—real estate.

People like the attention; they like to feel that they are special enough that we took the time to reach out. I wouldn't consider my financial person a life-long buddy outside of the business that we do together; I do like him, however, and enjoy his company. In this case, I'm the customer and he is the service provider. When he calls to ask me to attend a dinner or have lunch or just to say hi, it makes me feel good. I do recognize it's business for him, but frankly I like the attention. We all like a little "sucking up to" every once in a while. Like Richard Gere says in the movie *Pretty Woman*, "We are going to need a lot more help *sucking up to us*, because we are going to be spending an obscene amount of money in this store."

Do a short swallow on your pride and ego. Stay in touch; show your clients, friends, and family some attention and love; and watch your business explode.

Go get 'em!

27

When the Customer Is Ready

———◆———

Everything is plainer when spoken than unspoken.

SOCRATES

ILISTED A HOME; I placed an ad in the local paper and a resident from that same community called and wanted to see it. The buyer did not have a real estate agent and ended up buying the property, so, yes, I represented both parties in that case. All good, right? Here comes the bad part—and also the lesson.

I quickly formed a pleasant relationship with the buyers and everything was just dandy. The buyers owned another home that they wanted sold after moving into the new one. Great. They softly mentioned/asked me to list their home, first on Tuesday, then again on Thursday. Mr. Cool (that was me) was noncommittal, busy, busy, slightly aloof to the request, "glowing," distracted with other stuff, and was planning on getting around to it when he was ready, which was Monday. Too late, bud. By Saturday, they were getting nervous, so they called around to their friends, got a couple of names of real estate agents, and had it listed by Sunday night—$30K, poof, gone. Painful.

I thought they knew that I wanted to list their house. No. I didn't speak those exact words—but I thought they knew nonetheless.

Everything is plainer when spoken than unspoken. And by the way, in this case, everything is more profitable when spoken than unspoken.

To be fair to myself, I was a little swamped trying to do a good job on their deal and several others. I was planning on working like crazy through Saturday, taking a breather on Sunday, and starting to work on their listing on Monday. Well, my plan was not their plan. *They were ready to do business.* Both the husband and wife told me, independent of one another, "Jim, you were our first choice; we honestly thought that you were not interested." I'm dying a slow death as I'm hearing this.

We have to be ready when the customer is ready. In retrospect, I could have taken one hour out of "my busy schedule" on Tuesday or Wednesday just to get the process moving. That would have made the customer very happy and we would have locked in the business. Think about it this way. Has this happened to you on taking loans or listings or buyers? You are on vacation and slightly difficult to reach. Your client is ready to do business. You come back to work and start moving through e-mails and voicemails. And the conversation goes something like this:

"Hi Client, thanks for the call, supersorry for the delay, I was on vacation, but *I'm back in action* and happy to help you on financing," says Jim.

"Ummmmmmmm, hi, Jim, I feel terrible but I needed to get things going, so I already started the process with Johnny at Happycurbside Lending," says Client.

"Uhhhh," says Jim.

"Yeah, you know how it is, Jim, but I still love ya," says Client.

"Uhhhh," says Jim.

"Yeah, but for sure I'm going to get you on the next one, for sure, promise. You da man and I hope you had a good vacation," says Client.

"Uhhhh, okay, thanks for thinking of me, Client," says Jim, as he is feeling quite nauseated at this point and is ready to hurl one in the trash can under his desk.

"Well, Jim, my clients *always* wait for me." I don't think so. If you have been in this business for more than three minutes, you have had something like this happen. Why? Because...

The customer is ready to do business—ideally with you, but if not with you, then someone else will do. Be ready to jump *when the customer is ready*—and tell him or her clearly and plainly that you accept the job.

Go get 'em!

28

Clean House

———◆———

Business prosperity requires consistent diligence in
upgrading systems, employees, and customers.

A BUSINESS FRIEND

M Y DATABASE RANGED FROM ONE hundred to thirteen hundred
people, just depending on the mood I happened to be in at the
time. There were years when I would wake up one morning and say,
"That's it, I only want AAA names in my database, no more than one
hundred fifty." Then, there were times when I said to myself, "But what
if So-and-So needs to do business? He'll forget about me if I don't mail
or call or e-mail him," so I would expand, expand, expand. After talking with colleagues about this topic, up and down is pretty normal. We
get bored and want to shake it up; there is nothing wrong with that. In
fact, shaking it up usually reinvigorates us and our production.

First, who should go into your database? Past customers, people
you think could become customers, and people that you think may
refer business. That gives you a broad runway in which to work. It also
gives you the latitude to make life decisions and eliminate names from
the list. For instance, my wife and I own a dance school. Naturally, the
customer base knows my name even though I'm not around every day.
From afar, this looks like a great target market for my real estate business. There were some rare exceptions, but I never felt comfortable

doing "crossover marketing" into that business. My real estate colleagues told me all the time that I was crazy; I just wouldn't do it. I didn't want to dilute the dance school or the real estate business. So I kept them separate. I also coached a lot over the years. That was purely in my fun bucket, so I did not market to this group. Those are personal decisions that I made—for me. *Let's read the above definition of a database again:* 1) past customers, 2) people you think could become customers, and 3) people that you think may refer business. This will give you tremendous freedom and flexibility. Yes, I know. Some people might advise placing every living soul on the planet that you know in your database. That's up to you. I'll stand by my recommendation because it gives you freedom to make business decisions on a case-by-case basis.

Your database is a moving, breathing entity. It has a heartbeat all its own. If you are smart, you are looking at it and working on it daily. If your database is healthy, your business will be healthy. If your database is wounded, your business will suffer.

Let's be real. Are there times when we neglect our database? For sure; call me a guilty party. During those moments, we need to jump back in and *clean house.* Look at these moments as an opportunity to *upgrade your customer base.* Find out who is in and who is out. Every time you clean house, you are upgrading and improving your business. It's an attitude as well as a business reality.

Recommendation for cleaning house: Start sending everyone in your database an e-mail blast weekly; do this for eight weeks straight. Trust me, the skies will open, the dust will be gone, and the cobwebs wiped away. Some people will say, "So glad to hear from you, good stuff." Others will say, "Please remove me from the list." Celebrate either response. You will be reengaging with your fans, and also eliminating those folks that will *never* do business with you or refer business.

I know what you might be thinking; don't think it and don't worry. Your friends are your friends and will be your friends forever. You could send your *true friends* something daily for a whole year; they don't care.

There have been times (often) when I am purging my database and, frankly, I'm looking at the name on the list, and I have literally no idea who this person is. "How can that happen, Jim?" It happens. In those expansion phases, you are adding a whole bunch of people that you may be in contact with at that moment in time. That's how it happens. Clean house. Shake it up. There is no better feeling (well, maybe a couple) than removing twenty names from your database. It's a fresh start for you and your business. Cleaning house = upgrading your customer list = upgrading your business.

What else happens when you clean house? You generate business from all your AAA fans that you have neglecting for six months. *Correlate cleaning house with generating new business.* Have you ever purged your whole entire house and been shocked what you found? Twenty packages of unopened batteries; five brand new pairs of unopened scissors; five thousand unopened pens; fourteen shirts that you have never worn; and seventeen DVDs still in the wrapper. There is *gold* in them bushes—you need to trim the bushes to *see* the gold. Clean house.

Go get 'em!

29

Marketing versus Bragging

What a grand thing it is to be clever and have common sense.

TERENCE

VERY FEW PEOPLE IN THE world need to address business marketing on a daily basis. The average Joe has a paycheck job and doesn't need to deal with it regularly. A medium-sized business owner usually has a team that he or she can lean on to discuss marketing. In real estate, however, we are the vice president of marketing, and we are marketing *primarily ourselves*. Hi, I'm Carol, integrity is my vow. Hi, I'm Doug, you can trust me. Hi, I'm Cleve, I'll do you right. Hi, I'm Dave, experience is my thing. Hi, I'm Julie, I'm honest as a day is long. Hi, I'm Yael, I'm loyal and smart. Hi, I'm Jamie, I'm a great negotiator. Hi, I'm Shawn, I will help you win. Hi, I'm Rebecca, I'll fight for you. Hi, I'm Steven, I'll get it done. Hi, I'm Frank, I'll lead the way. Hi, I'm Mike, hire me and I'll do a cartwheel for you.

Real estate is a unique industry relevant to marketing. We are not marketing the processing speed of a computer or the efficiency of solar panels or the story of a movie. *We are marketing a service.* You can't reach out and grab what we have to offer. You can't take it off the shelf, put it in the trunk, and take it home. It's an intangible. So we need to paint the picture. We need to "write the story" for our target market, and possibly a different story for our past customers. After all, there is different messaging associated with, a) people that have already done business with us versus b) people we would like to do business with.

There is a fine line between good marketing and bragging. There is nothing worse than a bragger; someone who is bragging about their kids, about their job, about their money, about themselves, or about their business. At the same time, I admire those folks in real estate that are walking the tightrope between bragging and good marketing. They haven't yet done a belly flop into the pool of bragging, but pretty close. They have skillfully managed to send the message of "I'm your guy" or "I'm your girl" without saying that. That takes thoughtful intention, and frankly that takes a little skill as well.

I don't think I'm the only guy (or girl) that is uncomfortable with the "personal bragging" aspect of real estate. In fact, I believe it's a very small group that *is* comfortable with bragging.

Some real estate professionals market the team rather than the person. The Jalopy Team, consisting of Mr. Jalopy and his accountant. The Bentley Team, consisting of Mrs. Bentley and her dog. The Sonata Team, consisting of Mr. Sonata and his bookkeeper. The Ford Team, consisting of Mrs. Ford and her turtle. The Chevy Team, consisting of Mr. Chevy and his truck. The Impala Team, consisting of Mrs. Impala and her lender. The Rambler Team, consisting of Mr. Rambler and his cat. The Dodge Team, consisting of Mr. Dodge and his lizard. The Camaro Team, consisting of Mr. Camaro and his wheels. The Plymouth Team, consisting of Mrs. Plymouth and the one deal she did five years ago. I'm joking, of course, on the team names. In fact, if I were to go back and do it again, I would brand as a team even if I didn't have a team.

The team branding is good in many ways. We depersonalize it ever so slightly. We can market a person or a company. Hi, I'm Jim. I'm marketing Jim. Hi, I'm Coca-Cola. I am marketing a company called Coca-Cola. When you market a team in real estate, you are dancing somewhere in the middle. Everyone knows you are not a company, that's obvious. But at the same time, the word *team* has a tendency to communicate structure, stability, staff, and texture. So, good for the teams!

Many real estate professionals live in the same community in which they work. Okay. So how do you market (or borderline brag) in your own community? It's tricky. I talked this over with my real estate mentor when I entered brokerage. My mentor was still actively listing and selling homes at the time. When you are out and about in real estate, you get a feel for other agents. The reason I chose this one gentleman as my mentor is because I respected him. He was humble, low key, smart, and his clients trusted him. Actually, a man of few words, really, but what he did say, he made count. He was (is) a trusted businessperson in the community. I knew early on that I wanted to build my business model around his business model. We worked for different companies. We competed head to head many times, and frankly he won most of the time! But I took those opportunities to try and understand what the customer thought of him, his team, his brand, etc. *Trust* is the word that was always talked about. He was an avid marketer. But you would not call his marketing bragging. You would call it good marketing, consistent marketing, and professional marketing. He said to me early on, "Jim, I live in the same community in which I work. I never want to duck and hide when I see someone at the store. I want to be able to stand tall and not be embarrassed by my own marketing, so I'm careful on my messaging and content. Bragging is out for me. I come close, but I don't do it." He continued to tell me that he wanted people to call him because they trusted him to take care of business. They did; and he did.

A note on trust. Trust is a combination of being capable and doing the right thing. My mentor, for instance—people trusted him to take care of business. They also trusted him to do the right thing. The two go together and are rarely separated.

One final note on Skill. You will improve with time as a marketer. Experience will teach you a lot. Yes, there will be some people that have an instinct for it, but it's a learned skill nonetheless. You'll have to stumble your way through the bragging-versus-marketing mountains for a while. But know this: you'll improve with time. Give it some time. In the meantime, include lots of people in reviewing your marketing—your manager, colleagues, family, and friends.

You'll have to figure it out on your own regarding that fine line between bragging and good marketing. I'll leave you with a couple of questions on this topic. Do you want people to call you because they think you are the King Kong lender or the King Kong real estate agent? If they think of you as King Kong (or Kongess), can you sustain that required energy—day in day out—to maintain that image? Or do you want people to call you because you are a trusted member of the community? You answer that question for yourself. I know my answer. Whatever your answer is, make sure your marketing is consistent with your answer.

Go get 'em!

30

Speak

Men trust their ears less than their eyes.

HERODOTUS

WAKE UP LIKE A REGULAR person. Put your clothes on like a regular person. Eat breakfast like a regular person. Drive to work like a regular person. Enter the room like a regular person. But the second you take those two steps up the ramp and over to the podium, you are no longer Regular Joe or Regular Jill. You are Super Jill, the speaker, the orator for the moment, with supernatural powers. You are Super Joe, able to leap tall buildings just by thinking about it. Just the word "Hello" carries a ring of intelligence and elegance. Wow, she is soooo smooth the way she said "Hello." I wish I could be like Super Jill and say "hello" just like she does. I'm fainting with adoration, and Super Jill hasn't even said more than ten words yet. But wow, is she amazing. And Super Joe, what a stud. I wish I could walk to the podium just like Super Joe! You see the way he swings his knees as he walks. Wow. Every movement of Super Joe and Super Jill is closely watched. Step off the podium and you are back to Regular Joe and Regular Jill. Speaker Power.

In college, one football player per week was voted by the coaches to be Player of the Week. I was fortunate enough to win that award once, my senior year. One of the responsibilities was to address the Rotary Club that following workweek. My individual coach and I made our way over to the Rotary Club for the lunch meeting. There were about fifty or so people in attendance. The agenda was always lunch, the player speaks, and then the coach speaks. The coach always speaks second just in case he needs to do cleanup for his player. I spoke, then my coach. After the luncheon, I had people tripping over themselves telling me how much they enjoyed my talk. Are you kidding? I was terrible. Coach not only needed to do cleanup, he mopped the floors, did the dishes, and turned off the lights behind my ridiculous talk. I bumbled and stumbled and blabbed my way through it. I had no skills or experience speaking to a group at that time. But they apparently thought I was great, or at least good. What was that? *That was speaker power.* It's that little extra halo that circles your melon when you have the floor.

When we have the microphone, we become the expert. Even if we don't know anything and are a fumbling, mumbling nincompoop, we become the expert nonetheless.

I knew a real estate agent that was an average producer. I'm not sure how he started, but he ran these free buyer seminars. He did these seminars weekly. Sometimes he had ten people, sometimes zero. He couldn't list a house to save his life, but he always had a stable of buyers from those seminars. I was curious about his seminars and asked him if I could drop in sometime. He said yes. It was like meeting him for the first time. He didn't say anything or do anything all that special; in fact, I would say he was a very average speaker. But he had the floor nonetheless. He was the speaker. Yes, he was the speaker of his own seminar and invited himself to speak, but that didn't matter. He was the speaker with supernatural powers, a golden glow around his thinking cap. The knower of all to be known—the speaker.

Whenever you have a chance to speak, *do it*. It's a well-known fact that public speaking is one of the biggest human fears. Do it anyway.

The ancient Roman playwright Terence says, "Fortune favors the brave."

Speak as often as possible, and you and your business will grow.

A client of mine was in the media industry in Northern California. She was organizing a panel for a symposium for Asian real estate buyers in the San Francisco Bay Area. It was a good-size event; there were about two hundred people in the room. She asked me and three others to be on the panel. The event happened on a Saturday. By Sunday, I had three e-mails, by Monday twenty, and I was fielding questions for a month from that one event. I can't say I did a specific deal right away from that event, but I added about ten people to my database, and over the years two of them became real live paying customers.

Even if you are nervous, if you have a chance to speak, do it.

I taught a class one time for my company. There were about twenty-five people in attendance. The class was primarily about residential brokerage, but we actually tiptoed into a discussion on commercial. I am the first to admit that I'm a residential broker, not commercial. I do, however, know my way around the commercial math and can talk that language when necessary. So we started talking about commercial. After the meeting a lady pulled me aside and said that she had a commercial deal she wanted to talk with me about. Great. We decided to talk the next day. It was not a complicated deal, and I told her several times that she really didn't need me to be part of it. She insisted and said that the only thing that she wanted from me was for me to coach her through the deal. She said she would give me a 25 percent referral fee for that service. I told her one last time that she didn't need me but then agreed. The deal closed without a hitch, and everyone was paid, including me. What was that? That is speaker power. It's that rainbow around your thinking machine when you have the podium.

Grow your revenue line—speak.

Once upon a time, we tried to provide real estate services as a job benefit for a local university. The idea was to provide real estate education to the employees of the university, free of charge, of course. Frankly, it was a flop. The college representative did a great job, it just never happened the way we had envisioned. I did about five seminars over a two-month period and then we called it quits. A funny thing happened, however. I can link five closed deals to that failed attempt. I was exposed to literally no more than thirty university employees, but that is enough when you are *the speaker*. Speaker power.

You never know—speak whenever you can.

"Well, Jim, I'm brand new to the industry and don't have a clue—what am I going to talk about?" Don't make it complicated. Prepare some things that you are comfortable talking about, and go! Be honest. "Hi, I'm Sam. This is my first year in real estate, and I am so excited about being in this industry and talking with all of you good people. I'm not going to know everything naturally, but I'm excited to be here and we'll have fun." You'll be fine. Just do it. And bring a seasoned veteran with you if necessary.

When you get a chance to speak, do it. Even if you are nervous, do it. You will walk away a slightly different person and probably with some business. Here are some ideas and possibilities for speaking engagements: your kid's school, elder care facilities, home buyer seminars, the office meeting, a corporate setting, a class for your colleagues, your alma mater (high school and college), the business school at the local college. There are others.

Speaking periodically will give your business a good shot of adrenaline. And you might even find that you enjoy wearing the golden helmet for an hour or two.

Go get 'em!

31

Competing with Colleagues in Your Office

Always take hold of things by the smooth handle.

President Thomas Jefferson

IT CAN BE CHALLENGING WHEN we are competing for business with other people in our company or office, people on our own team. Two thirteen-year-old wrestlers are buddies and on the same junior high school wrestling team. They also happen to be in the same weight classification. The coach says, "You two get in the center ring for a wrestle-off, and winner gets the job against Serrano Junior High School tomorrow."

"But Coach, we are on the same team!" says Michael, who is slightly nervous about beating up on his buddy.

"I understand that, but we can only take one guy per weight class, so get in there and compete for the job," says Coach.

Stephanie and Maria are on the debate team at their high school. They are competing against Ventura High School next week. Six people are on the team but only four go with two alternates. Stephanie and Maria are of roughly equal talent and have been best friends since preschool. Coach says, "Stephanie and Maria, your ability and talents are very equal and I can only take one of you, so you two will compete for the job. You will debate each other tomorrow for the starting job. Be here at 3:30 p.m., ready to go."

Back to real estate. One of my favorite phases of my real estate career was when I was doing VA loans. Our lending office was small but fierce; I truly enjoyed everyone in the office. The manager was a warm-hearted, big-personality guy—the boss. I loved this guy and his wife worked in the office as well. We had a total of about fifteen mortgage brokers; five superseasoned people, five green peas (including me), and five mobile agents that did a deal here or there. So on a relative scale, we were a small team, but we did big volume, huge numbers at times.

There were only six closed-door offices with views when I arrived, which was only year two in my career. There were about eight cubes. Boss didn't know me from the Man on the Moon, so I got a cube, but I was determined to move into an office, fast. At that time, I was the number one/two/three producer month in, month out, in my previous office, but in this office, I started at roughly producer number five. These guys and girls were pros; they knew what they were doing and had been around. Boss knew I was an athlete in college and must have figured there might be a competitor buried in there somewhere. A bell was installed shortly after I arrived. So, when you took a new loan application, you were rewarded by walking over to the bell and ringing it. That thing drove me crazy. I could literally feel my heart race when someone else rang that lousy bell. It was somewhat subtle but it was like hanging a piece of steak three inches from the nose of a dog. But I wasn't the only competitive spirit in that office; there were several.

A few months into my new job, I noticed this guy that was always busy, busy, busy and ringing that bell constantly. He had a cube just like me, about ten feet away, and we were both quickly on our way to being promoted to an office. He was gone one day, so I took the opportunity to ask the processor how he was so busy. She said, "Oh, he is doing VA loans. He originates four to seven per week, and on a lucky day, three per day." Wow. That was it. I was literally off and running that week becoming a VA loan specialist. As soon I figured out what VA meant and how to do it, I was certain I would be the Northern California VA champion.

Within one month, *my office mate and I were competing for the same business,* day in, day out. I'm telling you, between the two of us, we dominated Northern California once upon a time. It became a little uncomfortable, however, in the office. He and I finally sat down one day and decided that we would continue to compete, and compete fiercely, for the business. But we would have a cooperative partnership of sorts; so when it was clear that we were going to lose the business, we would endorse the other guy and help him win. That was our deal and it worked. Boss was happy for the volume and also happy that his racehorses were calm, for the moment.

Now to real estate brokerage. When I started as a real estate agent, several people in my company were targeting expired listings. Some of those people were doing a lot of expireds. I figured as soon as I figured out what an expired was, I would start doing them too. So it began…

There were a few agents within our company that were particularly good at fishing for these expired people. I wasn't very good at it at the beginning but improved with time. In fact, I met with the CEO of our company one day to review my business and sourcing thereof. I had everything tightly organized on a spreadsheet, so it was easy for him to read. Just reading his body language, his jaw dropped slightly when he looked at closed transactions from expired listings: twelve, and it was only August—I had five months to go. That may not sound like a lot, but trust me, that's no easy task in the Silicon Valley. And frankly, I never really thought I was very good at it. I was successful because I made the call, asked for the appointment, and went on the appointment. I did that day in, day out, for a couple of years, and every once in a while the customer said yes. But frankly, I had to go on about five of these to get just one—terrible close rate, really. There were a few agents in my company, however, would go on two and get one. It started driving me crazy. Not only that, we were all going on the same appointments 80 percent of the time—you know, the ones that we are not supposed to target, the customers that interview five to eight people just for the sport of it. The 10 percent of the market that, trust me, you never want to target. So there I am, competing day in, day out, with my office (and company) mates chasing these expired listing people. Chasing them all over town and burning gas by the tanker load.

One day I was meeting with an expired listing gentleman at his home. The customer did not sign a listing agreement with me, however. I jumped in my car and started driving down the road. As I'm about four hundred yards down the street at this point, I see this oddly familiar car in my rear mirror. Yep, it's one of the lead dog expired listing people that also happens to work at my company. At that moment, I had lost about five in a row to this lead dog, and my competitive spirit was at a level ten. I needed to take a left to go back to the office; I decided to go right. I stopped. Thought, simmered, stewed. No way—not again. I strategically parked my car where I could see clearly when the lead dog left the house, but the lead dog couldn't see me. I waited. Finally, thirty minutes later, the lead dog was on their way back to their office. This was my moment. My plan was to make up some lame excuse that I forgot something or forgot to ask the client a question, or this or that, I don't even remember what it was. But I had a plan and it made total sense to me at the time, and I was also on a mission, so it really didn't matter. The only way that my plan would fail is if the client had already listed the home with the lead dog. So back to the house. Knock knock. Meet with the client, pour on every bit of charm that I could muster up, listing signed within twenty minutes. Wow, a ton a work. Not worth it really.

I do not tell this story because I am necessarily proud of it. In fact, it's a little embarrassing, and I think I let my competitive spirit get the best of me in this case because I was tired of losing. I relay this story as an example that it can get tricky at times when competing with office mates and company mates. "When the debate is lost, slander becomes the tool of the loser"—*Socrates*. If you lose to an office mate, sometimes it's hard, but have dignity in losing. One deal is not worth discord in the office. For me, the quote by Thomas Jefferson at the beginning of this chapter means *keep it cool*.

It's going to happen. Even if you are 100 percent working a referral business, from time to time you will run across one of your office or company mates.

Go get 'em!

32

The Chosen Few

———◆———

The level of our success is limited only by our imagination—
and no act of kindness, however small, is ever wasted.

AESOP

THIS GROUP IS DEFINED AS those folks who have the capacity and desire to refer more than one deal yearly. I refer to this group as *the Chosen Few*. Now let's make one distinction before we move the cart too far down the road. When we are providing service to a customer, there are no Chosen Few. A current customer is a current customer is a current customer; we do our best in all those cases to provide a good service and complete the task before us. We do not rank our current customers. We work our butt off for them; they have paid us or are paying us to do so. The Chosen Few are outside of current-pending deals.

I'll explain. We have current customers; we have hot leads; and then we have everyone else. We are talking about everyone else in this case. Who is everyone else? Everyone. Your database: past customers, friends, old colleagues, family members, social contacts, etc. This is a referral business. So we want to drive as many referrals as possible from the "everyone else" list. The first step in doing so is to spend some time categorizing. The first category for me was, the Chosen Few. Why? Because the Chosen Few will be your biggest bang for the buck (and effort).

The Chosen Few will include only those people that have a (realistic) *capacity* and *desire* to send you more than one deal per year. Would my mom be in the Chosen Few Club? Maybe, but maybe not. Would my best friend be in the Chosen Few Club? In some cases, yes, in some cases, no. Would a past customer be part of the Chosen Few? You'll have to decide that on your own, customer by customer. Would my CPA be in the Chosen Few? He or she could, as long as you manage that relationship. Could my wife or husband be part of that group? Wow, that's an interesting one. Could my contractor be in the Chosen Few? Sure, but is that realistic, and has he or she demonstrated a desire to be? Could my family law attorney be in the Chosen Few? Now, you are catching on. Could my client that I did business with eight years ago that consistently sends me a deal yearly be a Chosen Few member? You are improving. How about that girl that I have never done business with that just seems to *love* sending me deals—could she be part of the Chosen Few? Now you got it! Anyone could be in the Chosen Few. Remember the definition: those people that have a *capacity* and *desire* to send you more than one deal per year.

There are some people that *love* to send referrals. They absolutely dig it. I am actually one of those people. I will literally go out of my way to send a referral, for lots of reasons, but mainly because it makes *me* feel good that I'm helping someone else.

Capacity and desire. You might run across someone that would *love* to refer you a deal, but for whatever reason, they don't have the network or the capacity to do so. We still love them for it, but they are not part of the Chosen Few. On the other hand, someone might be in a position (have the capacity) to refer you more than one deal yearly, but again, for whatever reason, they don't have the desire to do so. No problem, we are not trying to force a square peg in a round hole. Just move on. Make numbers your friend.

Don't *guess* who you would like to be in the Chosen Few. My old workout partner was an executive at a large company. We trained together for many years. If I sat down and analyzed who I know, and then made a list of who I thought would be perfect for the Chosen Few, he would be at the top of the list. It just made sense. He never referred me a deal, not a single one. I know that he could have done it. I also know that he had the network to do it. And furthermore, a referral coming from him means something (based on his business status in the community). But for whatever reason, he never did it, and frankly I never pushed it. I made a conscious decision to leave him alone; if he wanted to refer business, great, and if he didn't want to refer business, that was fine too. But I wasn't going to push it either way. I was happy to be his friend and workout partner; that was enough. This is an example of a person that had the capacity but not the desire to refer.

On the other hand, for several years I had a lady in the Chosen Few that I had never done business with. I don't even remember how we came in contact, I think she called on a listing one time. Anyway, there was a period of three to four years that she consistently sent me one to three deals per year, all in her own neighborhood, a good neighborhood as well. She loved to keep an eye on the neighborhood, and she loved to send me referrals. I never would have guessed that this person would be in the Chosen Few. Just let it happen. Don't assume.

Don't push it too hard. Capacity and desire. The Chosen Few will rise to the top naturally, organically. Not everyone is going to be in this club; in fact, this is frankly a small, elite group. These are your VIPs. We are going to be spending time, energy, and money on this group down the road. Don't get yourself overextended by making this group too big.

Okay, I hope I have given you some ideas on how to identify the Chosen Few. *Now what are we going to do with them, and for them?* Before we get there, let me ask you something.

How many deals are you trying to complete this year? Write that number down. Now divide that number by two. Write that one down as well. That is the number of people you need in your Chosen Few. I want to do twenty-four deals this year; when I divide by two, that is equal to twelve. So that means I need twelve people in the Chosen Few. Can you manage twelve, can you spoil twelve, and can you maintain strong relationships with twelve people? I always had roughly twenty to thirty in the Chosen Few. No, I didn't have aspirations of doing seventy to eighty brokerage deals yearly, but hey, I'm not a gambler. I wanted to hedge my bet and make sure I had enough in the Chosen Few to ensure the numbers worked. Make numbers your friend.

This is not hocus pocus. It's simple, it's good business. And take a look at these twelve people. They like you, you like them, you are helping them, they are helping you. You can go chase after a bunch of people that you don't know and that don't like you; that is fine, go for it. I suggest making it easy, making it fun, making it rewarding. Build your team.

"Well, Jim, that's not going to work because in my specific industry, inventory is so tight, tight, tight that no one on my list can send me two deals yearly; they would be lucky to send me one." Then you have the wrong people on your list. Think harder. Work harder. I have been active in residential lending and residential brokerage. I can tell you with 100 percent certainty that you can build the Chosen Few in those industries. No, I have never been an active commercial lender or broker, but I guarantee that I could spend thirty minutes with you and we could identify (profile) people that have the capacity and desire to send you two or more deals yearly. Think harder. You can do that, or you can make cold calls for the rest of your life. Your choice. Many of my colleagues have chosen the cold-call route, and unfortunately those same folks are literally looking for another career every two years because they are a spent cannon—a tired horse. They are cooked, burned out, and wasted. Cold calling can be good in the short term, but is not sustainable long term.

Things to do with the Chosen Few. 1) You are having an ongoing conversation, over e-mail, over the phone, over text, over social media, in person, just you and that one person. 2) Don't forget the Chosen Few's birthdays and their family's birthdays. 3) Have good manners, say thank you, say please, and say you're welcome; trust me, you will separate yourself from the pack just by this one item. 4) Make ongoing, truly ongoing, contact; don't jump in and out or you'll lose credibility. 5) Ask each person to coffee or lunch at least every other month, I know people that meet for coffee on the same bat channel weekly. I'm not a big fan of that because I don't think that is sustainable long term. 6) Send them and their family a card for all the holidays; there are many, as you know. 7) Be a pro. Don't dabble into recipes and dog walking; stay in your world, real estate. Tiptoe on the edge if you want, but don't start sending your customers pie recipes—what does a pie have to do with real estate? 8) You will need to build up to this, but get the Chosen Few together and have them meet each other. From five to seven on Thursday evenings was my favorite time for cocktails and light snacks. 9) Be strategic. Add value to their life, real value. Build it into a strong business network. I can't tell you how many times the Chosen Few hired other Chosen Few members. 10) Send them something special over the winter holiday break. Use your own good judgment on this and stay within the law. 11) Know what is going on in their life, and anticipate their needs. For instance, you know that Kim and Jeff are going to be doing an add-on/remodel within the year, reach out and see if they need someone to talk with. Anticipate their needs and help them. 12) Recognize that any good relationship is reciprocal in nature. It can't be one sided. I can't tell you what to do on this, just recognize that fact and be considerate thereof. 13) If you forget all of that, just remember one thing: keep the conversation moving, and keep it natural and smooth.

If you are new to real estate, don't worry, you too can build the Chosen Few. It will surprise you how quickly you will build this group. You will likely have five people from day one. Be tenacious, but be patient. I call it pleasantly persistent.

You can make a good living by spending time with only the Chosen Few. You can also make a fortune if you completely commit to this group.

Go get 'em!

33

Endorsements

———◆———

Everything in excess is opposed to nature.

HIPPOCRATES

I'LL JUST SAY IT SO you know I understand: "marketing is tricky." What is too much and what is not enough? Five pages of "look how great I am"—that is clearly too much. Try this: no more than half a page on you and one and a half pages of endorsements. An endorsement means something; people care what others say. Even if the endorsement is canned and prepared, it stands for something.

An endorsement brings a third party into the conversation. And yes, let them talk with your endorsements. In fact, there was a time when I put the cell phone numbers of my endorsements right next to their name. I asked for permission to do this, of course, but wow, talk about being fully exposed. Clearly your endorsers are fans, but even so, you never really know how that conversation is going to go. That's a complete unveiling, a somewhat naked look at your business.

I will admit I borrowed this idea from a colleague at a different company. I stumbled across my colleague's marketing piece one day. It was simple and almost 100 percent focused on endorsements. There was a little about him: name, contact info, years in business, and some miscellaneous items; but honestly, it was limited to no more one page

on him. Then, the other side of the paper was 100 percent endorsements. I suggest keeping it to a single sheet of paper, front and back
side. You on one side and endorsements on the back side.

If you are starting in real estate and have never done a deal, you
still have endorsements. Be smart, be creative, you will find people
who will put their name behind you. When I started in lending and
the customer wasn't sure he or she wanted to hire me, I would say, "I
have a couple of references you could call." I changed the word *customers* to *references*. I gave them the phone numbers of my best friend, my
mom, and my college coach. No one ever called. You won't have to do
this for long after you have done a few deals.

Don't get discouraged by past customers that are not comfortable
endorsing you. "Wow, they must not like me or think I did a good job."
No, no, it's not that. Some will, some won't. Don't take it personally.
Think about it; if you did a crummy job, you are the first to know you
did a crummy job. Are you really going to be calling those people for
an endorsement? Of course not. You are going to call the remaining
99 percent of your customers—the happy ones. So if he or she is a
happy customer and says no, don't sweat it. It's just that he or she is not
comfortable with it for whatever reason.

Script. "Hi, Customer, this is Jim. I was hoping I could list you as a
happy customer on my resume list. Would that be okay?"

"Sure, of course, Jim, no problem."

"Great, thank you. Does this sound okay: 'Very reliable and professional...way to go, Jimbo.' Sound okay?"

"Perfect, Jim, good luck with everything."

"Thank you, Customer. Also, from time to time, and it will only be on a rare occasion, someone may want to do a quick background check on me. In that case, would you mind talking with him or her?"

"No problem, Jim. Have a good one, Jim."

Pretty simple. Modify the script as you deem fit.

One obvious note, when you call for an endorsement, have the endorsement prepared in advance and simply read it to them. No more than one sentence. Make it easy on the person that you are asking for an endorsement.

And smart people are smart. Sometimes people will be worried about "the liability" associated with endorsing a product or service (in this case). Consider this as you design the text. I'll give you an example. This one is bad: "Jim is the greatest. I highly recommend his services, and he'll do a good job you." This one is good: "Jim did a great job for us. We had a positive experience and will use him again." The second just simply makes representations on their own personal experiences; they are making no guarantee on how it will go with anyone else (no liability).

Here are some sample endorsement statements that I've collected over the years:

- ✓ Nice job, Jim!
- ✓ Jim did a first-class job for us from gate to wire!
- ✓ I truly believe Jim's instincts helped us make more money when we sold our home.
- ✓ Very reliable and professional...way to go with the house, Jimbo!

- ✓ Jim made it happen for us. He is a get-it-done kind of guy!
- ✓ Jim is a trusted real estate advisor for us. We think very highly of him.
- ✓ Trustworthy to a fault and extremely competent and capable. Great job, Jim!
- ✓ It was a pleasure doing business with Jim; he followed through on everything!
- ✓ The process is a bit intimidating; Jim was there for us every step of the way.
- ✓ Jim successfully guided my family and me through two life-changing deals. Thank you, Jim!
- ✓ My transaction took a good bit of time…Jim was very patient with us.
- ✓ Jim did a good job with the house…we're glad we had him on our team.
- ✓ Jim took great care of us and was a good guardian of our privacy and equity.
- ✓ It was a good feeling knowing that Jim was on our side and had things covered.
- ✓ Jim did a great job for us in a very difficult real estate environment.
- ✓ In my book, Jim's judgment and integrity are second to none.
- ✓ I wouldn't dream of doing a deal without Jim involved!
- ✓ I have always been impressed with Jim's ability to find a creative way to get it done.
- ✓ I needed someone that was 100 percent in my corner. Jim was there for me and got it done!
- ✓ Jim has a great eye for finding the "diamond in the rough." Thanks, Jim!
- ✓ Jim honored my confidentiality and privacy; he did a good job for me.
- ✓ He is a trusted friend and business mentor.
- ✓ It was great knowing I had someone good taking care of things.

- ✓ "Trustworthy" and "smart" are the words that come to mind about Jim.
- ✓ Jim saw it before we did; he really has an eye for seeing past the clutter.
- ✓ Jim truly fought to make it happen for us. Thanks, Jim!
- ✓ Jim displayed great people skills and was very professional.
- ✓ Jim was there for me every step of the way; I learned to trust his instincts.
- ✓ He did a great job for us and has become a trusted advisor.
- ✓ Jim has done such an amazing job for us on multiple transactions.
- ✓ Jim did a first-class job for us.
- ✓ I can't imagine having a better team help me purchase my first home.

Here is the exact format I used:

Nice job, Jim!

Xxx Xxxxxxx, retired advertising executive, 650.xxx.xxxx

One page on you—and one page of endorsements.

Go get 'em!

34

Whales

———————

The words of influential people mean something.
Unknown

A REFERRAL IS ARGUABLY THE biggest compliment that we can receive. "Jim, we trust you will take care of our friend; here you go." That's a compliment. All referrals should be defined as such, and naturally we should be appreciative of all of them. But...the reality is that not all referrals are created *exactly* equal. As your business grows, you will notice that one or two (or a very small group of) people are doing a *giant* amount of referring. Not only are they referring, but the people they are referring are actually calling. These are the Whales. People that 1) love to refer and 2) also have *street credibility. People listen to the Whale.*

When I was doing veteran loans, I had the opportunity of working with a fairly high-ranking officer at a base in the San Francisco Bay Area. We successfully completed his transaction. He sent me no less than twenty of his colleagues and subordinates over the next year. "Hi, Jim, Officer Johnson (that wasn't his name) said to call you. He said that you could help us save money on our mortgage." That was it. They were not about to shop around or call other lenders. Officer Johnson said to call Jim, so that is what they did. *People listened.*

I was recently reviewing this topic with one of my lender friends. His Whales are financial advisors, not so much real estate agents. Interesting. Why? Well, the financial advisors have an ongoing relationship with the client. The real estate agent has a short-term transaction with the client. Yes, as real estate agents, we try to stay in touch, but the task at hand is complete after the deal is done. In addition, real estate agents sometime have a tendency to refer two or three lenders, whereas the financial advisors typically refer one. So when he gets a referral from a real estate agent, he knows that he has about a 40 percent chance of doing the deal. When he gets the referral from the financial advisor, he has a 90 percent chance of doing that deal. Hence his game plan: maintain strong relationships with two to six financial advisors. *The client is listening.*

My friend from college referred me roughly ten loans the first two months in my real estate career. He was young at the time, no more than twenty-seven or twenty-eight years of age, but had climbed the corporate ladder quickly. He had accomplished in five years what would normally take fifteen. His status at his company, within his family, and within our friend group was very high. When he said, "You need to get your loan through Jim," people listened. It wasn't even a question. They were going to get their loan through Jim as instructed. He referred me roughly 25 percent of all my loan production that very first year. That's a giant-big-swimming get-out-of-my-way Whale—which you love.

For a period of time, I represented several Secret Service agents coming and going from/to the Bay Area. But there was one guy in particular that was doing *all* the referring. Oh, you have to use Jim. So that is what they did. No questions asked. They trusted him, so they trusted me by association. *They listened to The Whale.*

For a period of time I worked with a lot of attorneys, roughly five or eight at any given time. As a team, they accounted for over approximately 40 to 60 percent of my business for many years. When the attorney referred me to a client, there was a high likelihood that I would get the deal. *The customer listened.*

How many Whales do you have right now? How many people that you currently know could you turn into a Whale? Know your numbers. Do you have one Whale? Yes? Then great. Do you have five other people that you think you could turn into a Whale? Then great, get to work on the five. You need less than a handful of Whales in any segment of real estate (sales or lending) to be successful. Don't confuse the Whales with the Chosen Few in this book. The difference is that 1) when the Whales refer someone to you, that someone actually calls you, and 2) you will likely have only one to five Whales at any one time, The Chosen Few will be a larger group.

Remember, Whales are always on the move, cruising through the ocean (life). So your Whales will be in constant flux. Love the ones you are with (at the moment), but always be looking to date more. Make numbers your friend.

Go get 'em!

35

Active Customer Referral Strategy

—————◆—————

*Give me a lever long enough and a fulcrum on
which to place it and I shall move the world.*

ARCHIMEDES

WHEN I WAS DOING VA loans, about 30 percent of my customers
were current military and the rest retired. Almost without exception, I would receive a call during the loan process from my client,
usually active duty, referring me to one of his or her military colleagues that needed to do a refinance. "Jim, I was talking with Kevin
today at work telling him about the interest rates, and he said that he
wanted to do the same thing. Can you talk with him?" People know
other like-minded people.

I represented a young couple early in my brokerage career that
wanted to buy their first home. He was a policeman and she was a doctor still in residency. Forty-five days into the process, she referred me
to her colleague, another female doctor. I represented a college football coach in the mid-2000s, and as the deal was closing, he referred
me to another coach. People know other like-minded people.

People know other like-minded people; birds of a feather flock
together. My goal was to always make one deal turn into two—the one
I was doing plus one more. A two-for-one special, a two-fer.

To do a two-fer, we need a referral from the person we are working with. Sometimes referrals just "happen," sometimes we have to gently push the process along. During my entire real estate career, I would be the first to admit that I was reluctant to be constantly asking for referrals. Yes, I knew what to say and how to say it, and I even practiced what to say. But I was always slightly uncomfortable with it. When the shoe is on the other foot and I am the customer, I don't like working with anyone too "cooked up" or robotic. You can smell a salesperson that is about to ask for a referral from a mile away. The salesperson usually does one of two things: he or she gets either uncomfortable/nervous or overly aggressive. In either case, his or her body language is usually terrible and impossible to hide.

An active customer referral strategy nonetheless has to be part of your business. Here was the starting point for me: 1) Do a good job first and foremost, and 2) Make the referral conversation, conversational. Here is what I would say, paraphrased: "It's important to me to work with top-quality people, and you are certainly included in that group of VIP customers. I have found that by working with only top-quality people, I am able to provide a better service. And let's face it, quality people know other quality people. Therefore, as I grow my customer base over the next year or so, please reach out if there is anything I can do for you or if there is a friend or family member that needs assistance." You see what we did here? A) We complimented them a few times, B) There is a benefit to them personally, and C) We paid them one last and final compliment before we asked for a referral. That was roughly the message as paraphrased. I never delivered this message as a speech. It would come up when it came up. In fact, sometimes just pieces of it would come up when natural and appropriate; it's a conversation. And frankly, my objective was to have it come up when we were chatting about business in general, not my business, just business, business philosophy, business concepts, business strategies. I found "the business strategy conversation" to be a natural segue into the referral conversation.

The real estate coaching companies have a million scripts that you can consider using. I say this: use whatever works for you and whatever you are comfortable with. Here are three rules of thumb to consider, however: 1) For sure you need an active customer referral strategy, 2) Be yourself (don't be a robot or you won't make it), and 3) Be sincere about what you are saying, say what you mean, and mean what you say. Whatever you do, the end result needs to produce one additional deal—the one you are doing plus one more.

Go get 'em!

36

Lovers

———◆———

We entrust the most serious matters of life to our spouse.

SOCRATES

IMODIFIED THE THOUGHT BY Socrates above to the language of today. When we are really in a tight spot, who is there for us? Our spouse. When our back is (or isn't) against the wall, our spouse should be and is our only business partner. Spouses (partners/lovers) could play and should play an important role in your real estate business. I modified the details a little, but my colleague told me the following story many years ago.

His wife was having lunch with some friends. One of her friends said they were moving to the East Coast and may or may not need to sell their home. The home was roughly $3,000,000, total commission of $180,000 plus/minus, $90,000 to each side. When the friend mentioned this at lunch, the wife failed to mention that her husband was a real estate agent. A week later, the wife shared this story with her husband. After he came to from fainting on the kitchen floor, he asked his wife to please reach out to the friend. "It's easy, honey, just remind her that your husband is in real estate and that he would be happy to speak with them, no obligation," he says.

The wife called right away as requested. They had hired a real estate agent three days prior.

More salt in the wound. The friend says, "Oh, my gosh, I completely forgot that your husband is in real estate. I feel terrible, I would have hired him for sure, no doubt about it." So $90,000, poof, gone. No big deal, it's only $90,000, after all. The exact same amount of money needed for the wife to quit her job and take care of the kids full time for two years. That's all. No big deal. All in a day's work. Who's to blame on that one? It's definitely not the wife's fault. That one is on the producer, the husband in this case.

Let's dissect it and help you make money.

Our friends forget. We like to think that "everyone knows" that we are in the real estate business, doing loans or selling property. Not so, as it turns out. Most people are running their own lives and not necessarily focused on the nitty-gritty of this person or that person. To make matters more challenging, sometimes people know us (only) within a certain "context." Think about all the hats that you wear on a weekly basis: possibly you are a parent, son/daughter, coach, colleague, boss, volunteer, president of this or that, customer, client, friend, community acquaintance, and more. I volunteer coach, and those kids and that community know me as "coach." That's it, I'm coach. They don't know me as business owner or boss or manager or dad or son or business partner or real estate person. They know me as coach. And frankly, that's all I want them to know me as, because I do that for personal reasons, not business reasons. Coach is the context in which they know me.

Here is a real-world example. As a producer in real estate, I am naturally asked, often, "Do you know a good contractor?" I know a ton.

We all know a ton. And I also have a very close friend that works for a midsized (good) construction company. I love this guy. His family is almost family to me; therefore, he is almost family to me. I have literally almost never referred him business (because I forget), and I probably make a contractor referral at least weekly. Yeah, I know. I just don't think of him within that "context." I think of him as a friend. For some reason, my brain has never defined him as "contractor." It happens. Our friends forget that we are in the real estate business sometimes. "But men are men; and the best sometimes forget"—*Shakespeare.*

Know that and recognize that as a starting point, and then explain that to your spouse.

Our spouses forget. As a producer, generating business is on our minds 24/7. We are "living it" day in, day out. We can't expect the same from our spouse. They forget. "I am looking to hire a real estate agent, do you know anyone?" It could happen like that, but it usually doesn't. It happens like the story above. Some chitter chatter going on among friends:

"Carol took a job in Nashville."

"We are going to buy one of those condos downtown."

"I'm tired of managing that lousy property, what a headache."

"I guess we'll have to tap into the home equity to pay for college."

On the first one: "Is Carol going to be selling her home?"

On the second one: "Are they going to be selling their big house and downsizing?"

On the third one: "Are they going to be selling their rental property?"

And on the fourth: "Do they need to do a cash-out refinance?"

Work with your spouse to understand "the conversation" and pay attention to the dialogue.

Coach your spouse. Don't make it complicated and don't make it hard. Manners are important—right! So it might not be the right time or place to mention it; later might be better. *First step:* Upon hearing about the lead, the spouse should bring the information to you, the producer, immediately. Time is of the essence in many cases. Look at the story above as an example. *Second step:* Reach out. As a team, you can decide, on a case by case basis, how you want to approach the person. You decide. The good news is that you are doing it together, as a team. After all, *we only have one business partner—our spouse!* When push comes to shove, he or she cares the most.

If your spouse can generate two deals per year, what does that mean to your revenue line—$4,500, $7,000, maybe $15,000? I have some friends that are tenant rep producers; two deals could mean roughly $100,000 to them. Whatever the number is, it's more than you had before.

Go get 'em!

37

Trust

Be courteous to all, but intimate with few, and let those
few be well tried before you give them your confidence.

PRESIDENT GEORGE WASHINGTON

I WAS PUTTERING ALONG IN my loan business that first year, doing just
fine. But I noticed there were instances where I couldn't get a borrower a loan because he or she didn't "fit" into any of the lender guide-
lines. One of my colleagues said, "Check with lender JJ. He works with
a couple that does second trust deeds."

Second deed of trust. Someone wants to buy a house for $100K;
they don't have $100K in cash; they do, however, have $15K. They
borrow $80K from the bank because that's all the bank wants to give
them, and they borrow the remaining $5K from someone else. That
someone else could be a bank or a private person. The $5K they bor-
rowed is called a second deed of trust. Other common terms that all
roughly mean the same thing are *second mortgages, seconds, second trust
deeds, second money, seller carryback, piggyback,* or a *junior loan.*

In those days, which were the early to mid-1990s, not a lot of banks
were doing second deeds of trust. Frankly, I don't even remember any
banks doing seconds. The go-to methodology of buying a home back
then was a 20 to 30 percent down payment. Not everyone had 20 to

30 percent, however, so there was a real need for private-party second-money lenders.

JJ had been working with this retired couple. For retirement income, they liked doing seconds. They could get a higher-than-market interest rate and have their money backed by hard assets as well. For instance, let's say the going interest rate on a first mortgage was 8 percent. Depending on the circumstances of the deal, they would charge 11 to 13 percent, roughly 3 to 5 percent above "first mortgage money." That was normal, and that was the market. In fact, I bought a home in 1992 and had to borrow "second money" from a friend of the family. First-money interest rates at that time were 8 to 9 percent; I borrowed the second money at 13 percent. That could very well sound outrageous, but it was very normal stuff at that time.

This couple also loved the fact that their money was backed by hard assets. I call this *collateralized lending.* The collateral could be anything; a boat, a car, a bank account, ownership in this or that; but since we are talking about real estate, the collateral will be real estate. So on the above example, if the $5K were not repaid as agreed, then the lender (private party) could begin the process to seize the asset (house) to force the borrower to fulfill the obligation. In summary, private parties were (are) willing to loan second money because 1) the loan is backed by hard assets and 2) the interest rate is attractive.

One final note before we continue with the story about trust. In the event of a default, the lender in first position gets his or her money first, and the lender in second position gets his or her money second. Who has more risk? You got it! The person in second position has more risk. Risk and reward. So the additional 3 to 5 percent helps to compensate that lender in second position for the increased risk.

"Jim, I'm nervous about putting you in touch with this couple. This is *all business*. You have to understand this couple is very discerning. They are very good businesspeople," says JJ.

I called the private-money retired couple; we will call the husband, RC. "Hi, RC, I might have a deal for you." He turned me down flat. I tried again one month later. No again. This was a problem because my business was growing and I needed a private second-money relationship. In fact, I had stumbled into this grouping of people that were coming from the United Kingdom, taking technology jobs in Silicon Valley, one after another. And I needed a private-money second relationship to complete those deals (in addition to others).

"Hi, RC, it's me again. I'm starting to understand what you are looking for, so could you please review a new file for me?"

"Jim, first of all, tell me their story." Okay, I passed that test on the phone; I was prepared after the first two strikeouts for that question. "Second, I want to see all the same information that you are sending to the first-money lenders. In addition, I would like to see this, and that, and more; and also, I would like you to write a cover letter for me summarizing everything."

"Okay, got it, anything else?"

"No, that will do it," says RC.

My friend was right, this was all business. I learned more from RC than I did from many of the first-money lenders I worked with. It was military inspection time, and no surprise if you knew their vocational background. Thank God they liked the deal. *Funded!* I finally did a deal with RC.

Peeling back the onion. RC wanted to loan money to quality people. He was not necessarily an "equity lender." An equity lender makes a decision to lend money (in large part) based on the loan to value. An equity lender would probably not lend on 80 percent LTV, but he would lend on 60 percent LTV. It's safe to say that an equity lender would be looking at LTV first and the borrower second. RC, on the other hand, was looking at the borrower first and the LTV second. It was great if the LTV was favorable as well, but first and foremost, RC wanted reliable borrowers. He wanted to do business with responsible human beings. He didn't want to lie awake at night wondering if the borrower was going to pay him back.

You see, RC was not in the business of losing money. If there was any doubt in his mind of losing his principal, he was out! No further discussion was needed. President George Washington said, "*Worry* is the interest paid by those that borrow trouble." RC was not interested in borrowing even an ounce of trouble or spending one second worrying.

RC ended up working with a handful of lenders and real estate agents over the years, but eventually just limited it to JJ and me.

Building of trust. Deal by deal their confidence in me grew. We did a deal, then another, then another. I only brought them what I knew they wanted. And now that I understood what they wanted, I simply underwrote the deal myself before I ever sent it to RC. Not right away, but I would say by roughly year five, they *started* trusting my opinion. "Jim, what do you think?" Year one and year two they couldn't have cared less what I thought, thank you very much. My opinion would have been completely immaterial to the business at hand. All of a sudden my opinion mattered, ever so slightly, but it mattered nonetheless. It matters because they started to trust my judgment.

Here is the other side to it. I was piecing together unconventional deals based on the relationship with RC; I had my reputation on the line in many instances. My confidence grew in them as well. There were no absolute guarantees they would have funded the deal at the final hour. But I learned to trust what they were saying. If they said yes, they would follow through. There wasn't a doubt in my mind that they would not follow through if they gave me their word. Because of that bond (trust) that we developed, I think we were able to help a lot of people that would have otherwise struggled to buy a house. I did business with RC for about fifteen years as both a lender and real estate agent.

We all (lenders and real estate agents) need those types of relationships to maintain our strength in this business.

Think of RC as a vendor. Remember, for the sake of keeping it simple, the players in the industry are management, producers, and vendors. A vendor could be RC or a stager or anyone and everyone else that helps you complete the transaction. A real estate transaction can be a wacky process at times (most of the time, really)—we need our vendors. We need people that will jump in and help us close deals in a pinch. And in some cases, we need them to go out on a limb for us—they will do so, however, only if they trust us, if they believe in us.

I could have made a case to include this chapter about trust in "Operations" or "Finance" or "Attitude" or even "Getting Started." I chose to put it in "Marketing," however, because so many deals would been a bust without that relationship with RC.

Go get 'em!

38

Sneak Peek

———◆———

Things done well and with care exempt themselves from fear.
SHAKESPEARE

W E ARE GOING TO BE talking about softening the brand by introduc-
ing our personal life to the customer. Successful softening of
the brand in real estate will have a direct correlation to your revenue
line and therefore your profit for the year.

What are you going to show your customers regarding your personal life? Is it smart to give them a glimpse or a sneak peek into your
life outside of real estate? For the longest time, I showed my customers
next to nothing regarding my personal life. My attitude was, I am here
to do a job, and I plan to do it to the best of my ability; that is enough.
My customers don't need to know about my house, my car, my kids,
my wife, or really anything else, for that matter. That attitude softened
over the years.

Should the customers have a right to see that part of your life?
Well, they don't really have a right to see anything; it's your personal
choice, of course. But how much should they see? Is it smart to show
them a little? Remember, we are providing a very *personal* service, a
service that is mainly delivered by us—personally. The customer won't

separate the person from the service. They are linked—one and the same. Sometimes we would like to think they are not, but they are one.

When I was a lender, I noticed several of my colleagues sending out holiday cards with the whole family at Disneyland or Thanksgiving greetings with a family picture prominently displayed. I just wouldn't do it. In fact, the thought of it sounded so cheesy to me.

A few years into lending, we were having a party at the office. It was casual and you could invite your friends, clients, family, really anyone that you wanted. So I invited some clients, several of whom showed up. We had three very young daughters at the time, all under the age of seven. Our babysitting plans fell through at the last minute. I told the manager of the office what happened; actually, I told the manager's wife. She said, "Oh, bring them, we'd love to see the girls." Even so, I still had the good sense to not bring kids to business functions, but this was different. This was a true family-feel office, small, tight, and cozy—and this was more of a meet-and-greet setting than a formal venue. So we headed over to the party (office).

Softening the brand. I had never seen my clients so joyous. They were never that joyous when I was around. In fact, they pretty much ignored me at the party and talked with my wife and cooed over the kids. Where did that person go that was beating me up on the interest rate yesterday? Why are they so happy? It's really the first time any of my clients (other than close friend clients) had met my wife and kids.

The next week I needed to lock the rate for one of those clients that was at the party. Ring ring. I gave her the story about locking the rate. My client says, "Yeah, yeah, yeah, that's fine, Jim, do it, we love the girls, it was so fun seeing…" And on and on she went about the girls. I don't even think she even heard me on the rate that I quoted her. So I said it again and her response was, "Fine, Jim." And then she started back in again about the girls. Is this the same person that told me last week she was considering another lender if I couldn't get her the *exact* rate she wanted? Wow, I needed to think about this.

Is it smart to give your customer a tiny glimpse into your personal life?

As a real estate agent, I was competing with another agent on a listing. He went first, then I second. He was in a different office, but I always liked and respected him. We both came from referrals so it was going to be either him or me. The clients were transparent with us and told us as much; nothing hidden, which was great. I showed up at the meeting. After a little chitter chatter, they said to me, "Oh, yes, and we met with So-and-So yesterday." And then Mrs. Client started talking about my competitor's family. As I'm listening to this I'm thinking, "Did they even talk about real estate?" I mean, Mrs. Client rattled off so much personal information about my competitor; I could only presume they spent one hour on personal stuff and ten minutes on real estate.

Normally, I wouldn't think anything of it, but I really respected this guy. He was a good operator, modest, reserved, successful, and smart. You wouldn't describe him as a chatty person. In fact, I would describe him as professional, *strategic*, and mostly all business. He got the deal, roughly a $47,000 commission check.

Will your revenue line be the benefactor if you soften your brand?

By the way, you do have a brand. Your brand may not be by design, but we all have a brand nonetheless. Think of your brand as your image; the word *image* might be easier to digest. In fact, the words *image* and *brand* are used interchangeably in many cases; overall it's the "personality" of the product or, in this case in real estate, the service.

As your business skills grow, you will be able to modify your brand by design. Your brand should be authentic but at the same time it should be intentional; intended to drive revenue to your business.

The big picture. We wear a certain hat as real estate agent or as lender. We are there to do a job. Yes, we are. But could the experience be enhanced for the customer knowing who we are beyond the lender or beyond the real estate agent? Can it be a richer experience for all parties if they (the customers) know just a little about us personally?

Tactful. Is there a tactful way of doing this? Of course. Use good judgment, maybe a holiday card in December or a Thanksgiving card in November. This is not an every month kind of thing, just enough to let your customers know that you are more than just real estate agent or lender. You are simply softening the brand.

It's a business decision and also a personal decision in this case.

Remember, we are talking about only a glimpse, a half a teaspoon. I do believe there is a direct correlation between softening the brand and your annual profit.

Go get 'em!

39

Magic

———◆———

The greatest ability in business is to get along
with others—and influence their actions.
JOHN HANCOCK

HERE IS THE *MAGIC*—WE ALL know that word is fantasy, so don't ever buy into those headlines; flush that down the drain before we even start the boat. Let's do a supersized simplification of the real estate business as a lender or real estate agent: 1) finding deals, and 2) doing deals. Okay, I'm going to make an executive decision for us and say that finding deals is slightly harder than doing deals. I know I'm going out a limb on that (not really), but I think that's a pretty safe bet. Since we have now established that finding deals is harder, let's move on to step number two.

Finding deals. If someone asked me to pick one and only one "Finding Deals" topic in this book to reemphasize, which one would that be? I would have to think for a minute, but ultimately I would respond by saying, "I'd like to expand the discussion we were having in the chapter called "Do a Lot of Business Quickly." It was at the end of the chapter when we were talking about some of those fine-line distinctions relevant to referrals. I am choosing this topic because I believe it has a direct correlation to success in this business. This will be the only time I do this in this book, but I'm going to cut and paste that section below.

Here we go—cut and paste...

Work through referrals. A referral is a lead that comes from someone that you know—period. "Well, Jim, I have never done a deal, so how am I going to get referrals?" I'll say it again. A referral is a lead that comes from someone that you know—period.

"Hi, Steve, this is Jim" (I have never done business with Steve, but he is a friend from my previous job). After a little bit of chatter, "Steve, is there possibly anyone you know that needs assistance? Yes, great. Can you make that intro for me? Yes, great." Now I am talking with Adam through Steve. Adam and I talk. He is ready to sell his property in six months. Great. "Hey, Adam, I'll send those comps tomorrow over e-mail. Also, just by chance, is there possibly anyone else you know that needs assistance? Yes, great. Would you mind making that intro for me? Yes, great, thank you, Adam." Now I am talking to Susan through Adam. Now I have two warm referral leads to follow up with, Susan and Adam. I go back to Steve and say thank you very much and send him a $5 Starbucks card or write him a note. Steve is rich, but when is the last time someone gave him something tangible as a thank you? Now I have three "friendlies" in my hip pocket, two of whom are going to do business in the next six months.

Let me give you another example. I am at an open house and meet Glen and Stacey for the first time. We have a little chitter-chatter and then right then and there or later through e-mail or by phone, "Hey, Glen and Stacey, is there possibly anyone else that needs assistance? Yes, great." Now I am talking with Carlos through Glen and Stacey.

Which lead is more likely to close? Carlos or Glen and Stacey? Carlos. You got it! Why? Because Carlos is a warm referral lead and Glen and Stacey are a cold lead. "Hey, Jim, that's not fair, you didn't you *really* know Stacey and Glen." Yes, I did, I knew them for five minutes. *Remember, a referral is a lead that comes from someone you know—period.* It's a fine distinction and you'll probably want to work Carlos like crazy and completely drop Glen and Stacey. One generates income and the other does not. One is a warm lead and one is a cold lead. One will successfully drive your life and business, and the other one will drive you out of the business.

I am telling you right here and right now, that is how I was able to do so much business so quickly both in loans and then when I switched to real estate brokerage. It's one of those *Key to the Kingdom* type of concepts. If you can figure out another way to go from ground zero to the moon in one year, then that is fine. But the above is my recommendation nonetheless.

Now that you have had a chance to read that again, I am going to expand on it. It's common knowledge that we should be primarily working through referrals in this business; that's nothing new for sure. The point I want to make, however, is *the nitty-gritty definition of a referral.*

Please look at the example above, and specifically the one on Carlos and Glen and Stacey. So let's ask each of them this question, "How did you meet Jim?" Glen and Stacey would say, "We met Jim at an open house." Carlos would say, "I met Jim through Glen and Stacey." Now, the definition of a referral again is: a referral is a lead that comes from someone that you know—period. Which one is a referral? Yes, that's right, Carlos is the referral. Good.

In the definition of a referral above, was there any distinction relevant to how long I needed to know the person? No. I knew Stacey and Glen for five minutes. I could have known them for one minute, five minutes, a year, or twenty years. It doesn't matter. I know them now. That's all that matters. We hit it off at the open house; we are friendly to one another, so I know them now. And if they would like for me to talk with someone that they know, then I am a referred vendor to that new person. See?

I can't tell you how often the following has happened: "Jim, thank you for all the help on the transaction. I'm going to tell Jack o'Lantern (Jack o'Lantern was the person that referred them) you did a good job." I would literally be standing there for a couple of seconds trying to jog my brain on who Jack o'Lantern is. I eventually would remember, but after all, I might have only talked with Jack o'Lantern maybe two to three times in my whole life. And don't forget, I've never done business with Jack o'Lantern either. And no, I didn't forget to call Jack o'Lantern and thank him for sending me the referral.

Don't ever limit yourself. The world is a referral.

What to say. Over time, you'll figure out how to make it conversational. It's not the intent of this book to be teaching scripts; there are a million scripts you can find on the Internet. Find something that uniquely fits your DNA, and make it conversational to you. For me, it was simple, I felt comfortable saying something to the effect of, "Is there anyone you know that needs assistance?" I recognize that's a closed-end question/comment, but it fit within my DNA, so that's the way I did it. What kind of assistance? They knew. And if they did say, "What kind of assistance?" That's even better because now we are having a conversation—back-and-forth chitter-chatter. The hardest part of the conversation is just those first few words out of your mouth. Once that part is over, it's easy.

I'm expanding this topic in excruciating detail because I want you to know that you have options—*lots of options.* Even if you drop into a new city from outer space for the first time, you can generate some business from referrals—referrals from all those new friends that you have known for one minute, three minutes, or ten minutes.

That's the best I can do for a magic trick.

Go get 'em!

40

Gold Mine

Not what we have but what we enjoy
constitutes our abundance.

EPICURUS

THERE ARE VAST, WIDE-OPEN, UNDISCOVERED gold mines available for real estate professionals that would like to work the attorney market: for real estate agents, for lenders, and most areas of commercial. In large part, the attorney market has been completely ignored by real estate professionals; it's an unharnessed and vast *gold mine*. The calls come in to the attorney, and we are not there with our glove open to make the catch.

Picture this scenario as a real estate professional: you are working with a businessperson; he or she is referring you multiple deals per year; your competition is not competing for his or her attention; *you like him or her; he or she likes you*; and you are given autonomy to do what you know needs to be done as a professional. Sound completely unrealistic? Today, if I had the objective to send my brokerage business to the moon, I would focus on this area, the attorney market, almost to the exclusion of all others.

I was introduced to this market almost by accident.

I was doing a loan for an attorney and her husband. They were buying their first home, and the loan was a little tricky because they were young, didn't have much a down payment, had lots of student loans, had a minimal income, etc. They had been trying for a couple of years to get a loan with no luck. I actually met them through a direct-mail piece that I was sending out to renters. They called me and we met. I didn't want them to be disappointed again, so I asked them not to look for a house until we had formal loan approval subject only to property-specific conditions, such as appraisal, title report, and purchase contract. They agreed.

The loan took a bit of doing and wasn't a great loan, frankly, but we got them a loan nonetheless. They started looking with a real estate agent and successfully bought a house. Great. They were thrilled to have purchased their first home, and they recognized how difficult the loan was in this case. So they were appreciative, which is always a good feeling. I said thank you (we'll call them Fred and Elma) and congrats and really didn't think much it, and then moved on to the next deal.

About a year later, I had made that switch to real estate sales (as a real estate agent) and got a call from Elma, my client and the attorney. She said that she was working on a family law matter and there was a property that needed to be sold. She didn't much care that I had little to no experience at that point selling property. She was representing the husband and wondered if I would be interested in pursuing that matter. Naturally, I said yes.

Now, when you are working a divorce matter, you are working equally and 100 percent for the owners of the property, in this case, husband and wife (who weren't real fond of each other at the moment). It's very important to remember that. However, I came into the picture as a referral from the husband's team, so naturally the wife and the wife's attorney were a little leery of me. I walked into the door for the first time, and I could just feel that it was going to be tricky. The husband showed up too. I realized quickly that I needed to be sensitive to how difficult this was on each of them, but that I needed to be an independent and impartial voice in the room and mainly stick to the business at hand. We got through that first meeting okay, but it was too soon for them to make a commitment to a real estate agent, so we continued the process. Remember, it's a process.

As I stayed in touch with both of them over the next couple of months, I realized that the wife was leaning on her attorney and the husband on his. At that point in their life, the attorneys were their trusted advisors, possibly the number one advisor for each of them at that second. The husband was ready to hire me; the wife, however, was not. I asked the wife one day if she would like me to reach out to her attorney to give her a summary of things. She said yes. In fact, she was thrilled with the idea. I called her attorney and had a good, quick chat. Then I started to realize that I almost had four customers; the husband, the wife, and their two attorneys. Four, that's a big team.

After talking with the wife's attorney, the wife called me shortly thereafter and was comfortable moving forward. Do you think the opinion of the wife's attorney mattered? For sure, her attorney felt good about me, so she felt good about me. We got the property listed and sold. By the end of the transaction, I had a good professional re- lationship with the husband, the wife, the husband's attorney, and the wife's attorney. What they wanted more than anything else was equal and complete communication.

The climax of the story. Reminder, I came into the picture through the husband's attorney, Elma. The wife's attorney called me about a month later and said that she was pleased with how I handled things, and would I be willing to look at another matter that required a piece of real estate to be sold. Wow! That's what I said. Wow! What would happen if I actually *tried* building those relationships instead of just dumb luck landing in my lap? Could I actually build a good, solid referral business from primarily attorneys?

And so it began, one after another after another.

Trusted members of the community. I know what you might be thinking; we are only talking about divorce cases. You would be wrong if you are thinking that. Attorneys are trusted members of the community; people come to their attorneys for all kinds of business and personal matters. I do; I almost never make a decision without involving my attorney team. And we are not only talking about family law, trust, and probate attorneys. I have had attorneys send me deals that were involved in patent law, corporate law, criminal defense, and more—things that have nothing to do with real estate.

Think about it: when someone needs help and has a trusted friend/advisor in the legal profession, that person is likely to reach out to him or her. That attorney might be an expert at coal technology litigation and the person might need help with a complicated commercial building, but he or she is likely to reach out anyway as a starting point. I had an attorney that was an expert at microchip piracy issues that called me one day out of the blue; she said that her colleague, another attorney, needed an agent referral for a bread-and-butter buyer client. Awesome, great, thank you—I'll take care of that!

And yes, there are a lot of divorce and death cases. Recognize, however, that those cases will come from more than just family law, trust, and probate attorneys; they could come from every specialty of law under the sun, as a starting point. And finally, in those unfortunate situations of death or divorce, should there not be a good, solid, strong real estate professional involved in that process? You bet, for sure, even more so in those instances.

Good and bad deals. When you are working the attorney market, you need to be willing to get your hands dirty. Sometimes you might get to work on a home-run-smooth transaction, and other times it might be a nightmare. It's a must to maintain a good attitude and perform well either way. You have to be willing to take the good with the bad and give it your best effort either way. In addition, there might be some that are $100,000 deals and some that are $2 million deals. Again, it doesn't matter—people will be counting on you in both instances to get it done and get it done well.

Servicing. When you start building those strong relationships, your attorney clients will lean on you for lots of things. "Hey, Jim, can you run comps on a property, check that rate for me, can you look at this issue, or can you evaluate that?" There is a servicing aspect to working with attorneys in addition to "doing deals." It's not a problem; I'm giving you a heads up to be prepared for that and be willing to jump in when you are needed. And you do have to jump in and be responsive and helpful.

Who is working this market? Rest assured, practically no one is working this market. It's safe to say that many folks don't even recognize that this is a market to be worked. You will be all alone for the most part. "If that's true, Jim, then who is handling these deals right now?" They are falling through the cracks, landing in the hands of your competitors, one by one on a fragmented basis.

Attorneys could be referring a large volume of business. All you have to do is be clear in your intention about it. You want to catch the person (the customer) at the point of contact, when the customer makes the call to the attorney. That's the time to put out your glove and make the catch. Later, down the road, is too late.

One to four. If you are working a divorce case, really focus in and do a good job. *Your customer list went from one to four.* On a normal transaction, we have one customer and one possibility to generate more deals and referrals from the one customer. On a divorce case, we have four, and those numbers grow exponentially. Mr. Seller may want to buy a house; Mrs. Seller may want to buy a house; the attorneys may have more business for you. The possibilities are exponential. Use numbers to your advantage. Make numbers your friend. For that to happen, you have to do a good job.

A bad market. I'm convinced that people lean on their attorneys more when things go bad then when things are good. So the attorney market is a good market when the economy is good and it's a good market when the economy is bad. People need their advisors in both instances.

My *business* real estate agent. I could have said *my business lender* or *my business commercial contact.* I have had attorney clients that send me two deals yearly just like clockwork. But when they listed their own personal residence, they hired someone else; I have had that happen more than once. Before you feel sorry for me, think about it. I was not their *personal* real estate agent in their mind; I branded myself as their "business" real estate contact. They associated me with their business, their place of employment, and the other real estate agent with their personal life. So over a six-year period I would do twelve deals with them and they did one deal with someone else. No problem.

I'm thinking about all the attorneys that I worked with; I'm guessing only two to three would hire me to help them buy a house or list their personal residence. But all of them would hire me to take care of a piece of business they were working on within their firm. See the difference? Once you understand the difference, you'll understand the power of working the attorney market.

Five good attorneys. You don't have to go crazy here; how about start by building strong business relationships with five active attorneys over the next few years? If they are successful and you are skillful about embracing that relationship, it's realistic to produce two deals annually from each attorney, ten total. You can change the assumptions if you like, but based on my experience you will be able to do one to three deals yearly from each relationship. Two is a good number. In some markets, a real estate professional can base his or her entire existence on ten deals yearly.

Building relationships. I can't give you step one, step two, and step three on this. I will give you some ideas, however. These are professional people. You have to be thoughtful. I have sent out letters over the years in an attempt to build my attorney client customer base, with absolutely zero response. And well-written letters, I must say; but even then, no response, not even a ripple. Personal touch is the key. Think about who you may know right now that is an attorney, and start there. And for young people brand new to real estate, think about parents and even grandparents of your friends that might be an attorney. Ask to have coffee or stop by their office for a minute. The messaging is simple, for now: you just want to be there as a real estate resource for them. Remember, this not an in-and-out deal. You are building a relationship. It's not going to happen overnight. These are serious matters, in many cases; they are handling them within their law firm. It's going to take awhile for them to trust you. Be patient and be available as a resource. And then, when you finally get a chance to do a deal with them, *kick butt.*

Go get 'em!

Operations

A Guide to Making It in Real Estate

41

Lead the Process

———◆———

If your actions inspire others to dream more, learn
more, do more, and become more, you are a leader.
PRESIDENT JOHN QUINCY ADAMS

NATURALLY, WE ARE ALL CURIOUS about what people do for a living.
When asked that question, I usually answer something to the effect
of, "I'm in real estate" or "I'm a broker" or "I sell real estate" or some vari-
ation thereof, depending on my mood at the moment. But if someone
were to rephrase the question and ask me, "How would you characterize
what you do on a day-to-day basis?" I would say, "I lead and manage the
process."

A real estate transaction has hundreds of moving parts. It's a
project that has to be managed. Someone has to take complete responsibility to complete the task at hand. That person has to monitor,
encourage, manage personnel (directly and indirectly), educate, and
lead the team to victory. Think about the people that touch an average real estate transaction: the selling agent, the listing agent, the assistants of the agents, the managers of the agents, the escrow officer,
the assistants of the escrow officers, the appraiser, the appraiser's assistant, the lender, the lender's assistants, the clients, possibly family
members of the clients, the client's attorneys, the client's tax professional at times, inspectors (up to six or seven in some cases), and on

and on. A real estate transaction is a process. It's a process that has to be managed. There should be and can only be one leader that takes complete responsibility to complete the task at hand.

When I moved into real estate brokerage, I was able to complete a transaction in the luxury market within about three years. One of my first customers was an executive of a local technology company. I am not going to lie, I was a little intimidated and nervous. But he told me early on, "Jim, you lead; I don't have a lot of time, so you tell us what we need to do to get this done." No one had ever told me that in the way that he said it, but then again, I had never worked with anyone at his level of success in business. Without exception, he and his family did everything that I asked when I asked. As an aside, my experience is that successful people know when to lead and when to follow. Can you imagine how much fun this business would be if everyone respected the leader and actually let the professional lead the transaction? Digressing even further, here is a little secret I'll share with you about the luxury market: *the bigger the price point, the more financially successful the client, the easier the deal becomes.* You can make your own conclusion on why that is. Here is mine: successful people know when it's time to lead and when it's time to follow.

I built a home in 2006. My contractor had been around a long time. The owner of the company was frugal, experienced, confident, and in his late 50s (at that time); a true no-nonsense type of personality. He told my wife and me early on that he was going to manage the process and also educate us on the steps as we were moving through the process. Of course we wanted him to manage the process; that is why we hired him. We were not quite sure what he meant by *educate*, but the process started nonetheless. He called me early on and said (I am paraphrasing), "Jim, excavation is complete and we are going to pour the foundation. Before I do that, however, I am going to install a layer of material on the ground to prevent moisture and other intrusions. Any questions?" He did that the whole way through. He kept my wife and me fully informed. He knew the process; I didn't know the process. He had done it hundreds of times; I was on repetition number one. As a customer, I appreciated the education. In fact, from that moment forward I installed "the education steps" into my own real estate business.

As real estate professionals, we need to lead the process. The client doesn't know the process; we know the process. Sometimes we forget that when we are working on transaction number 345, the client might be working on transaction number one. They don't know. We know. We need to educate people along the way. "Mike and Julie, just a friendly reminder that we are performing a crawl space inspection on your home on October 5. Please ensure there is clearance to the crawl space. My assistant will be there and the inspector is bonded, so don't worry; this is all part of the process. You might be thinking, why are we doing this? Good question. Well, the buyers need to know what they are buying, and frankly you want them to know what they are buying. Very normal stuff, all part of the process. Any questions?"

The client wants leadership. The client needs leadership. He or she is paying us to lead and manage the process. In many cases, the next phase of his or her life depends on our willingness and ability to lead. Can you imagine the following?

"Wow, Jim, I can't believe there is standing water under my house. Oh, my God, what do we do?" says Client.

"Ut oh, I hope they don't back out. This is terrible. See, I knew this was going to be a bad day." says Jim in a wimpy voice.

"Is the buyer going to back out of the deal, Jim? What do we do? I'm so nervous," says Client.

"Gosh, I hope not. This is terrible, oh, no," says Jim as you hear the nervous crackle in his voice.

No way! Here is what the client deserves and is paying us to do: "I know you are nervous, Client, but this is very common. Stand by, Client, I am going to call the selling agent and we are going to get a game plan together to move forward. Either way, we are moving forward. I'll call you back within forty-five minutes."

What happens if we don't lead the process with strength? Well, just like in any setting that involves human beings, whenever there is a vacuum or gap, someone will fill it. Guess who will fill that leadership gap if you don't? You got it, your client. Guess who is now flying the plane with absolutely no experience in the cockpit? You guessed it again, your client. Guess who will be in the copilot's chair or even in the back of the plane as a passenger or, worse yet, in the storage compartment as a piece of luggage getting knocked around? You (the person that should be leading). Guess who is now the boss? Your client. Guess who he or she is bossing around with no clue what he or she is doing? You. Now that your client is the boss, do you think he or she is willing to give up the reins and give them back to you? No way. Just hang on for dear life at that point and hope that the plane doesn't crash.

Tell the client he or she is wrong when he or she is wrong? No. Don't be that person that is too abrupt and self-righteous about being direct. Use some people skills, soften the edges a little, but be forthcoming nonetheless. They can take it—tell them when you are going astray. And there may be instances where you do need to say things in a more direct manner. Use your people skills, tell the truth, and lead the process.

The customer hired us to take charge and *lead the way*. So do it.

Go get 'em!

42

The Fallacy of Service

I do the very best I know how—the very best I can—
and I mean to keep on doing so until the end.
President Abraham Lincoln

I WENT TO A SEMINAR when I started in real estate given by a hot-shot, bigger-than-life real estate guy from another state. He was talking about this, talking about that, mainly how great he was. Then he talked about service. He said, "If you are not providing exceptional, over-the-top service, you might as well quit." As I sat there as a young person starting in the industry, listening to this guy, I felt defeated before I even started. How in the world can I compete in an industry in which everyone else is doing it at such a high level? I have heard this same/similar kind of statement a thousand times over the years. "Oh, you have to give amazing service. You need to 'wow' your customer. Your service has to be an unbelievable experience."

I like what President Lincoln had to say above: "I do my best."

Now that I have been in this business for a couple of decades, there are not a lot of things that bother me, but this is one of them. It drives me up the wall when I hear that kind of "perfect service" talk. It's akin to a coach saying to a player, "You have to be perfect or you might as well quit—you loser!" I hate hearing that, and I hate hearing the knuckleheads that talk about perfect service in real estate. Don't make it complicated. Service is simple. The customer hired us to do a job, so do it to the best of your ability. Okay, that might be a little simple for some—so here it is expanded: 1) Run the project, 2) Tell the truth, 3) Be reliable, and 4) Do your job.

Run the project. We are not running a company or a long-term venture. A real estate transaction is a short-term project with many moving parts. Every project needs a leader. There can only be one leader. So lead. Run it. Take the reins and go. That is what we have been hired to do. That is the expectation.

Tell the truth. If you want to be looking over your shoulder for the rest of your life, then fine, lying is an option. But if you want a good life and business, then simply tell the truth. What is there to lie about anyway? "Mrs. Customer, there are a lot of moving parts to a real estate transaction, and at times it may get a little bumpy, but honestly, don't worry, we'll get there nonetheless, as a team." Look, things happen during a real estate transaction, unexpected things. I recognize there are possibly people reading this that have done over one thousand real estate transactions of some shape or size; me too. I have never had a twin transaction or an exact look-alike in all those deals. They are all a little different. There are bumps in the road. Things happen. Over time and over our careers, we are able to see the curves in the road before they appear. But variables exist nonetheless. Tell your customer the truth. Tell them that it is a process and that you will successfully get to the other side of the river. Word it however you want to word it, but be forthcoming and work through the bumps.

Be reliable. I am going to overlap reliable and responsive, because in my view they are cut from the same cloth. My friends that are super-successful are some of the most reliable and responsive people that I know. I could send them an e-mail right now, and they would get back to me within the hour. If you ever want to guarantee failure, then be superunreliable and unresponsive. This is a career killer. If you ever want to really make your customer mad, take two days to get back to them on an e-mail. The more reliable we become, the more money we will make. The more people that count on us, the more money we will make. Can I count on Jim to get back to me in a timely manner? Can I count on Jim to do his job? Can I count on him to run the project? Can I count on him for this, count on him for that? Over time, the more people that honestly can count on you to be reliable and responsive, the more successful you will become and the more money you will make.

Do your job. Ultimately we need to complete the job that we have been hired to do. If we don't, no referrals, no growth, no income, no life. Sometimes the customer will be really happy with us and sometimes he or she will not. But that should not affect our responsibility of doing our job. I have had deals where I have literally worked like crazy and the customer was so, so happy; I have also had deals, however, where I gave myself a C grade and the customer was thrilled. Go figure. We need to do our job in spite of the current emotions of our customer. Emotions have a tendency to change over time. If we don't do our job, however, that will be the only thing the customer remembers. He or she will remember that we fell down on the job and didn't get it done.

Aristotle said, "We are what we repeatedly do. Excellence, then, is not an act but a habit." And if you forget everything about service, just remember what President Lincoln said: "I do my best."

Go get 'em!

43

Atten-hut!

———◆———

A superior person is modest in speech but exceeds in actions.

CONFUCIUS

I DO RECOGNIZE THERE ARE many versions of *atten-hut*, but we all know the rough meaning nonetheless. My wife is a dance teacher and was reared by a three-war veteran. There are times when she needs absolute attention from her students—*atten-hut!* The students drop their hands to their sides, chins up, eyes on teacher, and quiet as a mouse. She has their *full attention*.

The customer wants our attention. Yes, they want something done, that's obvious. But they want our attention as we move through the real estate process. The customer is buying our time, energy, and attention. Remember, we are not in a getting-deals-signed-and-disappearing business. We are in a service business that requires us to get things done. Give them what they want: your attention first and then ultimately the successful completion of the job. Many of us are constantly concerned about what we are saying and how we are saying it (me too). None of us can say and do everything perfectly all the time. What we can do, however, is be there for the customer and give him or her our *attention*.

I have had deals where quite honestly I thought I performed at about a level B at best, but the customers were thrilled to death and tripping over themselves to refer me to their friends. I'm thinking, "Wow, I don't quite get it." But then thinking back on the process, they could reach me by phone or e-mail, I did a pretty good job of antici-pating their anxieties, I handled their concerns, and I was reasonably responsive the whole way through. Basically, they could count on me day in, day out. No: not to be perfect; just to be attentive.

Think about it this way. If you have been in the real estate business for more than a day, on occasion we have all seen brand new lenders or brand new real estate agents go to the top of the list in one year. Clearly they don't have the skills or experience of a seasoned person. Why would so many customers trust those who are so green? Well, their head was in the game, their attention to detail was obvious, and they were enthusiastic—and all that comes oozing though their pores like booze the morning after.

Build a strong business that will stand the test of time. *Give the customer your attention.*

Go get 'em!

44

Be a Team Player in the Office

If we do not hang together, we shall surely hang separately.
BENJAMIN FRANKLIN

BEING A TEAM PLAYER IN the office makes you strong, the office strong, and the industry strong. In addition, being a team player in the office will make you money. "Well, I'm an independent contractor and own my own business and don't really have a boss and don't entirely need the office."

Well, let's talk about that.

As producers, we own the job. Technically, most of us do not have a boss and we can control our schedule, that's true. We do run a small business, that's true. But I like to say we "own the job." We can choose to take the job to this office or that office because we have ownership of the job, as opposed to a corporate job at Apple Computers, Apple owns the job; that job requisite stays at Apple, period.

Here is the distinction: a more traditional business is something that would and could continue to operate without the principal. In real estate, 99 percent of the time, when the producer stops, his or her production stops as well. If you really want to own your own traditional small business, then open up your own (lending or brokerage) shop, which would include capital, personnel, leasing an office, licensing, insurance, heavy risk, managing, and on and on—then, the difference between owning the job and owning the business will became glaringly obvious. As independent lenders and real estate professionals, we run a small business and own the job.

So whether or not you are convinced we own the job in real estate, let's continue. What do we need to survive in this business? Naturally we need strong marketing, strong finance, and strong operations. We are talking about operations in this case. I am guessing that in most or all instances, your office does not hand you home-run, cash-the-check leads on a daily basis. That's just not the way the business is structured. Therefore, we generate our revenue/income through our own efforts and ingenuity as independent real estate professionals. Fine; that's why we love this business—because the sky is the limit.

Now, we need to take a portion of that revenue and purchase operational support and services (i.e., the split). What kind of services? Office leadership, management, culture, insurance, synergy, and energy that comes from being part of a team, a roof over our heads, technology, administrative support, furniture in most cases, copiers, HR in some cases, and more. We are asking the office to provide all those services short of us doing our job, which is 1) finding deals and 2) successfully closing deals. Embrace the fact that the office (or the company) needs us and we need the office. Just a fact, Jack! It's a codependent relationship. Be a team player within that office. It's in your best interest to do so.

I believe it's an interesting topic, and I will be the first one to admit that I always struggled with this codependent relationship. Why did we get into this business to begin with? I believe freedom and limitless income would be at the top of the list for most of us. "Well, Jim, I don't agree. I just love reading about subterranean termites. It's so much fun to understand how they crawl around in the dirt." Okay, cool, but for the rest of us, freedom and limitless income. Who is attracted to this type of business? In many cases, entrepreneurial-type personalities that want to run their own show and not have a boss. *Therein lies the rub.* We are asking free-thinking, independent, entrepreneurial-type personalities to be team players, to take a back seat in some instances, and to root on the team. Interesting cultural dynamic. Understand it. Accept it. And do it. It's in your best interest that the company does well and colleagues in your office do well.

By nature I have always been a relatively positive, happy person. The only time I had a bump in the road emotionally, however, was when I worked from my house. I was building my personal residence at the time and the house had been completed, but now came the landscaping. I wanted it done right, so I moved my office to my house for six months so I could keep my eye on things. Bad idea. After about two months I was dragging myself from this to that. I would say to my wife, "What in the world is wrong with me?" And then it finally hit me. It was the first time in my career that I had worked in the house and from the house on a day-to-day basis with little to no face-to-face interaction with colleagues, friends, etc. I know that can work for a lot of people. But wow, not for me. I quickly got my butt back into the real estate office and was cured. There is just something about the hum of the office. Even if my door was shut, I could still feel the daily chatter, deals moving, and people trying to achieve. That experience reminded me of the importance of office team energy—an invaluable service that the office/company provides for us.

You *will* make money by being a good team player in the office. Wow, where do I start on this one? First, what characteristics could be consistent with the definition of a good team player? Quite possibly being trustworthy, reliable, loyal, honest, friendly, skillful, inclusive, and others. When I started in the loan business, there was a lender in the office that was skillful and friendly to everyone in the office. I literally walked in off the streets for the first time with ten to fifteen leads that I had no idea what to do with. The manager said, "You work with Lender C on these deals." So that's what I did, and we decided to split all of them, since I had no idea what I was doing at the time. I did all the work and she coached me. She earned roughly $10,000 on those deals just for having a good reputation and being a good sport in the office.

Several years later, management in my office was involved in a small real estate development deal. I was asked to participate along with a handful of other people. I know, every deal has risk, but if you knew the details of this deal, risk was very low and upside was high. This was really a tangible reward for being loyal, reliable, fighting the battles when necessary, and being a good team player. That investment required $50 (add some zeros). In the last ten years, I have received an average of $1 monthly from that investment, and the $50 has turned into equity of roughly $500. I would have never been asked to be part of that deal if I was not a good team player for management in the office. Being a good team player can pay well.

Let's talk a little further about how being a good office team player can grow your revenue line. Why? Because at the end of a day, we are in this business to support our families by providing a good service. And also, people pay attention when we talk money. So here is another example. It's naturally just the right thing to do to be nice to everyone in the office, but I can say with all sincerity, I always did my best to reach out to the administrative staff in particular (i.e., secretaries, helpers, runners, receptionists, admins, etc.). One day a call came in to the office from a person in the community that wanted to talk with an agent about listing their home. The receptionist rang through to my office. "Jim, you are always nice to me. Do you want this lead?" I can probably count on my hands how many times over twenty years I have closed deals through office leads, but this was one of them. Yes, for sure I wanted it, and thank you. Listed, closed—and drove $21K to my revenue line. Be nice, be a good team player, and possibly make a little extra money.

There is a tremendous amount of business that can be sourced to loan processors. When I started out in the loan business, we had four total processors on site and a manager that chipped in when things got busy, so five. My manager at the time was a seasoned real estate pro and told me early on, mostly in frustration, "Our loan processors have huge personal networks, and it's crazy that no one reaches out to them!" Hmmm, that's interesting. When you came in the front door of our mortgage office, you walked straight ahead to go to the agent desk area but had to take a hard left to get to the loan processing area. In other words, the processors were off by themselves in the corner of the office. As often as possible, I would come in the front door, take the hard left, and say hi to everyone as I walked by; I did the same thing as I left. Hey! How about just paying attention to people, being friendly in the office? Pretty simple, really. I probably generated roughly $25,000 that year just through processor networks, and they made money too. Starting to be convinced that being a team player pays?

Are you approachable in the office? There are deals that will happen in the office and stay in the office. But if we are cold, standoffish, naturally, we are not going to be part of those conversations. That's fine if you don't want to be part of those conversations; I know people that are not such good team players that do a lot of business and are not part of those deals. But if you want to be part of that "deal flow," then you have to be in the office and approachable. And every once in a while, you may just pick up a pearl and make an extra $10,000 to $50,000 yearly—not bad for just being a good sport.

This can be a lonely business without the support of the office. As independent contractors, we are part of a team within a very competitive industry, an industry that attracts some doggedly competitive personalities. It's nice to have a group of people in your corner to help fight the daily battles and share in those successes and occasional setbacks. For business advice, I lean on one of my most successful college teammates from time to time. When advising me, he always starts it off with, "Jim, what can I tell you, the world is competitive." It's better to take on the world with a team.

A united real estate office will make everyone in that office more money.

I could have put this section in "Marketing" because, as indicated, your willingness to be a team player will have a direct correlation to your revenue line. In other words, you will do more business by being a team player in the office. But again, we are mostly on our own in this business to produce our own leads, and the operations side of the business is equally important to marketing. The quality of the relationships that we build in the office will ultimately affect a) the quality of service we are able to provide for our customers and 2) our ability to serve more people over time (i.e., make more money). Therefore, marketing and operations in this case are forever interdependent.

Go get 'em!

45
Finishing Produces Results

———◆———

*Affairs are easier of entrance than of exit, and it is but
common prudence to see our way out before we venture in.*

AESOP

DRAW A DIRECT CORRELATION BETWEEN finishing and your revenue line. The finish will produce a good financial return. The finish will put you in a position to help a loved one or friend. The finish will help you buy a home. The finish will send your kids to college. The finish will eventually help you retire.

We can do everything right, go 99 percent of the way there, but if the finish is bad, the results are bad. Leave your collegiate efforts two classes short after committing five years of your life, and produce no diploma. A soccer team plays well for eighty-eight minutes but falls apart the last two, walks away a loser. The efforts to write a book are nearly wasted without the ability to push that extra 1 percent and finish. The plane crashes because the copilot was momentarily distracted when checking that one last (and final) item before takeoff. Run twenty-six miles but stop short of the last 385 yards, and no accolades for completing a marathon.

On the other hand: write that thank-you note after a successful transaction and produce a $30,000 referral; handle that small little item at the end of the deal (which is driving your customer crazy) and produce a happy customer that refers you $100,000 in business over the next five years; ask for the business at the conclusion of a great presentation and drive $15,000 to your revenue line; personally attend the signoff and generate $7,000 in new business. Our business is dependent on our willingness to finish strong.

As customers, we expect a lot; we are demanding, and rightly so. We have paid a vendor (a real estate professional) to produce a result. What have you done for me lately? *Lately* is the operative word; correlate *lately* with *finish*. We can do a great job, hit the target on all marks, and if we fall down at the end of the deal, the customer will remember. His or her most vivid and recent memory will be that we didn't do this or didn't do that; basically that we didn't finish and take care of him or her. "But wait, Jim! I worked my butt off for five months and spent two hundred hours on this deal; won't they remember that?" That was yesterday. The customer needs us today.

Ninety percent of the goodies come from that last 5 percent of finish work. The difference between winning and losing in business is very small. You don't really even have to know *how* to finish—you just have to be *willing* to finish. Those folks that are willing to finish will be successful. I have seen colleagues literally spend thirty hours working on a flyer, talking about it, designing it, reviewing it, proofing it, thinking about it, and laboring over it! And then they never send it. Thirty hours invested with no return. A flyer will never be perfect— just finish it and send it. Finish the project and generate a $10,000 transaction from the flyer, a great return for *the finish*.

The majority of profits are in the finish; that last little bit of effort. I had a client that was referred to me by an AAA customer. I did my best to always provide a good service, but I was particularly on my game in this case, given the AAA status of the referring party. The customer gave me an A grade on that deal, both husband and wife. The deal closed. The client called me roughly three weeks later regarding an issue he was having with the house. The client was a level-headed, successful guy, but for whatever reason I could quickly see this issue was driving him up the wall. Upon receiving his call, bam, I jumped right back into action. I had his issue fixed that very day. I know this guy. If I had fallen down on that issue, all the hard work I had done prior to that would have been nullified—cancelled—wiped out! In this case, it was just a loose end; button it up. Finish. That guy has sent me over $100,000 in business over the years. The finish equals $100,000 in that instance.

I recognize sports analogies are repulsive to some people, but allow me to give you a personal one on this topic of finishing. I tell my young offensive lineman at my volunteer job, *"Finish your blocks.* Yes, we can get five yards by doing a good job for two seconds, but we'll score touchdowns by blocking for four (seconds)—it's just a little more effort to go from five yards to six points."

Go get 'em!

46

Offense and Defense

No problem can withstand the assault of sustained thinking.

VOLTAIRE

SOMETIMES WE STUMBLE ONTO IDEAS out of necessity. About year two in lending, I had built a solid business but was still feeling a little unorganized. I don't consider myself to be an operations expert, but I do like things orderly, and it bothered me that things weren't tidy. I was managing twenty to forty loans at all times, so I needed an epiphany. One day I started writing down things that I do during the day, everything. Then I wrote down the words *finding deals* and *doing deals* (hey, I'm a simple thinker). And then I looked at my task list and realized that nearly everything can go into one of those two buckets. I started breaking up my day into finding deals and doing deals. When I arrived at work, I would write down: 8:00 to 9:00 a.m. = finding deals; 9:00 to 10:00 a.m. = doing deals; and so on all the way through 3:00 p.m., at which time I would leave the office for appointments or get a workout.

This plan was working, but something was missing. The problem. By about 10:30 a.m., the phone was ringing like crazy, and by 11:30 a.m. I was completely off my schedule and just reacting to this or that. Reacting. Hmmm. That sounds like defense to me. Executing a plan, that sounds like offense to me. So I modified my game plan from *finding deals* and *doing deals* to *offense* and *defense*. From the minute that I woke until about 11:30 a.m., I could control my world—I could play offense. From that point forward, however, don't fight it, Jim. I needed to accept the fact that I needed to play defense and react to this or that.

You can also think of offense as marketing and defense as operations.

Offense: What do we do on offense? We plan. We scheme. We dream. We attack. We anticipate. And then we ultimately execute our plan. We have an advantage because the defense doesn't know what we are about to do. There is an element of sophistication to offense; that's why the O-lineman in football are the smartest guys on the team! Sorry to you defensive people out there. We have an element of control when we are playing offense. We know what we are trying to accomplish. For me, it was crystal clear, this was my marketing time.

Defense: We are mostly reacting. Yes, there is an element of planning, but the planning is different. You need to "read" what the other person is doing. Read your key. React to this or that. It is a secondary reaction based on the movement of the offensive player. React to what the offensive player is doing. "But Jim, there are times when the defense runs an attack." Yes, but rare. And think about it: If we attack when we are reacting to a customer, does that go well? Defense was the time when I did operations.

In my mind, I needed to split it up because my day was running together like a jumbled-up pudding mix with several ingredients bleeding into one another. In summary, offense = finding deals = marketing; defense = doing deals = operations. So here is an example of how I would utilize this strategy on a daily basis:

7:00 a.m. = Defense, plan for day, and give the task list to my assistants

8:00 a.m. = Offense

9:00 a.m. = Offense/defense, see if anyone needed me, and keep playing offense

10:00 a.m. = Offense

11:00 a.m. = Offense/defense, transition to defense

12:00 p.m. = Lunch

1:00 p.m. = Defense

2:00 p.m. = Defense

3:00 p.m. = Offense

4:00 p.m. = Offense

5: 00 p.m. = Go home and check in on things and turn it off by 7:00 p.m.

Aesop said, "After all is said and done, more is said than done." Maintain control over your day and get things *done!*

Go get 'em!

47

Office Jumping

———◆———

He that is discontented in one place will
seldom be happy in another.

AESOP

THERE ARE RISKS ASSOCIATED WITH office jumping. I am using the
words *team*, *office*, and *company* synonymously. In my view, they are
all one and the same. What is office jumping? It is moving from this
office to that office on a regular basis. If you have been in this business
for a while, you have seen this. Let's study this topic, and more specifically *let's review the economics and risks thereof.*

The office exists to support us, the agents, and our production.
The office is there for us; it's the team that we have selected. We have
hired the office to provide us with all those services that we don't want
to deal with, such as the building lease, insurance, managing, personnel, etc. We compensate the office for those services through our
revenue split. When we leave, to the manager, it feels like a shot in the
nose. It feels like he or she has been fired, that we don't want to be part
of his or her team. Why? Because the manager is working his or her
butt off to keep us happy and provide a good service for us.

Now think about it on a macro level, the industry as a whole.
Excessive turnover compromises the services companies can provide,

services intended for the agent. For instance, the manager would like to allocate $100 monthly per agent to be used on advertising at the agent's discretion. How can the manager budget that line item if he or she has no confidence about who is coming and going? So what does he or she do? He or she cuts or modifies the service. Who does it hurt? The agent. Who is responsible for turnover? The agent. Who is therefore responsible for the service being cut? The agent—there you have it. Turnover is bad for the agent and bad for management.

When we switch offices, our revenue drops. Consider this. You are going to move offices. You spend three to six months thinking about it and researching the move. Then you spend another month terrified about telling your manager about the move. Then you spend another two months getting familiar with the dynamics of the new office. I believe we lose six months of income when we jump, but since I'm a team player I'll concede and say we lose four months, minimum. Why? Momentum! So if you make $6,000 monthly, you will lose roughly $24,000 by jumping offices. Maybe you can justify this loss of income for some reason. But I believe it's wise to recognize nonetheless that there is indeed a financial cost to office jumping.

Here is a real-world example of switching offices and the income hit thereon. When my first mortgage company shut down, I spent several weeks with no office. I didn't office jump in this case but was forced to find another office nonetheless. I drove around in my nine-year-old red MR2 with files jam packed to the sunroof hunting for a new office. I labored over the decision (on selecting a new office) because I don't like switching once I'm settled in. I finally found a fantastic fit, unloaded my boxes, and off to work again. It literally took me four months to get back up to a complete stride. I say I lost six months of income, but again, I'll compromise and say *I lost a minimum of four months from this transition.* Painful. I said, "Never again if I can help it."

The grass is not necessarily always greener. You've seen it, a well-intended parent overly involved in his or her child's sports career. He or she is moving the child from this team to that team, all in an attempt to advance the child. I'm not saying it's wrong, I'm saying it's risky, and in many cases the risks outweigh the possible benefits. Will children like their new teammates? Will they like their new coach? Will they be challenged too much or too little? Is it a stable environment or will we be looking for another team a year from now? By leaving, is the child learning the right life skills? *There are risks associated with trying to find that perfect fit.* Are we better off taking responsibility for everything and making the best of what we have and digging in? Just a question to consider.

Now, there may be instances where office jumping is prudent: immoral or illegal business practices; an impossible relationship within the office; a management change that is unacceptable; and other possibilities. But short of those, is it wise to change our environment on a regular basis? If you just need a change to shake it up or for your own mental health, then fine. But call it what it is and understand you are going to lose efficiencies.

I can't tell you how many times I have seen people leave and then come back three to four months later. So that person just lost eight months of income looking for the pot of gold. That's almost one year of income for one bad decision—risky.

Are we pointing the finger at the manager or company too much? As producers, we entered real estate largely because we wanted freedom, independence, no boss, and limitless income. Well, then, get going. Make the best of what you have. Take responsibility for everything and kick butt!

Go get 'em!

48

Waking Up in the Morning

———————

He that rises late must trot all day.

BENJAMIN FRANKLIN

I MADE MY LIST FOR the following day. I know my schedule. The alarm is set for 6:00 a.m. I'm going to bed on time. I'm ready to dominate and attack the world when I rise for the day. Yes! Alarm rings. Snooze. Alarm rings again. Snooze. Oh sh234890t—it's 8:15 a.m. Panic—scramble—and immediate sense of failure. Sound familiar?

Those first few minutes of the day will steal our ambitions. All that drive and determination that we felt the night before—gone. Our desires and dreams for the day—gone. Our success—gone. A great life—gone.

My father-in-law was in the military for twenty-eight years and gave me the best advice on waking up. Set your alarm somewhere so that you must get out of bed and walk several paces to turn it off. Ideally, set it somewhere that is between your bed and the shower so you can walk like a zombie from bed and keep walking straight into the shower.

I started using that advice, and it was working. After a few months, however, I found a work-around to the plan. Walk like a zombie and turn off alarm, walk like a zombie back to bed, get in bed, pull covers over head, go back to sleep.

I had such a problem with this for so long that I needed to redefine that moment for myself; that dangerous moment in the morning (in some cases it's just seconds) between success and failure. Sound dramatic? But it is quite important. For me I said, "I am not going to let five minutes negatively affect the outcome of my life." I needed to *redefine that moment as an enemy*; an enemy that wanted to steal the success of my family (wife and kids). I had to throw the family in there for obvious reasons; I think most of us would go the mat if our family were being attacked. I knew that if I could get mad at it, I would want to fight it and attempt to win. For me, it worked, and I still use that trick to this day.

Additionally, you may want to consider making an appointment with someone in person. "Steve, I will meet you at Starbucks at 6:30 a.m." I did this for years with my assistant(s). Trust me, the only thing that got me to that coffee shop most days is that I didn't want to let them down and be a flakey-Jake no-show. I'm not a big fan of phone appointments at 5:30 to 6:00 a.m. in the morning in an attempt to wake up, because it's drag self to phone, drag self back to bed! I met a friend at 5:20 a.m. twice weekly for racquetball for many years. No choice. None of us wants to be a no-show and let down our friends. So I had to get myself there, bleary eyed driving to the gym; five minutes of racquetball and I was at level ten awareness with zero chance of going back to bed.

Aristotle, Benjamin Franklin, and wise people before, after, and in between have advised, "Early to bed, early to rise, makes a man healthy, wealthy, and wise." Maybe there is actually something to it. All I can tell you is that I can find some of the most successful people that I know at Starbucks between the hours of 6:00 and 7:00 a.m.

Summary: 1) Define that moment as an enemy. 2) Place your alarm where you must walk several paces to turn it off. 3) Make an appointment with someone in person.

Get up.

Go get 'em!

49

Working with Seniors

———————————

Good people do not need laws to tell them to act responsibly,
while bad people will find a way around the laws.

PLATO

WHO QUALIFIES AS SENIORS WHEN seventy is the new fifty and eighty is the new sixty. What the heck does *seniors* mean anyway? People are running marathons at eighty-four, climbing high mountains at ninety, water skiing at eighty-eight, and living healthy lives over one hundred. Average life expectancy for a male in America is roughly seventy-nine, and for a female it's eighty-two. That means there are a ton of people living into their eighties and nineties and doing business with real estate professionals.

I was at a neighborhood meeting recently with an eighty-nine-year-old man. This guy was sharp, physically imposing; he looked and sounded like John Wayne at fifty. There is another gentleman in my neighborhood that is ninety-five and stretches daily, cuts wood, drives; you would honestly think he is sixty years old, no more. My grandma and granddad both lived to ninety-two and both were 100 percent capable and sharp. Hey, wisdom certainly comes with age and experience, and this group has it by the bushels. And frankly, I have always loved working with the retiree group; a superhonorable and enjoyable part of the job in my view.

With all that said, there are reasons to be especially thoughtful when working with seniors; and there are a couple of things that we need to discuss, namely elder abuse and mental health.

Elder abuse. Elder abuse is a problem in America. I know seniors that receive calls regularly from sharks trying to intimidate them into giving them money. They say they are from the IRS or the state or some collection agency and try to scare them into wiring money. One of my college friends that is currently a senior executive is looking into an early retirement so that he can form a company to go after these sharks. His parents were victimized several times by these bottom-sucking lower-than-whale sh#$&*#t turds! That's pretty low, in case you are wondering. The sensitively to elder abuse is high, and rightly so. What is our responsibility as real estate professionals in the event we see signs of elder abuse? I'm not an attorney and am therefore certainly not qualified to react to that question. At the very least, bring it to your manager for discussion.

Mental health. The following is a made-up story but very real nonetheless. Jack, the real estate agent, listed a gentleman's home. The client was roughly eighty years-of-age at the time. Jack listed his home on Tuesday, met with his staff on Wednesday to get things going and placed the property on the market on Thursday. Jack received a call on Friday from the client's son. The son was nice and cordial but explained to Jack that the family suspected their dad was experiencing some form of mental decline, illness, dementia, Alzheimer's, or some combination thereof; they weren't sure, but they knew there was a problem. The son further told Jack that he was concerned that his father was no longer capable of managing his own business affairs. Jack had never had this happen and technically his dad was Jack's client, but at the same time the son sounded completely legitimate and reasonable. What should Jack do?

I believe it's our job as real estate professionals to pay attention. *Use common sense.* If you suspect you are working with someone that does not have complete mental capacity in your view, bring it to your manager immediately. There is no exact playbook on what to do next. But bring your suspicious to your manager for sure.

"Rashness belongs to youth; prudence to old age"—*Cicero.* And I'll close this chapter on working with seniors with a statement by Thomas Jefferson: "Whenever you do a thing, act as if the whole world were watching."

Go get 'em!

50

You're Glowing

Mountains will go into labor, and a
silly little mouse will be born.

HORACE

WOO HOO! YOU JUST LISTED two houses or took three loan applications. You're back from the bottom of the ocean and unstoppable! On a roll. Look at you…yeah! You're lead dog and this time you're going to remain the lead dog! You have this unbeatable bounce to your step; a golden glow around your helmet; and a fearless mindset, the envy of all your office mates. And then two months later you're dead in the water, flat on your back. Why? Because we sometimes confuse the signing of the deal with the completion of our job and forget the process. High as a kite is no good: bad plan, lumpy income, poor service.

In many ways, the job of real estate agent or loan agent is a very dysfunctional business model. As producers, we are required to wear many hats: CEO, CFO, VP of advertising, VP of operations, and of course the front-line salesperson, *getting deals signed.* In the above example, the front-line salesperson got the deal signed. Good job on that piece; you don't have to go crazy, however, it's just a step in the process. Now that deal needs to be handed off to the operations team, which in most cases is the same person that signed the deal—you!

Just remember the simple functions of the business: marketing, operations, finance, and attitude. All pieces need to be working for your income to work.

I hate to admit it, but there was a time in the mid-1990s that I had over ten signed loan applications sitting in my desk drawer, and they had been sitting there for a few days (okay, maybe a week). I was glowing, taking roughly two to three applications daily, intoxicated with the "getting deals signed" part of the business. I could hunt with the best of 'em but was not prepared to deliver that volume of service. I was too young and scared and uninformed to realize that it was a process. Things had to almost fall apart for me to finally install some simple systems/personnel around marketing, operations, finance, and attitude.

Like the coach says, "Keep your emotions between the lines." The higher we get, the harder we fall. Pace it out, enjoy the wins, but don't forget the *process*. Any knucklehead ding-a-ling can get high as a kite for an hour or a day or a minute, but professionalism is maintaining a steady pace day in, day out—that's toughness! That's being a pro in real estate.

Go get 'em!

51

Waiting by the Phone

While the mind is in doubt, it is driven this
way and that by a slight impulse.

TERENCE

BUYING OR SELLING A HOME or doing a refinance is an all-consuming process. When the customer is going through it, it's all he or she can think about. "What is happening with my listing? Did anyone see my house today? I wonder if he or she liked it. Maybe no one will like it. Uh-oh, what will happen if no one likes my house? Well, I guess I can't move after all and take that great new job in Ventura. Or maybe we can rent this one for a while and then sell it later. But if we do that, can I afford to buy the new house if I don't sell this one? Maybe we should just stay. But that's ridiculous, someone will like my house. But what if they don't like the dingy carpet? Shoot, I knew I should have replaced those carpets before we sold. Maybe we can pull it off the market, replace the carpets, and then put it back on. But if we do that, will we lose momentum? No, we're fine, it will sell. But what if it doesn't sell for what we want? Then what do we do? Well, I guess we'll just stay and not move." And it goes on and on and on...

When people are buying or selling a primary residence, it's all they can think about. Why is it so top of mind? Because it is a "structural change" in their life. The customer's life cannot move forward until this deal is done, one way or another. We are dealing with where people sleep at night. It's an instinctual, all-confusing thought when your bed is in flux. Where will I (and my family) be sleeping in two months? Will we need to separate the family for a little while? Will we be here or there? *The customer is waiting by the phone for information,* sometimes literally. He or she wants information, and the more the better. Even if there is no information, customers want to hear from us, their representative. No, they don't need to hear from us verbally all the time; text or e-mail is fine too. But they need and want information nonetheless.

The biggest complaint about the real estate community is communication, and I don't even need to read a study on this. It's not what we say or how we say it or that we are slick or not slick—it's simply that *we don't communicate enough.* The customer is thinking about this transaction 24/7. As a real estate professional, we might be thinking we are doing a pretty good job if we touch base every two to four days. Let's cut it in the middle and say that it's been three days since we have communicated with the customer. What could have happened during those three days? Take a look at the first paragraph of this section; the customer walked to the edge of the cliff three times. And that whole paragraph only took the customer about 60 seconds to think those thoughts. Can you imagine how many times he or she walked to edge of the cliff in seventy-two hours? Maybe a hundred—or more likely a thousand plus.

Let me give you an idea to consider.

Early in my real estate brokerage career, we were working extremely hard. I say *we* because I like to use the word *we* as much as possible, but number two, I had two full-time assistants that were on my own personal payroll and some independent contractors as well. We were a team. Many times, between current listings and current pendings and hot-hot leads, we were managing roughly twenty transactions. That's a lot for Silicon Valley. How do you do a good job and keep your customers updated with that level of volume? As the volume picked up, I needed to do something to improve customer service and communication. One of my assistants was an early riser. She loved to work the 7:00 a.m. to 3:00 p.m. shift. I asked my early-rising assistant to start meeting me at the coffee shop at 6:00 to 6:30 a.m. We usually did this four days per week and sometimes five, Monday to Friday, no weekends. These meetings were informal; we simply talked about all twenty deals, what she should be doing, and what I should be doing on that day, deal by deal. And, by the way, customers usually love talking with an assistant, but they love talking to the person they actually hired even more. Not-so-subtle *hint*. We made our lists and were ready to take on the day. These meetings usually took about one hour, and she would leave first to get a jump on things. I would hang around and goof around for a while and stroll into the office by roughly 8:30 a.m.

The magic. There were exceptions, but on an average day, I contacted all twenty people by 9:30 a.m. to 10:00 a.m., and frankly, most of the most of time, by 9:15 a.m. and sometimes by 9:00 a.m. How is that possible? First of all, I (I say *I* because I am ultimately responsible for everything) am running the deal, not the customer. They hired me to lead, not follow. They don't know what they are doing; I know what we are doing. I am the project leader, so I lead. Be a follower, be a leader, I can do either one, frankly. The average person does both on a day-to-day basis. But if you are going to be leading, *then lead!*

"Mrs. Rodriguez, Rebecca (that wasn't her name) is going to be calling you today to coordinate that termite inspection, all normal stuff. Call if you need anything."

"Hi, Jeremy, Rebecca will be sending that counter by at roughly 2:00 p.m. If you don't get it by then, please call me."

"Hi, Sue, we had one showing yesterday. I talked with the agent. They are going to take another look in a few days, and I'll keep you posted."

"Hi, Ruth, I think we need another landscape bid. I'll have a guy swing by tomorrow."

"Hi, Joe, nothing to status you on today, same as yesterday. Have a good one, we'll stay at it."

"Hey, Don, that package we mailed should be arriving today. Call me when you get it. Thanks," etc.

Don't forget, I'm calling at roughly 9:00 a.m., so more than half the time I am getting their voice mail; the other half of the time, they are just trying to get their own day going. So they usually say something to the effect of, "Great, thanks for the update, Jim." And that was it. And of course I would do these updates by e-mail as well, just depending on what was needed for that day for that deal. I'm telling you, most days, I contacted all twenty clients by 9:15 a.m. in the morning. I just simply executed a tight plan for three hours; I had the rest of the day to focus on marketing and reacting to this or that. I got up early. I made my list. I contacted my customers. Simple! I touched base with my customers about what was happening in the process. A real estate transaction is a process. I would remind my customer of that fact a hundred times per day. So when they would hear from me, they would understand that it was simply just another small step in the process. *I'm training the customer to be calm.*

I'm not saying we were perfect or even close to it. There were days that we missed. And there were days where I ended up talking with a client for an hour and didn't get down to the bottom of the list. But most days, I was able to communicate with all customers. I'm not a night person. I literally have little to no creative juice past 3:00 p.m., so I wanted get it all done early. And I hate reacting to things and frankly like to run things. I guess at the Freudian level, I didn't want the customer telling me what to do, or even implying that I should be doing this or that. I always felt like a bum when the customer was trying to tell me what to do. I wanted to be in charge of the transaction, produce a good result, and provide a good service all the while. This was the best way I knew how to do it.

What happens if the customer contacts us before we contact him or her? It's the difference between hot and cold, night and day, oil and water, dirt and air. When we call them, we are demonstrating that we are running the project, have *already* reviewed what is happening for the day, know what needs to be done, and are doing it. When they call us, we are on our heels reacting to their questions. When the customer is asking all the questions, you are dust! Just zip up your tent and wait for the storm to pass. You don't want your customers peppering you with questions 24/7. You want to run the project and status the customer on what is happening. That is what he or she hired us to do. Take charge, lead, get it done, and communicate.

Go get 'em!

52

Selecting a Price

———————

Tell me and I forget—teach me and I
remember—involve me and I learn.

BENJAMIN FRANKLIN

WHEN I ASKED MY NEIGHBOR what she would like to learn about in this book, selecting a price was her number one answer. We could naturally write volumes on this single topic, but we will be only scratching the surface in this case. Let's start with residential and then tiptoe into commercial. Here is the summary in advance for residential: *involve your customer and work as a team.*

I told my clients, *"We are going to select a listing price together, as a team."* I have literally never had a significant objection to this approach. Why should there be? I just made the customer part of the process. Yes, I roughly know where we are going (at the very least I know the range), but I believe we should let customers get there on their own, in their own time, at their own pace. It's their money and their house, after all. I would often give the seller(s) an assignment. For example, "Mrs. Seller, you please drive by these five, and Mr. Seller, you take these, and I will study the rest of them. Let's talk in two days and compare notes." Who am I to come in like God and say, "This is the price"?

"Well, Jim, I tell them the price."

Okay, fine, if you feel good about that and that works for you, then okay. But be prepared to deal with the consequences if you are wrong. And you will be wrong 100 percent of the time because pricing property is guesswork at best. *It is not humanly possible to determine an exact price for a piece of real estate.* I don't care if someone has done 10,540 transactions for 114 years in the same neighborhood. Determining a final sales price can be done only by placing a product in the open market and seeing what a buyer is willing to pay.

Make the seller part of the process. The seller can be the number one analyst on the team. Think about it. As real estate professionals we are studying probably ten to thirty properties daily, all with unique characteristics. The sellers are studying *one* piece of property—theirs—several hours daily, for six months straight, looking in the paper, looking on the Internet, comparing this, comparing that, talking to friends and business associates. Can they be objective? When the customer is not objective, then it's our job as the real estate professionals to point that out. Does the fact that the customer is helping with pricing devalue the role of the real estate professional? Of course not. We are experts at the running the project (and process) and ultimately getting the job done. The client needs our experience to skillfully lead the way. And consider this: How about recognizing and managing the hard work of the seller? "Hey, Mrs. Customer, great job determining the per-foot number on Apple Dumpling Lane." Lead the team. Don't get defensive. Make the seller an important, valued, and needed part of the team. Decide the price together. *Do it as a team.*

"Well, Jim, I listed a property for $220,000 and it sold for $220,000; I hit the number—exactly!" Not really. How do you know whether if you had listed it for $226,000, someone would have paid $224,000?

The customer lost $4,000. How do you know whether if you would had listed it for $209,000, you would have created multiple offers, thereby driving that final sales price north to $228,000? The customer lost $8,000. How do you know whether if you had listed it for $239,500, someone would have offered $222,500? The customer lost $2,500. We don't know the number for sure. Work as a team. Decide the listing price collectively as a group, a number that the seller can own and that the real estate professional can support. *The price range will become glaringly obvious if you study it enough.*

It's not our job to come in like Moses from the mountain and etch the price in granite. It's our job to educate, to lead, to run the project, and to complete the task. If you choose the price, you are hanging yourself out to dry and eroding the cohesiveness of the team. If there is a stupid chess move to be made by a real estate agent, this one takes the cake. Early in my career, I made the mistake of saying, "You should list your home at X." Dumb. "Jim, you told us X, what happened?" Are we working together as a team anymore? No more team. No more cohesiveness. No more love. Now, it's us versus them. Real estate agent versus seller. A real estate transaction is a two- to six-month marriage. It's no fun to be on different teams for six months. Look. Make it simple and be honest.

"Mr. Customer, we are going to be studying the price together as a team, and together we will make a good decision."

"Well, Jim, what do you think? I know that you have to be thinking something regarding the value of our home."

"Sure, of course, here are the comps. See right here? There is so much more to consider, however, and frankly it's going to take all three of us working at it for two to three weeks to make a good decision."

"I understand that, Jim, but you need to give me something to go on for now."

"You bet," and then I simply read them the comps again and make some comments along the way, but I'm very careful not give an exact number. A range, maybe, a number, no way. Am I dodging the question? No. I'm being honest. I am telling them that it takes time to make a good decision.

Don't forget. When people study value, they typically study comps; those properties that have sold recently that are similar to the subject property. That's easy, that's important to do, and that's what everyone does. What's equally important, however, is to study what is for sale. For instance, I'm studying a property and the comps are indicating that the neighborhood is selling for roughly $350 per foot on average. Both the seller and I agree that the subject property is clearly on the average side, so using the average number of $350 is valid in this case. I look at what is currently for sale. On the low end, there is a beat-up home on Cupcake Lane in very poor condition listed at $354 per foot; the next home is listed at $392 per foot (in below-average condition), and the rest are above $400. Let's also assume that all of these homes have been for sale for over thirty days. Can we take advantage of the fact that everyone is asking too much money for his or her home? Of course we can. My job is to represent my client and help my client to the best of my ability. So, when I see a possible strategic advantage, I want to mention it for his or her consideration. "Mrs. Customer, it would appear that all the other sellers in the neighborhood are asking too much for their home. There might be a way to take advantage of that fact. I think you should consider asking $370 per foot. We are probably asking a little too much but may look like a bargain compared to these other overpriced homes." If I only studied comps, I would not have seen that move. That move would have possibly made the customer an extra $20 per foot. This is not a fantasy move. I have done this move; my colleagues have done this move. This is a bread-and-butter move. This move is nothing special. Again, work as team and make good decisions as a group.

An honest approach from a seasoned veteran. I know a seasoned real estate agent in the San Francisco Bay Area that has been around for over twenty-five years. He has an honest and open conversation with almost all of his seller clients that goes something like this: "Mr. and Mrs. Seller, I have been doing this now for over twenty-five years, and if there is one thing I know, it is this: it is very difficult to determine the price a buyer is willing to pay for a piece of property. There are so many intangibles to consider. I have seen swings as large of 40 percent plus or minus off the average, just depending on the particulars of the home, lot, and location. Therefore, I am here to run the process for you, advise you, etc. But the reality is that this is your money and your house, so I need you to be intimately involved in the pricing process. Sound okay?"

A giant swing. All the details have been changed, but here is a real world example that has happened several times. I took a listing. I started looking at the comps right away. I did my whole spiel about "the team," and that "we are going to do it as a team." My clients were crystal clear, however, that they wanted $1,320,000. They were okay with "the team idea" as long as the team decided on $1,320,000. Hmmm, okay. My gut was telling me that the number was high, and quite possibly very high. However, the property was tricky to price for so many reasons. We needed more feedback, professional feedback. I had an idea. "Mr. and Mrs. Customer, could I have a handful of my colleagues stop by and give us some independent feedback on a listing price strategy?" They agreed. I had seven colleagues come by. This was a seasoned group, no green peas, top dogs in the area. The numbers came in as follows: $890,000, $920,000, $950,000, $975,000, $1,020,000, $1,050,000, and one person thought maybe, maybe, if we were really lucky, it could reach to $1.1 million. The sellers were not impressed. They said, "We want to list it for $1,320,000." There was no use continuing the conversation; they were dug in. And to the seller's credit, the circumstances of this property were complicated. We listed the property at $1,320,000, and it sold within one month at $1,320,000. *Gotta work as a team and be flexible.*

The commercial side of the world. We own a commercial property with a group of investors. One of the partners wanted to exit the partnership. The operating agreement indicated how such matters should be handled, so we followed those rules. The departing party selected the appraiser; the appraisal came in at roughly $1.0 million (add some numbers). Several months prior to that, we were considering a refinance and the appraised value was roughly $600K. I was talking with one of my commercial friends several months after the partner exited the deal, and he was fairly certain the property would sell at $1.3 million. All this happened within a one year period in a flat market, no big ups and no big downs. These were all real estate professionals; this was not Johnny and his band of misfits, these were pros. These professionals were $700K in conflict, exceeding a 100 percent discrepancy on price.

A friend inherited some money, so he decided to start lending second deeds of trust on commercial buildings. His plan was to protect his investment by lending no more than 70 percent (total) of the value of the building; that is also called 70 percent combined loan to value, or 70 percent CLTV. CLTV means the combination of all debts (or loans) on the property. For instance, let's say a property was worth $100,000, and there was a first deed of trust of $50K; my friend, in that case, would be willing to lend the borrower $20K as a second deed of trust—$50K plus $20K equals $70K, and $70K is 70 percent of $100K, or 70 percent CLTV. When he told me what he was doing, I suggested he make sure that 70 percent is *really* 70 percent. What do I mean?

Well, reference the departing partner in the above story as an example. Is the CLTV based on $600K million, $1.0 million, or $1.3 million? If you are wrong (or the appraiser is wrong) on the value, your 70 percent CLTV will put you in a very vulnerable position. What would happen if the appraiser was wrong about the $100K valuation and the real value was more like $65K? My friend in that case is screwed if the borrower defaults. Sure enough, those values were a little generous; he didn't lose any money, but came close.

Here is a common problem that has happened several times. A non-real-estate guy sells his company for massive millions of dollars. He decides to buy commercial properties to generate income. He was conservative, so he bought everything with a 50 percent down payment. Pretty safe, really; he is bankrupt eight years later. All the money he borrowed at 50 percent LTV turned into a giant heavy anchor when the economy went bad and subsequently (and sadly) sank the ship to the bottom of the ocean.

Let's review it. He would buy a building for $1 million; put a down payment of $500K and take out a loan (debt) of $500K. When the economy went bad, he had a tough time attracting quality tenants, and the tenants he did have stopped paying rent. Within a short period of time his expenses exceeded his income, and he was running at a loss on all these buildings, losing $5K monthly on this one, $10K on that one, $4K on this one, and $20K on that one. He burned through all his liquid reserves trying to cover these losses and hang in there until things turned around. He couldn't hang in long enough, sadly. There was really nothing he could have done. *What's the message?* Number one, there is a correlation between the value of a building and the income that can be generated from the building and, more specifically, the *quality* of that income. And, number two, safe equals no debt. His LTV was low, but the loans were debt nonetheless. The debt was his enemy when things went bad.

"Jim, I'm depressed. Why are you giving me all these somewhat sad, challenging stories?" I'm trying to illustrate the wide range in which a single piece of commercial real estate can be priced, analyzed, appraised, and ultimately sold. Think about the possible categories of commercial: warehouse, strip malls, manufacturing, office, apartments, hotels and motels, farms, gas stations, storage facilities, churches, residential care facilities, medical buildings, hospitals, and garage/parking structures. There is no way I'm going to attempt to address pricing in all those categories.

Before we close this chapter however, we do need to talk about one piece of commercial math, *CAP rate*. If you had a big bucket of money, you would probably want to get the best possible return from your bucket. Business 101. Generating an acceptable return in real estate is called a capitalization rate, or a CAP rate. What is a CAP rate? For instance, if I buy this building for $1 million, what would be my return (not including appreciation) yearly from the $1 million (after expenses)? The result of that number is called the CAP rate. Secondly, generating a return in real estate is also a function of risk and return. In other words, how much risk am I willing to take to generate a CAP rate of, let's say, 7 percent.

So let's look at a real-world scenario.

I am interested in buying a shopping center. Do I take more risk buying a shopping center in Flagstaff, Arizona, or buying one that is four blocks from Stanford University? Both locations have a 7 percent CAP rate. Which one has more risk? Will I accept a smaller CAP rate (return) given the fact that Stanford is a better location? Flagstaff is beautiful, but come on. Let's name just a handful of companies around Stanford: Google, Yahoo, Facebook, and on and on. Of course I will accept the smaller CAP rate. How much smaller? Am I willing to accept 6 percent? How about 5 percent? How about 4 percent? Would I actually consider buying a shopping center by Stanford knowing that I am only getting 3 to 5 percent? It's happens every day. It's called peace of mind, a good night's sleep, risk and return, AAA real estate.

If someone were to ask, "Is there one piece of math that appears to drive commercial real estate?" it's safe to say the answer is *the CAP rate.* Even so, you could ask five commercial professionals to analyze a piece of commercial real estate and they will all produce conflicting CAP rate numbers.

I'll end this chapter the way we started this chapter: do it as a team and involve your customer. Benjamin Franklin said, "Involve me and I learn."

Go get 'em!

53

Bad to Good to Bad

———

It doesn't matter how slowly you go, so long as you do not stop.

CONFUCIUS

I LOOK AT THE ABOVE thought by Confucius, and I think about momentum. It's impossible to stay at 62.4 miles per hour our entire business life. Sometimes we are at 45.0, other times, 60.0, and others 94.0 mph. The key is to keep going. Maintain some kind of pace in your business. Even if you are slow at the moment, press on at that slow but steady pace. The pace translates to momentum, which affects deal flow.

Two to fifteen to twenty-five. Those were roughly the numbers when I would go from a bad real estate agent—to a good one—back to a bad one. What?

Years ago after a seminar, we were sitting around with a group of colleagues talking about the business and specifically production. The topic of deal flow surfaced, and then we digressed into a conversation about *the perfect number of deals to manage at any one time.* It was a little different for everyone, but everyone could answer that question for himself or herself: six for me, nineteen for me, eight for me, three for me, fourteen for me. And then someone said, "I noticed that when I'm in a slump and only have one to three deals, I quickly turn into this *crummy agent that I can't even recognize,* providing poor service, not motivated, just feeling somewhat like a bum. I can't get myself to do even the simplest tasks." Hmmmmmm. A foggy quiet hit the group, followed by a knowing nod from one to the other to the other. We all knew it to be true but had never heard in those terms.

Not enough business. Not enough deal flow is not only bad for you; this is bad for your current customers. Your customer will suffer when you are operating in the "not enough" range. I know, I know. It's counterintuitive. "Well, Jim, if I only have one deal, I can focus *all* my attention on them. I will give them amazing service." It's a good theory, but it doesn't work like that. Your business is a moving, breathing entity with you at mission control. It has to move, it has to breathe, it cannot sit still. It's a transaction business, it's a process business. Step one, step two, step three. I've never counted, but let's say there are seventy-four steps in the process. Each step has its own level of sophistication. Each step is a skill. Each step has to be maintained and tuned up. Use it or lose it. Use that step only once every six weeks, it will be like learning it for the very first time. You will bumble and stumble and fumble your way through it (just a single step in the process). Do that step once per week, and you won't even break a stride. So, the first thing that happens when you are operating in the Never Never Land of "not enough business" is your operations will get rusty and in some cases crumble.

Here is the bigger problem. The team doesn't feel successful when you are in a slump. And remember, even if you don't have an assistant (most people don't) on your payroll, you still have a team. Everyone that touches that transaction is part of your team; your manager, the receptionist, the administrator, the escrow officer, your appraiser, your inspectors, possibly your mentor, your office mate, and more. They are all affected when you are operating in "not enough business" range. "Wow, volume is down; Jim, do you have anything new coming up? Gosh, will we ever do a deal again in our liiiife?" It's a downhill spiral.

When you find yourself in the "not enough business" range, fight your way out as soon as possible.

Just right. If fifteen is the number, then you and your operations team are hitting on all cylinders between thirteen and seventeen. That's the sweet spot. That's the rhythm. You are in a groove. And when one deal falls off, you have another one to take its place. It's flow. It's chemistry. You and your staff are in harmony relevant to operations and marketing. You can plan effectively when you are in your sweet spot. Your staff has plenty to do, you have plenty to do. As discussed, a real estate transaction is a process. The process needs to move, flow, progress. Talk about the price; sign the listing; meet to sign disclosures; put the sign up; check the interest rate. When you have adequate deal flow, you are feeling successful and your staff is feeling successful. It's the same as a ball club that is out of sorts. Half the time no one can figure out why it's out of sorts, but it's out of sorts nonetheless. And then the ball club wins ten games in a row. Why? Who knows? Rhythm, chemistry, confidence, it's all those team intangibles that are relevant to business, sports, or family. When you are in the "just right" range, the team intangibles are usually aligned. This is your time to pour it on.

Too much. There is a limit to how many deals you and your staff (team) can handle at the moment. Let's say that you have built the machinery to handle fifteen deals. You can't wake up one morning and expect your operations team to effectively handle thirty. It will break. Why are strong men strong? They have spent years building the infrastructure, the underlying timbers, the ligaments, tendons, and supporting mechanism to handle those heavy loads. A strong man can't go from a bench press of three hundred pounds to five hundred pounds in a week. His body will break in half. He can, however, go from three hundred to five hundred by building the infrastructure over a period of time. Maybe it will take two years to do that. Same in your business. Too much weight (business) will break the system, and customer service will suffer.

Fight like heck to stay in the "just right" range.

Go get 'em!

54

Off Means Off

———◆———

Beware the barrenness of a busy life.

SOCRATES

ASIDE FROM FINDING NEW BUSINESS, this is one of the biggest operational challenges for producers. You need to shut it down. Your family needs you to shut it down. And frankly, your customers need you to shut it down. Impossible! "My mortgage, car, and kids' tuition payments all depend on that deal closing next week. I'm screwed if it doesn't happen." You have to shut it down. Or, at the very least, you need to pull the throttle back from time to time—*mental health hangs in the balance.* Other parts of your life hang in the balance. And frankly, you'll do more business if you can find a way to consistently shut it down.

Before we jump to ideas and solution, this is a problem. It really is. I'm not going to sugarcoat this one. As the producer, you are a small-business owner. You have no safety net. You have no paycheck. There is no residual income to speak of in this business. Your revenue stream is 100 percent reliant on that deal closing, and then the next, and then the next. One by one. It's a transaction-oriented business. We have a lot of people around us in supporting roles; however, it's 100 percent on us, the producer, to score! No one else can do it or will do it. We are the ones that have to put it in the back of the net. Period. Our families depend on us to do that, management depends on us to do that, and supporting vendors count on us to do that.

"Jim, with that level of isolated pressure, how in the world do you expect me to turn it off?"

When I was doing loans, I worked with a real estate agent that took every Wednesday off. He loved to scuba dive. Somehow, he convinced a couple of his buddies to do it with him. When they didn't go, he went anyway. I worked with him for roughly five years and never knew him to miss a day. I did a few deals with him over that five-year period, and on all of them he completely vanished every Wednesday. Frankly, it drove me crazy that I couldn't reach him on those days, but life continued on nonetheless. The deal closed. Everything was fine. He would resurface (no pun intended) on Thursday, refreshed and ready to go again.

When I was selling real estate, I worked with a true superstar producer that took Fridays off. "Hi, this is so and so. Today is Friday, it's family day for me, so I will return all calls tomorrow." Now you see me, now you don't. Vanished. Gone. The lights were out and no one was home. The world (and his business) could be falling apart and he would still continue on with "family day." On a workday, however, he was all in, pedal to the metal. On and off. Now you see me, now you don't. I worked with him for roughly four years, and he never missed family day to my knowledge.

The wife of one of my lender friends was an Olympic athlete. During those Games, he disappeared. He told everyone that he was going to disappear, but at the very least I thought he would check e-mails, etc. Nope. Gone, poof, vanished. This guy, at the time, was probably one of the top twenty lenders in the nation with a giant bank. I never told him the following because I didn't want him to be a slacker on my deals, but I always respected his ability (mental discipline) to unplug and focus in on other areas of his life for a while and then step right back into business without even a ripple. *It will wait. The world will be fine. Relax and do what you have to do.*

Don't forget. Many of us entered the world of producer in real estate because we wanted freedom (and we didn't want a boss). Don't be a hostage to the business just because you are scared. Be your own boss. Would a boss require you to work twenty-four days straight? Only a terrible boss would ask that of anyone. *Be a good boss to yourself—give yourself some time off.*

There are people that like to remain plugged in at all times. I respect that and share a bit of that posture. If you are wired that way, you still need to find a way to bring the pace from a ten to a three a couple of times a week.

My personal routine. I was (am) consistently cooked by Thursday. I like to go like crazy Monday through Wednesday, sleep in a little on Thursday morning but still work that day nonetheless, power through Friday, but cut out early Friday afternoon. I shut it down (if you will) Friday afternoon through midday Sunday. But for me, on Sunday, I start thinking about the upcoming workweek. So I just make it a workday—a half day. I get into the office at roughly one o'clock, get in a good five hours, and am back home for dinner by sixish. I like to work Sundays because it's quiet and I get prepped for the upcoming week. That's me. That's roughly what has worked for me my entire career as a producer.

It's Saturday morning, you stumble out of bed at about seven thirty, get some coffee, the family is relaxed. It feels different than Friday or Thursday or Wednesday or Tuesday or Monday. Dirt is still dirt. The sky is still the sky. Air is still the air. Nothing structural has changed.

Why does it *feel* different? It's an attitude. It's mental discipline. When you are a producer in this business and responsible for producing your own revenue, you need to find a way to relax, disconnect, and recharge.

You can make any day your "Saturday." Throttle it back from time to time and your revenue line will be the benefactor.

Go get 'em!

55

Small Sips

———

One wanders to the left, another to the right; they
are both equally seduced by different delusions.

HORACE

I'M SAYING, "BE DISCERNING." STAY level headed. You don't need to jump
high as a kite and hit your head on the ceiling, rendering your melon
unconscious and yourself down for the count (from overconsumption of
the company Kool-Aid). There is a way to be a good team player in the
office, be business loyal, and at the same time be discerning. You have a
responsibility to yourself and your family to be thoughtful and to think
void of emotion.

I was a Spartan in high school, a Spartan in college, and now I'm a
volunteer coach for the Spartans (by choice). Am I loyal? Did I drink
the Spartan Kool-Aid on a personal level? The Spartan thing is part
of my personal life, not my business life. It's a personal comfort zone
for me. *Don't let anyone confuse you about personal loyalty and good business
decision making.* Socrates said, "I am not an Athenian or a Greek, but a
citizen of the world."

Look, you are the small-business owner—the guy or girl with no
paycheck. The real estate company exists to provide the necessary infrastructure for your production; that is why you pay the company part

of your commission. If your situation is completely intolerable at your current company, don't talk badly, just simply make a graceful exit—but when you are there, be there. Be loyal to your company brand and colleagues, *but take only small sips of the company Kool-Aid*. And if you happen to be at a different office in two years, then be loyal to that office, those colleagues, and that manager; again, small sips. That is your team at the moment. That is the team you have chosen. It doesn't have to be your team forever, but it is at the moment. Family is forever (personal) and business is business.

Large sips can be fatal. A guy who worked as an employee (in technology) was making roughly $40,000 that year. He was the primary and only bread winner of his family; they were struggling a little financially. He was offered a job in a different industry for almost double his salary. He *loved* his current company. He didn't want to leave, but he needed to make more money; his family needed him to make more money. His buddies suggested that he talk with his current boss about income; that's only fair. He did. The current company could afford to increase his salary by 3 percent with a soft commitment to increase it more later. He was emotionally attached to the current management group and declined the new job. Sadly, he went bankrupt two years later—root cause, insufficient income. His buddies were 100 percent convinced that he was hopelessly intoxicated on the company Kool-Aid. Small doses of Kool-Aid are fine; large doses, however, can be fatal—it clouds our thinking.

The coaching industry. The coach goes ten and three and is currently making $300,000. He gets an offer from another college for $1,000,000 yearly. The current school cannot meet that offer, so the coach takes the new job at $1,000,000 yearly. Some of the alumni at the previous school start grumbling about loyalty. Are you kidding? Look, the coach was loyal and did his job as coach at school A; and now he is doing his job at school B. It was a good business decision.

Small sips with school A and now small sips with school B. He did his job then and is doing his job now. There is honor in that. Family is family—business is business.

Remember something, you live and die in real estate through your revenue line. When push comes to shove, you are the only one that will be responsible for that line item (production)—the Kool-Aid will not help you. Your family relies on you to be discerning, to be logical, and to be rational—to be ever mindful that you are running a business and that everyone around you is helpful and supportive, but you are the only one that can drive it over the goal line.

Go get 'em!

56

Move

———◆———

Natural forces within us are the true healers of disease.
HIPPOCRATES

WHEN I STARTED MAKING NOTES, this was frankly the very first chapter that I wrote. Here is the original chapter the way I wrote it without edits.

When your tail is in a crack, move. When you are in a rut, move. When you are kickin' butt, move. No, don't get a new house. Move your body. Make a new list and move your body around to get going again—get busy. We are wired to move our body. Most of us think better on the move. Hippocrates also said, "Walking is the best medicine." Charles Dickens said, "This is a world of action, and not for moping and droning in."

As a lender, I took most of my loan applications face to face. I didn't need to do that; I could have easily used the snail-mail system. But I wanted to meet all my customers and stayyy onnn theee moveee. It's not for everyone. But it worked for me. Hated, hated sitting in an office all day. There were times when I didn't "technically" have a real business meeting scheduled for that day. So, on those days, I would call up a customer or two and go out and do a meet and greet. Get on my feet. Shake a couple of hands. Get face to face with someone. Go out of my way to do someone a favor. It almost never failed—within a month or two, that person would refer a client.

When you are kicking butt, move. When your tail is in a crack, move. When you are starting out, move. When you have been doing this since the beginning of time, move. Move your body—energize your mind.

Like the coach says, *move.*

Go get 'em!

57

The On-Off Switch

———◆———

Nobody can give you wiser advice but yourself.
Cicero

THIS CHAPTER WILL FLY IN the face of another section called "Off
Means Off." We do need a break from time to time, but as a re-
alist, I do want to cover the topic of *doing business on vacation*. Why?
Because that's life in the big city; it's going to happen. You are on
vacation and get pulled into a deal. And, more specifically, instead
of picking up our phone every time it rings, can we go from off to
on to off again? It's both an operational and quality of life issue, so
here goes.

When I was a lender, one of my closest friends in the world called
me on a Friday morning at eleven o'clock. "Hey, Jimmy, I bought a
house." We went to high school together, and at that moment in time
we lived about one hour from one another. He and his wife lived and
worked in downtown San Francisco. He had been casing this house for
about six months; studying it, driving by it, talking to neighbors. It was
in a perfect suburb of the San Francisco Bay Area. "I need a loan. The
only way I could get them to agree to my price was a fast close. It closes
two weeks from today, and they already told me they would boot me
out if I don't close on time." With an awkward pause.

I obviously know this guy; he is a rainmaker in every sense of the word. There is no such thing as "can't do" in his vocabulary; one of the reasons I love him. Show him an obstacle; he'll go over it, through it, or around it without breaking stride. He is one of my tightest friends to this day, and for sure I didn't want to disappoint him. I knew he went out on a limb to get this place. And I also knew that he promised that fast close knowing (hoping) that "Jimmy will find a way to get it done."

Now, as a short digression to this story, this is one of those tricky things about working in this business. This was nearly an impossible task to complete, I mean, truly challenging. If for some reason that deal didn't close, would he be sore at me? No way, not a chance in the world. He knew how difficult this was to complete. In fact, his own dad did loans for a time, so he knew how challenging this was. Even so, I would have felt terrible that I disappointed him and that would have affected me, which would have affected him. So, no choice, I had get it done.

I received the call in my car: my wife, my kids, and a bunch of their friends were in the car, and I was pulling the boat on the way to the lake for the weekend. The good news is that I had thirty minutes to game plan (with myself in my head) before arriving at the lake. I needed those thirty minutes. Upon receiving the call, I told my wife that my friend bought a house; I didn't tell her, however, that it was closing in two weeks. We arrived at the lake and I had a plan.

I told my wife the story and also told her how important this was and that I needed three hours. It happens sometimes. I was in complete off mode—and not only did I need to turn the switch to on, but the wattage needed to be fully engaged for three hours. *I knew that if I didn't attack this situation with everything I had, I would be thinking about it all weekend and it would ruin my trip.* It takes two to three hours to settle in and unpack anyway; we would be out on the lake by three thirty, no problem (I promised). I needed to do it, I wanted to do it. When people are in a pinch and really need something done, they are going to call people they can count on. And my friend was frankly in a pinch, and I wanted to personally make sure this happened. So I disappeared to go to work.

These kinds of scenarios are the ones that test a) your ability to run a project, b) the strength of your business relationships, and c) the quality of your team.

Step one: get organized. I called my friend and told him I needed all his stuff in my office in the next two hours—pay stubs, W-2s, tax returns, bank statements, purchase contract, prelim, and anything else he could possibly think of (he worked in finance and knew the drill). He also knew the request was coming and jumped into action immediately. I also told him that I would be back on Monday morning, and in the meantime, if he received a call from anyone in my office requesting more paperwork, then jump to and get back to him or her straightaway.

Step two: the appraisal. This was the most time-sensitive item at the moment. One small problem on that: the appraisers are approved with specific banks, and I had no idea which bank we would be submitting to. If the appraisal was not ordered that day, that second, no way this deal would close. I had to hedge my bet on this. I ordered the appraisal with 1) the person (appraiser) that I could count on to get it done and get it done quickly and 2) the person that was approved with the largest number of banks. Appraisal was ordered. Done.

Step three: try to find a bank that would do it. Going in, I already knew what everyone was going to say. "Jim, wow, two weeks, I don't think so. Maybe three, for sure four, but no way two weeks. We could try if you want, but no guarantees." I was prepared for that.

After several calls, I called my representative at the Big Bank. She said to me, "Jim we have done two-week deals before, but only a handful, and if there is even the slightest hiccup on the file, we are not going to make the two-week window." I made some more calls but decided to put all my eggs in the Big Bank basket. "And Jim, I need the file today," she said.

Step four: submit the file. This normally would happen on day seven to day sixteen. I called my team at the office, and they were happy to jump in and go, go, go. Sometimes the team loves these types of deals because they energize everyone and galvanize the group. I told them the story. By that time, my friend was already in the car on his way to the office to drop off all his paperwork to my team.

My three hours were almost up (with the boat, my wife, and the kids waiting): the appraisal was ordered, the bank was identified, and we had a plan to submit. That would get us through the weekend and I could turn the switch to off again. On the lake by three o'clock.

On again Monday morning. I rolled into the office and everyone was energized. The appraiser had already completed and dropped off the appraisal, the team had confirmed receipt of the package with the Big Bank, and my processor had already talked with Big Bank to convince them to underwrite that very day. I drove the appraisal over to the bank to be married up with the package. The package was complete and ready for formal underwriting by noon on Monday. Woo.

That completes my off-on-off-then-on-again story. You might be curious what happened, however. We closed right on schedule with literally one of the best rates in town. It was not easy, but we got it done nonetheless. Amazing what you can get done with a good team that is motivated.

It's just going to happen.

You'll be on vacation and in a blink of eye get pulled into an (important) deal. Here is my suggestion: if you jump in, jump all the way, pedal to the metal, turn the switch on, take control, look forward a few days, anticipate what will be happening, and then make arrangements for those possibilities—and do all that away from the family. And then, go back and turn the switch to off again.

Go get 'em!

58

Time Well Spent

Take time for all things: great haste makes great waste.
Benjamin Franklin

SPEND THE TIME TO DO it right. There is no such thing as wasted time if that time is spent doing it right. I have showed clients approximately sixty homes before they found one to buy. I have also had instances where I showed clients one and they were ready to go. I have had loans for which I spent no less than fifty man hours on that single transaction; I have also had ones that required only five man-hours. In either case, spend the time that is necessary to do it right.

Spending the time to do it right is good for the customer, good for you, and good for business.

"Time is arguably our biggest asset in this business, so why are you asking me to be so generous with such a valuable asset?" I didn't say *waste* it. I said spend the time that is necessary to do it right. Measure twice and cut once.

After retiring from Warner Brothers, my granddad sold some property for a few years, as a real estate agent. We talked a lot about real estate before he passed at age ninety-two. He said that every deal and every customer is a little different. He explained that he always had a plan, but he had flexibility built into the plan. Sometimes the customer would need him for an hour, sometimes for twenty minutes, and sometimes for one minute. He spent the time necessary to do it right. He transferred those lessons he learned at Warner Brothers, where he would plan, plan, plan for the upcoming movie; but he knew that the plan was only the plan and that the studio would spend the time (and money) to do it right, whatever that entailed and whatever that meant.

Consequences of rushing things. It's common knowledge that it's best to launch a listing when the listing is 100 percent ready to be launched. On this one deal, we had spent over one month meticulously preparing the property for sale; making it sparkle, ensuring all the paperwork was ready, educating the customer, etc. Time was ticking, however. Over a month had gone by and I needed to get it on the market that very day to ensure we made the broker tour the following day. One snag, I didn't have all the seller disclosures back in my office yet. I called my customers and they promised they would deliver everything to me the following morning. With that assurance, I decided to put the property on the market that day, with their approval.

The next morning, "Jim, sorry, Steve left on a business trip this morning and we forgot to complete the paperwork, but he'll be back Monday." This was on a Wednesday, and the property was live and on the market at this point. I know that probably doesn't sound like a big deal. It literally tripled the amount of work required for that one small mistake, my mistake. I spent the next five days backpedaling with colleagues and buyers, explaining that the seller disclosures would be online on Monday and also taking meticulous notes on everybody because I had to notify them when the paperwork was indeed online. It was a first-class launch with one exception—and that one exception caused me (and my team) countless hours of unnecessary work. That was on me. I could have pushed harder and ensured the paperwork was in my office on time; or I could have easily convinced the client to push the launch out one more week until such time as we were 100 percent ready to go. "Readiness" is important. I rushed it. I knew it when I did it, but I did it anyway. So, instead of comfortably sitting there at mission control running a first-class listing, I was on my heels backpedaling (and apologizing) the entire time. Not fun. There are consequences to rushing things. Spend the time to do it right.

Your customers will feel it if you try and box them in. "Well, I can talk with you, Mr. Customer, between 1:33 p.m. and 1:48 p.m., will that work for you? Oh, and I do have an appointment at 2:00 p.m., just want you to know." Are you kidding? The customer knows when we are trying to rush it; just like you know when you are the customer and are being rushed out the door. Take it easy. Slow and easy is good for business. Focus in. Maybe it will take ten minutes, maybe it will take forty minutes; not a big deal in the overall scheme of things. When serving the customer, take the time. If you rush it too much, you'll be prospecting for nearly 100 percent of your business for the rest of your life in this business.

Don't be an Everlast punching bag. That's not what we are talking about. Use common sense, and don't allow yourself to be pushed around. But when you are working, work! Spend the time. The customer is usually somewhat nervous about something the whole way through the process. Slow it down and explain some things here and there. I know you may want to race off to the next appointment, but be careful. I made that mistake a few times and paid the price. Race around from here to there and you'll be doing the same racing around ten years from now; and at the same time you'll be watching your colleagues, nice and relaxed, fielding all those AAA referrals (from happy customers) as they are landing squarely in their lap—seemingly out of thin air. Be careful, slow it down, take the time to do it right.

There are no short cuts. You'll pay the price, I'll pay the price, we all pay the price when we cut corners and don't spend the time. Nah, I don't need my client to proof the flyer before it goes to the printer; just go with it, they'll be fine, this is a "rush" transaction, after all. Ring, ring. "Um, Jim, the flyers just arrived at the house. It's a really nice flyer, it's pretty and glossy, buuuut we were hoping for some different pictures, and we thought it would be better to list this rather than that; and we want to mention the fireplace and the park next door."

"You are right, Mr. and Mrs. Customer. I have it right here on my checklist where it says *Client to Approve Flyer,* and I simply didn't do it. No excuses, sorry about that, I'll fix it right away." Someone has to go pick up all these junk flyers, dispose of them, call the graphic artist, and make the changes. I have to proof it (again). The client has to proof it and approve it. I need to send the approved piece to the printer, the printer needs time to print the new ones, and someone has to go shuttle them from the printer to the house. Short cuts don't pay. Spend the time to do it right.

There is no such thing as wasted time if you are spending the time to do it right. In all fairness, the customer is paying us to do it right. But on the other hand, if we cut a tiny corner here or a tiny corner there, do the customers really know? Sometimes they do and sometimes they don't. But you will know. You have to build your business one brick at a time so that it's rock solid in five years. Cut corners now and you may find your business blown down to the ground when the first big hurricane (economic recession) rolls into town. Take the time to do it right, and you'll be able to withstand some massive tidal waves that will hit the beach from time to time.

Go get 'em!

59

Supporting Cast

———————

Remember—upon the conduct of each depends the fate of all.
ALEXANDER THE GREAT

NOTHING HAPPENS IN A VACUUM. As producers in real estate, we need our team; we need our internal team and we need our external team. We can define our external team as the supporting cast or our vendor team. Your vendor team can make you money, or they can be a deal killer and cost you money.

What are vendors? Depending on whether you are a lender or real estate agent or commercial professional, there are many: appraisers, title personnel, escrow personnel, insurance agents, inspectors, painters, chimney contractors, plumbers, electricians, general contractors, specialty contractors, civil engineers, graphic artists, printers, videographers, photographers, handymen, architects, movers, attorneys, tax professionals, property managers, stagers, and more. These are all those people that play a supporting role to help us get the job done.

What do we want from our vendors? We want them to do their job. And we also want them to keep things nice and smooth. Remember, the customer is already nervous about something—it's a real estate transaction, after all, and there are about four thousand moving parts.

We need to surround the customer with thoughtful, capable, honest, and calm people. As a team, we are helping the customers get to where they want to go—body and mind fully intact. We want our vendors to do their job and remain calm.

Where to find them. That's easy; your colleagues. You can save yourself years of time and effort by simply asking your colleagues for vendor referrals. Your colleagues will have already done the vetting process for you in most cases. They will have worked with the vendor for years and can represent the quality of their work and the character of the person. "Jim, what if my colleagues are not willing to share their vendors?" Then you are in the wrong office.

A real estate transaction. If a vendor is already living in this world of real estate, he or she will understand the pace, intensity, and dynamics of a real estate transaction. Don't expect someone new to understand that, however. It's different. Everything is different about a real estate transaction. For instance, if a painter does ten deals monthly and only one of them is a real estate transaction, he or she might not be able to deliver what you need. On the other hand, if eight of those ten are real estate deals, then he or she "gets it." The pace is different. The dynamics are different. The attitude is different. A real estate transaction has a life unique only to itself. Make sure your vendors are living in that world.

Everything reflects on you. Everything your vendors do will reflect on you, everything! We live and die in this business by referrals, and the customers will remember how your vendors treated them. Were they nice? Were they capable? Were they professional? Were they timely? Were they respectful? Were they calm? Everything will reflect on you, and your vendors will ultimately have an impact on your referrals down the road; they are an overlapping piece of the service.

Feedback from customers. In most cases, you are placing your vendor team in touch with your customer. Listen to what your customer is saying about your vendors. And more importantly, listen to what he or she is not. Most people are not going to jump out with, "Wow, Jeremy did a terrible job." Listen to what customers are not saying and then ask questions. If you have a problem with a vendor, fix it before it festers.

How to manage performance. You manage your vendor group similarly to how you would manage an employee. You supervise, you support, you coach, you set clear objectives, and you hold people accountable. You have to get comfortable providing feedback, good and bad.

On deck. Nothing stays the same forever. Things will change over time with your vendor group. If it's easier, think of your vendor team as a sports team, let's just say a football team. If your wide receiver gets hurt or disappears unexpectedly, who can step in and play that role? It's the same with your vendor group. You might be happy as a clam with your attorney or your inspector or your civil engineer, but make sure you at least have someone in mind that is on deck that you can install into that position. Be loyal, but be smart.

Replacing a vendor. If vendors are not performing, you have a couple of options. You can talk with them and work with them and see if they will come around. Or you can replace them. It's up to you how you want to handle things. My mom was a teacher, principal, and then assistant superintendent of schools before she retired. She was always of the opinion that you don't help people long term if you don't provide feedback. So if you decide to replace a vendor, you can either do a fadeaway jumper or have that uncomfortable conversation. That's up to you. Personally, when I have had to replace a vendor, I simply faded away and didn't use them anymore. But that's your decision.

Deal killers. We want our vendors to do a good job and also be transparent with our customer. But human beings are human beings. Two people can be reporting the exact same fact, and one person will leave the customer scared to death and the other person will leave the customer well informed but calm. Be careful. Make sure that your demeanor is consistent with your vendor's demeanor. People skills are important.

Referring business. Our vendor list is quite large, as you can see above. It would naturally be great to generate referrals from this group. It may happen organically, but frankly, I never put that expectation on this group. First and foremost, I want them to do their job. And I want them to do it well. If they refer business, then great; if they don't, that's fine too. Number one priority, Mr. or Mrs. Vendor, do your job. Take care of the business at hand.

Use your vendor team to help secure business. On several occasions, I have asked my vendors to reach out to a client as I am interviewing for a listing. I will tell my client that my escrow representative will be calling to explain that part of the process. Or I tell the client that my inspector will be calling to explain the nitty-gritty dynamics of that piece. Or I might have my civil engineer call the client to start discussing the fence issue. I explain to the clients that they are hiring me, but they are also hiring my team; therefore, I would like to introduce some of the team to them before they make a final decision. I call this the "halo effect." The customer becomes more comfortable knowing that you have all the pieces covered.

Vendor party. I held a luncheon with all my vendors one time. I had about twenty-five people show up. I did this at Chevy's restaurant, and it cost me about $300. It was a way to say thank you and build up some goodwill. In a pinch, do you think those vendors were happy to get in and help Jimbo after I just treated them to lunch? You're quick! It's easy, it's cheap, and the benefits are exponential.

I am encouraging you to be discerning about who you place on your vendor team. You are working with this group of people on a daily or weekly basis. Are they enjoyable to work with? Are they quality people? Can you rely on them? Do they keep you calm or send your blood pressure to the moon? Will they run and hide at the first sign of trouble, or can they work through complications? Will they jump in and help in a pinch? Do they reflect well on you and your brand?

Carefully select your vendor group and then treat them like gold.

Go get 'em!

60

Anticipation

Preemptive, step-by-step customer education
will avoid potential conflict.

JAMES R. CARTER

WE NEED TO MAKE THE process smooth for the customer. Aristotle said, "The aim of the wise is not to secure pleasure but to avoid pain." Aesop said, "It is thrifty to prepare for the wants of tomorrow." I'll blend and modify the two for real estate: It is wise to prepare for customers' wants and thoughts of tomorrow to avoid pain and deliver a good customer experience.

"Mr. Customer, you are going to be receiving something called a good faith estimate. Nothing to worry about, call me when you get it and we will review it."

"Mrs. Customer, we will be placing your home on the market on Wednesday. I will be calling you on Monday to provide you a status. Now, during that five-day period we might get five people looking at the home or we might get one hundred people looking at the home. In either case, it's nothing to worry about—we only need one good buyer. Talk with you Monday."

The dictionary says that to *anticipate* is to predict, to foresee, to expect, to be prepared for. There are unexpected things that happen during a real estate transaction. Is a real estate transaction a process, however? You bet. And as professionals, we know the process (i.e., step one, step two, step three, etc.). Based on that next step, can we predict what the customer might be feeling or thinking? Almost without a shadow of a doubt—yes. The client goes through very predictable emotions and thoughts as we move through the process. It's part of our job to recognize that and smooth out the bumps (for the customer).

"Mr. Client, you will be receiving the inspection report shortly. Remember, the inspector is there to do a job; he or she is going to find and list those items that are not up to par. Every home, even a brand new home, is going to have some items listed. In fact, in my experience, there are usually about two to three pages of items that the report will define as *Immediate Recommended Improvements*. So don't worry, we will review all those items together, as a team, but expect there to be some items nonetheless."

What would happen if I didn't prepare Mr. Client for the inspection report?

"Jim, this house is a wreck. Did you see all these items under the section where it says *Immediate Recommended Improvements*? There are three pages of stuff that is broken on this house. Get me out of this deal."

Lead or follow. Lead (educate and anticipate) the process or follow (react and watch your customer take over). Be in control or be a punching bag. When you anticipate and lead, you are in control of the process. "Mrs. Seller, the next step is X; don't worry about anything else other than X, got it?"

"Yes, Jim, I got it."

Great. Lead the process; anticipate what is coming and explain it to your client.

When your customer is asking a million questions, that is a sign of a leaderless ship adrift in the ocean. It is our job to anticipate, to lead, and to educate. When you are anticipating and communicating, you are leading and therefore doing your job.

Let's look at the time and work involved with anticipating and leading versus reacting and following. Let's say I have ten deals going right now.

Here is the story on the Anticipating and Leading Team. I spend an hour in the morning planning what needs to happen that day on each deal. I make a few notes. I arrive at work and work on each deal one by one. I take action on what needs to be done through e-mail, phone, text, or some other means. And then I communicate that to my client; again, through e-mail, phone, text, or some other means. How long did that take me? It took me about one hour to plan and one hour to execute. I'm done by ten to eleven o'clock. The rest of day is relatively quiet because my vendors and staff know what to do and my customer knows what to expect—for that day.

Now, let's look at the Reacting and Following Team. I wake up (whenever), have some coffee, drive over and get a few (seven) donuts, fill up the car, and roll into the office at nine fifteen. Then I talk with some colleagues, daydream about what the day may hold, check my e-mail, go to the bathroom, daydream a little more, talk to some colleagues, and run an "emergency" errand. Now it's eleven fifteen and the phone starts ringing.

"Jim, the inspector is late, can you call him?"

"Jim, did anyone see my house yesterday?"

"Jim, what do I do with the paperwork?"

"Jim, do we need to lower the price?"

"Jim, did anything new come on the market?"

"Jim, how do I do this electronic signing thing?"

And on and on. I'm in panic mode now and it's only eleven thirty in the morning. I will be spending the rest of my day reacting and scrambling because I didn't anticipate.

The score is two hours for the Anticipating and Leading Team— and six hours for the Reacting and Following Team. *Low score wins.*

When we anticipate what the customer may be feeling or thinking and do something about it, we are providing a good service. They don't know the process, we do. "Mrs. Customer, when you arrive at the title company, you may find the stack of paper to be slightly intimidating. Don't worry, it's normal, and I'll be there to help you." Rather than Mrs. Customer arrives at the title company and *reacts* to the stack of paper. It's part of our job to make the process smooth. If the customer knows what is coming, he or she will be fine. If he or she doesn't know what is coming, you are asking for a train wreck. Anticipate and educate.

If you don't have the instincts to anticipate, then work to get the instincts to anticipate. Anybody good at his or her job or in business has the ability to anticipate what is coming. Sometimes it's an instinct and sometimes it comes from experience and sometimes both. If you don't have the experience yet, then create the habit by planning for an hour every night or every morning. If I simply take five minutes to explain to the customer what will be happening that day, I save myself thirty to forty minutes later in the day *reacting and fixing.* Multiply thirty by my ten deals; that's practically my whole day wrapped up in reaction mode. You can't effectively run a business that way.

And one final quality-of-life note. There is a direct correlation between anticipation and customer service; customer service and happy customers; happy customers and referrals; and referrals and your enjoyment of the business. Draw a direct line all the way from anticipation to your enjoyment of the business. *Anticipate!* It's good for the customer, it's good for you, and it's good for the real estate industry at large.

Go get 'em!

Finance

A Guide to Making It in Real Estate

61

Breaking Down Finance

———◆———

Rich people without wisdom and learning
are but sheep with golden fleeces.
SOLON

THERE ARE FOUR PIECES TO finance: the financial skills to adequately serve the customer; the financial skills to run a small business in real estate; the financial skills to run your personal life; and the financial skills to invest and build wealth.

Serve the customer. Real estate is a financial transaction both in lending and sales; we need some level of skill on Excel and the financial calculator. It would be hard to survive as a lender without a good working knowledge of the financial calculator. I do know some real estate agents that do quite well without a working knowledge of either one. My belief, however, is that some level of skill in both is in the best interest of the customer. I will tell you, there is no way I could have done what I did in lending and sales without a strong working knowledge of both Excel and the financial calculator.

Run the business. Out of the four areas, this one is at the top of the list—and the good news is that it's the easiest to execute *if* you build a team. Build a team that includes your business attorney, your bookkeeper, and your tax person (accountant). Spend the money. It's

worth every dime to have a team helping you run your business finances like a real business. Don't trip over dollars to pick up the pennies.
Focus on this one.

Run your personal life. I didn't cover this topic in this book. I
will tell you that good habits in one area have a tendency to positively
affect others. For instance, my bookkeeping team has become so inte-
gral to what I do that I use them to help me run my personal finances
as well. Are there similarities between running the finances of a family
and running the finances of a small business? In our personal life, do
we take in money (income)? Yes. Do we have personal expenses, such
as food, clothes, etc. (expenses)? Yes. Do we or should we have some
left over (profit)? Yes. Sounds pretty similar to running a small business to me. Could the same team that is helping us run the finances
of our small business also help us run our personal finances? You bet.

Invest and build wealth. This is not my area of expertise, so I did
not cover this topic. I will refer you, however, to a chapter I wrote called
"Invest or Work." Consider those thoughts.

Head in sand and hoping that it all works out leads to destruction
and misery. Remember, you are not alone here. Reach out for help.
Start by learning Excel and the financial calculator, then hire a good,
reputable bookkeeping company. Round out the effort by including a
great business attorney and tax person. Continue to build and learn
day by day. It makes you strong; you are unlikely to be fooled when you
have some basic financial skills and exercise discipline. Remember,
running a $5,000 budget is a warmup to running a $500,000 budget.
You have to be good at one level to graduate to the next.

It's not just about having money; you have to manage that money.
There are plenty of examples of people that had tanker loads of money but couldn't manage it—and therefore lost it. I tell my kids more

often than they want to hear it, if someone can't run a $1,000 budget, there is no way I would trust them to run a $100,000 budget. It's about the fundamentals, structure, discipline, and, yes, some skill development. Take it step by step, put the structure in place, be patient, concentrate on each level—and get ready to prosper beyond what you thought possible.

Go get 'em!

62

Bookkeeper

———◆———

Through discipline comes freedom.

ARISTOTLE

G ET A BOOKKEEPER. THIS IS one of the best gifts that you can give to yourself in the interest of your financial health. Even if you don't have any money, do it. It took me way too long to figure this out. I did it on my own for too many years; I had a family member do it, I had my assistant do it. Don't even attempt this. Hire a professional book-keeping service to complete this task for you. I actually think I could have progressed faster if I'd had a bookkeeper from day one. Even if you are only doing one to two deals yearly on a part-time basis, you will quickly see the benefits of a bookkeeper.

For $50 to $200 monthly, you can save your life, your financial life. Wow, I just got a check for $20,000—woo hoo. Here we go. Look at me. Pay this, spend on that, before we know it, poof—it's gone! And we haven't even paid the taxes on the $20,000. So we had revenue of $20,000, and now we are in debt to the state and federal governments to the tune of roughly $8,000. Do ten of those per year, and you are in debt $80,000. Sound familiar? If it doesn't, then you haven't done any deals in real estate yet or you are being paid as an employee (versus an independent contractor).

In the real estate world, we don't have cash flow. We have injections of large sums of sugar every once in a while. If you are doing a lot of business, then the gaps between "once in a while" are reduced. But it's still lumpy. You may be doing a King Kong volume or doing three deals yearly on a part-time basis; if you have been around for more than a day, lumpy, lumpy, and lumpy. A good bookkeeper will help you bring some sanity to this lumpy income stream.

A bookkeeper can pay your bills; provide a monthly profit-and-loss statement, balance sheet, and general ledger; and efficiently correspond with your accountant/tax preparer. Your bookkeeper should be an important part of your team. "Well, Jim, I can't afford to have one." You can't afford *not* to. Ask your friends that own businesses for a referral in this area. Then talk with two to three bookkeepers and get started. It will take two to four months to work into a rhythm/process, but give it some time and let it develop.

Here is my bookkeeping routine:

1) My morning routine consists of reviewing my receipts from the day before, making a couple of notes on them, and mailing them off to the bookkeeper. In addition, anything that needs to be paid goes in that envelope as well. Gone, out of my hair, I don't have to think about it for the rest of the day.
2) The bookkeeper mails me checks that require my signature; I review them, sign them, and mail them off. Done.
3) At the end of each month, my bookkeeper e-mails me the profit-and-loss statement, balance sheet, and general ledger for my review. We review them together, make changes where necessary, and he and I put a stamp of completion on that month.
4) Every quarter I have my accountant do a complete audit of the work that the bookkeeper has done for accuracy and

transparency. I trust my bookkeeper, but trust with verification. I do this a lot, where I have professionals double check other professionals' work. It makes me sleep better.

5) Then my bookkeeper sends the profit-and-loss, balance sheet, and general ledger to my CPA on a quarterly basis. I tell my bookkeeping team and CPA team to correspond directly with one another, but copy me on all e-mails.

6) In a nutshell, that's the process. It's actually similar to the process that big corporations use, just smaller numbers and staffing.

One note: I suggest maintaining signature authority on all checks. Get a bookkeeper. "Through discipline comes freedom"—*Aristotle.*

Go get 'em!

63

Business Bank Account

———◆———

Rather go to bed without dinner than to rise in debt.
BENJAMIN FRANKLIN

I ACTUALLY KNEW A LENDER when I started in real estate that ran his business as a niche form of a trust; he was also a CPA and certainly qualified to run that type of obscure entity. Don't worry, we won't get stuck in the mud and have a long conversation about complicated entity structures, types of bank accounts, and tax-related issues—we are pushing for common sense.

Common sense. You are running a business, so you need a business bank account. And no, you can't use this account to pay for Tommy's swim camp or Johnny's piano lessons or Mary's gymnastics club. This is a business bank account and will be used only for business.

In addition, are there times when we might not have our checkbook with us and need to pay a business expense? For sure. You'll need a business credit card as well. Same goes: *we don't get to use our business credit card to purchase dog food or pay the kid's college tuition bills or make a deposit on the upcoming family vacation.* Yes, I have been there. The card stays securely locked away in your wallet or purse. It only comes out *for an appearance* if you are in a pinch and need to pay for a business-related expense.

Moving money. If you don't have any money in the business account at the moment, then work with your bookkeeping and tax team, and they will show you how to correctly make an "owner's contribution" to your business. They can also show you how to accurately move money from your business to your personal account. Work with your bookkeeping and tax team in both those instances.

I ran my real estate operation as a sole proprietorship for twenty years. I told the bank, "I'd like the account to say *Carter Real Estate Business.*" They said *no.* They explained that it's a sole proprietorship and they couldn't do that. They said, "Just *list it* as James R. Carter and *use it* for only business purposes." I could have thought of that—I did think of that. That's not what I wanted, however. I wanted it to feel like and look like a business account. I needed the account to walk like, talk like, quack like, and smell like a business.

Why?

As lenders and real estate agents, we are free as birds to fly wherever our minds may take us that day; we don't have a boss, remember? *We need structure*—and the more the better. By having the bank account look like a *business* bank account, we reaffirm—to ourselves—the truth, which is that we are running a small business. This is not a hobby that allows us to goof off all day. It's a business. We need the business account to look like a business account. It's a constant affirmation that we are more than just the lead sales rep; we are also the VP of ops, VP of finance, VP of marketing, director of attitude, and CEO. *Structure.* All those functions need to work for your business to work. The labeling of the bank account is simply an affirmation of that fact.

By the way, the bank finally agreed to label my online banking "Real Estate Business." Small wins.

Go get 'em!

64

Cash to Run the Business

Nothing is enough for the man to whom enough is too little.

EPICURUS

How much money should I keep in my business account? What are the fundamentals associated with business cash reserves as a lender or as a real estate agent? Is there a standard percentage? Should it be a percentage of income, a percentage of expenses, or some other criteria? And by the way, when I say "cash," I am referring to money in the bank, not green bills.

A business friend and I were discussing this topic, and he made a good point when he said, "If the business is broken, cash reserves don't matter. It's about the structural integrity of the business more than cash reserves; income, expenses, and profit—and consistency thereof." I made note when he said it years ago. There are still some things to discuss, however, on this topic of business cash reserves. Instead of showing you graphs and charts, I am going to give you some things to think about so you can successfully manage your business cash reserves on your own.

Brand new to the business. Here is a rule of thumb: have six months of business and living expenses saved before you start. So, if your monthly business expenses are $2,000 and your monthly personal expenses are $2,000, then have $24,000 saved. If you are young and brand new to real estate, it is not likely that you have $24,000 saved up. Maybe a few people do, but I suspect not many. I know that I didn't start that way. It's my responsibility, however, to suggest a responsible way to begin—$24,000. But if you want to make this happen, then make it happen! Find a way to get it done.

Planning by the quarter. A business quarter is defined as three-month increments. So January, February, and March could be defined as quarter one, or Q1. The income in real estate can be rather lumpy on a month-to-month basis. But it can be equally predictable on a quarterly basis. For instance, let's say my plan is to generate $10K monthly from January to March. The actual income may happen as follows: January, $0K; February, $22K; March, $8K. We missed the goal on a monthly basis; but we hit the goal over a three-month time frame. So, once you are up and running, I'm suggesting that you manage your cash on a quarterly basis.

Personal business rhythm. You'll know this for yourself over time. Personally, I closed a large portion of my yearly income between January and June. It just happened that way. It happened when I was a lender, and it happened when I was a real estate agent. Here is my guess why it happened. When the kids were back in school, I would begin the push. This was roughly the beginning of September. Remember, there is a lag between work and income by about three to four months. I had no problem maintaining a nice pace from September to March; I could feel that I was running out of steam, however, by roughly April. So I closed a large chunk between January and June and a reduced number from July to December.

Over time, I knew how to manage my business cash based on those income dynamics. Personal business rhythm will be different for everyone. Once you determine what that is for yourself, you can use this information to make good decisions on how to manage your business cash.

Here is the key: regardless of who says what, when, how, where, why regarding how much cash you need, if you want to make this happen— *then make it happen!*

Go get 'em!

65

Managing Business Expenses

———◆———

Beware of little expenses; a small leak will sink a great ship.
BENJAMIN FRANKLIN

T HE VAST MAJORITY OF REAL estate agents and a large portion of lenders are paid as independent contractors. As such, it's safe to say most independent contractors in real estate are filing a Schedule C with the Internal Revenue Service (IRS). Let's review the first two sentences on the following IRS website, http://www.irs.gov/pub/irs-pdf/i1040sc.pdf, regarding a Schedule C. It says:

> *"Use Schedule C (Form 1040) to report income or loss from a business you operated or a profession you practiced as a sole proprietor. An activity qualifies as a business if your primary purpose for engaging in the activity is for income or profit and you are involved in the activity with continuity and regularity."*

I hope you are now convinced you are running a small business; the IRS explained it in fairly clear terms. The starting point in running a small business is installing the mechanism to manage expenses. Your bookkeeper can help you with this. It's easy to do and you will love yourself for it.

I have a college friend that manages an approximately $100 million budget with a biotech firm. I asked him how they approach managing their expenses. He said, "We budget and then we monitor the budget." It's as simple as that in real estate; we budget and then we manage the budget. We plan, and then we compare what actually happened to what we planned to happen.

I used some form of the following budgeting worksheet for twenty-plus years. And by the way, your budget is not necessarily directly correlated to your final tax analysis; that is between you and your tax person. A budget helps you manage your expenses associated with the business. And once you build the worksheet, you can easily move money from one category to another based on your objectives.

As lenders and real estate agents, we have *fixed costs* and *variable costs*. An example of a fixed cost is licensing. An example of variable cost for a real estate agent that is working a listing is advertising specific to that listing. *Step one:* plan your expenses for the month. *Step two:* keep that plan in mind as you are spending money for that thirty-day period. *Step three:* send all expense-related documentation to your bookkeeper at the end of the month. *Step four:* review the results thereof, plan versus actual. *Step five:* make necessary adjustments for the following month.

If you are uncomfortable with any of this or find it slightly intimidating, don't worry. Take it one step at a time. And I highly recommend that you retain the services of an experienced and reputable bookkeeping team, accountant, or both to help you and possibly coach you as well on this process. One step at a time, you'll be fine.

Go get 'em!

Real Estate Budget

March, 2020

Fixed Costs	plan	actual	delta
Automobile (business only)	$50	$75	-$25
Bank service charges	$5	$5	$0
Bookkeeping	$100	$100	$0
Business Insurance	$100	$60	$40
CPA tax service	$100	$120	-$20
Legal consulting	$100	$75	$25
Licensing and dues	$150	$150	$0
Marketing	$500	$500	$0
Meals and entertainment	$100	$50	$50
Office fees	$300	$300	$0
Office supplies	$100	$140	-$40
Payroll	$0	$0	$0
Professional development	$150	$100	$50
Postage and delivery	$200	$150	$50
Telephone	$50	$60	-$10
Technology	$200	$250	-$50
Taxes	$1,000	$1,000	$0
Unexpected contingencies	$300	$175	$125
Total fixed costs	$3,505	$3,310	$195

Variable Costs (assuming two sales as a realtor)			
Advertising	$500	$400	$100
Other deal specific costs	$1,000	$800	$200
Total variable costs	$1,500	$1,200	$300

Total Budget	$5,005	$4,510	$495
	plan	*actual*	*delta*

66

Profit-and-Loss Statement

———◆———

Measure what is measurable and make
measureable what is not so.

GALILEO

BOUT HALF WAY THROUGH MY master's program, the professor assigned an interesting project. He said we needed to meet with a
CEO, CFO, or both of a local company and talk with him or her about
how he or she managed his or her finances. I called a college friend
and he knew a CEO that was willing to meet with me. This company
was privately held, and I didn't have the nerve to ask too many detailed
questions, but I'm guessing they were doing roughly $20 million yearly
in sales. We set the date to meet.

We met in his office and he asked his CFO to join us. They were
both generous with their time and enthusiastic to help me complete
my project. The meeting was going great, and then all of a sudden
the CEO turned on a dime, red faced and noticeably irritated with
me. I definitely had hit a nerve. I was knee deep in my studies at
the time, and I had all these slick terms on the top of my head, such
as *commercial paper, treasury management, current ratio*, etc., and I was
young and lacked real-world business experience. Whatever I said,
he didn't like it. He said, "Bulls&$*&#t. I'm running a business, and

those terms don't mean squat to me. Money in, money out, cash in, cash out, and at the end of the day there better be some left over." I said thank you, moved on to another topic, and we continued.

I never forgot the lesson I learned from my CEO interviewee that day: money in and money out.

I'll make it sound complex and then I'll make it sound simple.

Complex: Profit-and-loss statements are accountants' way of calculating profits using a complex set of rules (Generally Accepted Accounting Principles) that mostly apportion income and expenses among accounting periods. While such statements are helpful to financial analysts and others who want to be able to compare financial information among many entities knowing they were prepared using common standards, such financial statements are not very helpful in managing the day-to-day financial affairs of most businesses. For those businesses, including real estate brokerages, "money in and money out" statements are more useful.

Simple: As lenders and real estate agents, we rarely deal with business assets or long-term debt, so we can simplify all of it. How much did I take in? How much did I spend? What is left over? That's all we are doing here. *We are counting.* The below worksheet is the summary of that counting process.

A friend of mine that runs a vast real estate business defines this principle as "what's left is mine!" Every month, money comes in from different ventures: commissions, sales, referral fees, rents, etc. The money hits the table and stacks up. Next, he starts paying the bills, mortgages, salaries, taxes, and any other expense that hits the company that month. When he is all done, he says, "What's left is mine." What's important is the tracking, the counting, and the management of income and expenses. The closer you look, the more you will find, so keep a close eye on what comes in and how it goes out.

Yes, you can get fancy on your expense categories if you want. I don't. My CPA tells me there are few exact requirements (there are some, however) on the names or number of expense categories. My rule is to use, at minimum, the categories required by the tax authorities and then add categories that may be meaningful to me to manage the business. I keep it simple. I mostly focus on money in and money out. You are accounting for money received and expenses paid, and as such it is relatively simple provided you keep your records current. By the way, if you are not a good record keeper—become a good record keeper.

The profit-and-loss statement should serve two primary purposes: 1) it will help you run your small business and 2) it can serve as one of your "source documents" for your tax preparer. For specific tax advice, naturally consult your tax professional.

Running the business. Personally, I would like to rename this document "Money In and Money Out." Why? Because I use this simple document as a cash management tool as well; how much money came in and where did I spend it? I want to see every last penny that was spent, regardless of how my tax person handles that line item. "Jim, what do you mean?" For instance, let's say I need to purchase a chair for my office that costs me $200. The tax person may or may not be able to "fully expense" that $200 chair within the calendar year that I spent the money. Fine. But how much cash did it take out of my business account to purchase that chair nonetheless? Yes, you are correct, $200. So, I want to see that $200 on this document. Money in and money out.

As lenders and real estate agents, we are not running a multinational asset-heavy business that is doing $200 million in revenue. Keep it simple.

Taxes. Your tax person will largely use the information contained in the profit-and-loss statement to compute your taxable income and prepare your tax returns. Yes, he or she will likely reference your general ledger and balance sheet; but again, let's keep it simple. All those conversations are between you and your tax person and possibly your bookkeeper.

The profit-and-loss statement may look somewhat familiar to your budget, which is located in the chapter called "Managing Business Expenses." There will be some similarities and some differences. For instance, income and net income are not included in the budget. In addition, the expense categories may or may not be similar. Why? Because life is life; unexpected things can and will happen over a 365-day time frame. You may need to adjust categories here and there.

My bookkeeper prepares the profit-and-loss statement for me because he or she is qualified to tie down all the pennies. I am not a tax person or a bookkeeper or a CPA; I am not qualified to do any of that. I am business person. I rely on those professionals to help me.

I have intentionally avoided a complex discussion of financial accounting in this chapter. In my experience, there is little to no correlation between understanding all the complexities of accrual basis and tax rules accounting, such as depreciation, amortization, allocation of car expenses, expansible percentage of meals, etc., and *being a successful real estate professional*. Keep it simple. *Money in, money out.*

I am encouraging you to think of your profit-and-loss statement with a renewed, positive energy. Think of it as a competitive weapon, something that can and will help you win. It is an asset; a useful tool. A surgeon has a menu of tools to get the job done, depending on the surgery. This is a tool to help us be successful in real estate. Embrace it as such.

Go get 'em!

Profit and Loss Statement
Calendar Year 2020

TOTAL INCOME	**$100,000**
EXPENSES	
Fixed Costs	
Automobile (business only)	$600
Bank Service Charges	$60
Bookkeeping	$900
Business Insurance	$900
CPA Tax Service	$1,400
Legal Consulting	$1,200
Licensing and Dues	$1,800
Marketing	$3,500
Meals and Entertainment	$750
Office Fees	$3,600
Office Furniture	$350
Office Supplies	$800
Payroll	$0
Professional Development	$1,800
Postage and Delivery	$1,800
Technology	$2,000
Telephone	$600
Total Fixed Costs	$22,060
Variable Costs	
Advertising	$4,500
Other deal specific costs	$6,500
Total Variable Costs	$11,000
TOTAL EXPENSES	**$33,060**
TOTAL PROFIT	**$66,940**

67
Personal Financial Statement

—◆—

A jug fills drop by drop.
BUDDHA

THERE ARE ROUGHLY 43,200 MINUTES in a month. Take thirty of those and check your personal financial health.

I am calling this chapter "Personal Financial Statement"; the below worksheet, however, is technically not a personal financial statement, nor is it a schedule of real estate. Those are certainly more extensive documents required by the lending industry. I needed something simple that I could update quickly and could easily visualize as my financial scoreboard. The below worksheet is the end result. I call it a net-worth statement. It's simply an accounting of assets minus liabilities, which equals net worth. I use some form of the following worksheet to this day. Without exception, I limit it to a single sheet of paper regardless of what may be happening financially at that moment.

Overlap. Why am I putting a personal financial statement in a book about becoming successful in real estate? Because there is a natural and normal amount of overlap between our business and personal finances, given the fact that we are running a small business. Good decisions in one have a tendency to affect the other, and vice versa.

Create good habits. Take 120 minutes monthly to review and update your 1) business budget, 2) profit-and-loss statement, and 3) personal financial statement. They can all be done together in one two-hour sitting. Do it by yourself, with your partner, with your bookkeeper, with your accountant, or with your manager. Set the date and do it.

One hundred twenty minutes. Look, we are talking about becoming financially self-reliant and possibly not needing to ask the boss for a raise—for the rest of your life. There is some responsibility that goes along with that song and dance. This is one of them. Keep track. It's simple. It takes me no more than thirty minutes monthly to update the below worksheet.

Burying your head deep in sand. Here is an extreme, unfortunate example of what happens when we don't keep track of our finances and instead bury our heads in sand. A lady was having some trouble financially and didn't want to confront the numbers or the problem. A few months went by, and she figured she would get to it at some point. When the bank took her house, there were eight months of unopened mail in the trunk of her car. Let's assume that this all happened in a good real estate market. If she had simply confronted the numbers, she could have maneuvered her way out of that problem. Confront the numbers; look at them once a month at a minimum. As a real estate agent or lender, business affects personal and personal affects business. Keep track of your money.

Be conservative and honest with yourself. I am fortunate to have a close friend in my life that is my personal real estate investment advisor; I love and respect this guy dearly. We were reviewing my net-worth statement over lunch one day. He said, "Jim, I love you like a brother, and I want the best for you. I have to tell you, however, your valuations are generous. Be honest with yourself."

Here is an example of what he was referring to.

Let's say I owned a fourplex and the value was somewhere in that $200K to $220K range. I was using the $220K on my net-worth statement, which was obviously the high side of the range. Not only that, but I was not deducting for transaction fees (when and if I sold the property). Instead of using $220K as the value, my friend was suggesting I use $184K: $200K minus 8 percent for transactions fees equals 184K. Did the $220,000 make me feel good? You bet. Was my friend right, however? Of course he was. Be honest with yourself when you analyze your numbers.

I hope it works out. How do we take care of our bodies? We eat right, get some exercise and visit the doctor every once in a while for a checkup. How do we take care of our finances? "Well, I hope it works out." That won't work. In real estate, we need to be constantly monitoring our business and personal finances. It doesn't take a lot of time, and it's something we must do.

Negative net worth. If you are young and starting with a negative number, then fine. Throw a party when you get to breakeven and then move forward from there. Even if you are older and have had a run of bad luck, keep track and celebrate when you get to that breakeven number. You are older and wiser now and can use that experience to make up ground quickly; keep track of the numbers. And hey, some of the most successful and wealthy people in the world had a negative net worth smack dab in the middle of their business career. It can happen to the best us. Move forward, keep going.

"I'm not a numbers person." First of all, stop saying that. Second, look at the numbers and you'll become more comfortable with them over time. It's a single sheet of paper. Fold it up, stick it in your purse or wallet, and pull it out and look at it as you are sitting waiting for your car at the car wash.

I have a company that tunes up my garage doors twice per year because I would rather pay $150 now than $2,000 later on. I would rather exercise sixty minutes daily now than have health problems in five years. I would rather pay $200 monthly for my landscaper to come twice weekly than face a $10,000 problem down the road.

Think of checking your net worth regularly within the same context of the examples above. Those examples are obviously relevant to avoiding a problem down the road, which may feel negative to some. But consider this: from Socrates to Plato to Aristotle and many great thinkers before and after them, all talk about avoiding pain. And just to make you feel good, on the positive side of the equation, *what you measure has a tendency to grow.* You may find tracking the numbers results in the growth of those numbers.

Go get 'em!

Personal Financial Statement

Jack and Jill Wentupthehill - March, 2020

ASSETS

Liquid

Bank #1 Checking	$1,000
Bank #2 Checking	$3,000
Bank #3 Savings	$7,000
Bank #4 Savings	$3,000
Bank #5 401K Plan	$12,000
Bank #6 Other Retirement Plan	$1,000
Bank #7 Stocks	$4,000
Cash	$1,300
Total Liquid Assets	$32,300

Not Liquid

7458 Mammoth Mountain Ct (primary residence)	$130,000	
Private Investment in Uncle Henry's Winery	$5,000	
Cars	$18,000	
Boat	$20,000	
Furniture	$12,000	
Total Not Liquid Assets	$185,000	
TOTAL ASSETS		**$217,300**

LIABILITIES

7458 Mammoth Mountain Ct (primary residence)	$95,000	
Car Loan	$10,000	
Boat Loan	$15,000	
Credit Cards Paid Monthly	$0	
TOTAL LIABILITIES		**$120,000**

PERSONAL NET WORTH	**$97,300**

68
Taxes

Paying your taxes serves a useful
purpose—it keeps you out of jail.
A Friend

Pay them.

69

Car Payment

You can take a chance with a person
who pays his bills on time.

TERENCE

WHEN YOU ROLL INTO STARBUCKS at six thirty in the morning (okay, nine thirty) on your way to work, what do you see? A construction team getting ready for the day; a middle-aged man in the corner on his laptop with a five-day beard; the neighborhood friendly guy in jeans greeting everyone; the twenty-something, out-of-college person, well dressed, frantically doing something on his or her phone; the mom or dad, wearing workout gear, that just dropped off the kids; and the well-dressed businessman/-woman.

We naturally judge other people—yes, you; yes, me; yes, everyone. "Well, Jim, I don't judge people." Some of us judge less, some judge more—we all do it to some extent. Your customer judges you. He or she will size you up: overall appearance, the clothes you wear, acceptable grooming, *the car you drive*, etc.

Buy a car that runs and looks good. It's easier to buy a newer car and take a payment (within your means). Look, a car is an expense, period. You can make a monthly payment on a newer car or come up with large sums of money every once in a while to fix an old beater—either way it's roughly the same, but way less hassle with the newer car.

Also, on those days when you have "poor me" disease, you will simply feel better driving around town in a nice car versus a beat-up piece of junk. Remember, we are in a service business. The customer usually will not distinguish the person from the service—the two are in most cases one and the same in his or her mind. Nice car, nice clothes, nice person, nice service.

Go get 'em!

70

Lumpy Income

———◆———

We must consult our means rather than our wishes.
PRESIDENT GEORGE WASHINGTON

LUMPY, DUMPY, AND FRUMPY. IF you are new to real estate or haven't quite started yet, it's possible the following chapter will just be words on a piece of paper. If so, you may want to circle back to this when you are up and running; it will be more meaningful to you at that time. To those folks that are active in real estate today, you will be living what we are going to talk about below.

Every industry has income dynamics that are specific to that industry. Education: it's mostly about a steady monthly tuition check. Utilities: monthly, some is fixed, and some is based on use. Retail and restaurants: they sell what they sell that day. Landscape maintenance: steady monthly income. Landscape construction: lumpy income based on one-off projects.

Real estate: as lenders and real estate agents, we get paid if and when we close a deal. Those are the income dynamics of the real estate business. It's a "transaction" oriented income stream. Here is an example of how lumpy it can be: January, $10K; February, $3K; March, $32K; April, $2K; May, zero; June, $54K.

Can we flatten our income? A notion exists that says, as paraphrased, simply make X amount of contacts daily, and that will likely do the trick. That is helpful, but that is an incomplete answer. You can generate a truck load of leads and clients, but if you don't have the operational infrastructure to deliver the service, you are wasting your time. Or go ahead and throw those twenty new clients at your operations department that has been designed to handle only five. You will have a mess on your hands from all the unhappy customers, who will also not be sending referrals down the road.

Marketing, operations, finance, and attitude—they're about flow and chemistry and all those intangibles that exist when you are running a well-oiled machine (business). So yes, make those contacts and put forth some effort on marketing, but pay attention to operations and finance and attitude. Some daily focus on each category will help to flatten your income stream. It won't be perfect, but it will help.

Here is how we could get in trouble when we run transaction-oriented businesses. Let's say that lender Joe is planning for monthly revenue of $8,000 in calendar year 2015. It's now June 2015, and Joe is more or less right on track. It's a little lumpy, but he is doing just fine. Joe closes a few giant deals in July that earn him $45,000 extra, above and beyond the $8K objective. *Giant lump!* After the hangover wears off from the celebration, Joe realizes he has $45,000 sitting in his business account. Hmmm, what does Joe do?

Step one: Joe decides to pull the trigger on the luxurious patio for his backyard that he has been wanting, $15K.

Step two: Joe recognizes he needs to save some for taxes, but he'll deal with that last; he's just making a mental note for now.

Step three: The kids need stuff, $2K.

Step four: Joe is feeling good with all that money in his pocket, so he blows another $3K on expensive meals and entertainment.

Step five: Joe decides it's time to buy that fancy car consistent with a man at his production level, and the deposit is $12K.

Step six: Steve, Joe's good buddy, has a "can't lose" stock pick. He knows he shouldn't do it because he still owes the taxes, but he figures he can get in and out quick, no problem—and he is also considering this money to be the tax money, and, who knows, maybe he'll be able to double his money quick, $8K.

Step seven: And what the heck, Joe decides to make a down payment on the boat too, $5K.

Within a blink of an eye, $45K went from Joe's hands to other hands. When money goes from your hands to another person's hands, you just lost control of that money.

And then Joe gets the phone call from his tax person. The tax person starts explaining these terms called *marginal tax rates* and *alternative minimum taxes.* "Wait a minute," says Joe. "That's not fair; I worked my ass off for that money." The CPA says, "Welcome to the world of making a lot of money, Joe."

Joe is now in debt to the state and federal government somewhere in the neighborhood of $15K to $23K. He is also stuck with a $1,000 per month payment on the expensive car and a $300 per month payment on the boat. *But he still has the stock.* His buddy Steve: "Ummmm, Joe, that didn't work out so well. It turns out it was a worthless penny stock. Yikes, hate to tell you this, but we lost all the money."

Live within or under your means. Bring your desires down to your present means; increase them only when your increased means permit, as Aristotle said.

There are some very smart people in the world that say, as paraphrased, "Take on a big mortgage payment and a big car payment and that will *push you* to perform." Maybe that works for some. It doesn't work for me. The problem is, it's not sustainable long term. How long can you run on that treadmill before you break down from exhaustion? And in the meantime, your balance sheet is loaded with debt. You cannot put a price tag on a good night's sleep and peace of mind.

Live below or within your means so that when that $45K hits your account, you can truly improve your financial standing. Your expenses have remained constant and your cash position has improved. Why do the rich keep getting richer? 1) They largely have their expenses under control, 2) They have very little debt, and 3) They have some money in the bank so that they are 100 percent prepared for the next *real* opportunity.

If you are living in a six-hundred-square-foot house and have three kids, then fine, crank up your expenses and get your family into an acceptable living situation. But short of that, keep your expense line flat as your income line grows. By doing so, you will become big, strong, and fast financially.

Lumpy income. Work to flatten it and work to manage it. *Flatten it:* Focus daily effort on marketing, operations, finance, and attitude. Don't allow any one category to overpower the other. *Manage it:* Live at or below your means. So if your revenue line was $100K last year, push for a 20 percent growth, so your new goal is $120K—but plan your life and business around $80K.

Do the above for three to four years and you'll find yourself sleeping like a baby with a whole bunch of cash in the bank.

Go get 'em!

71

Invest or Work

———◆———

*Riches: they are blessings to those who know how
to use them, and curses to those who do not.*

TERENCE

I AM WRITING THIS CHAPTER to stimulate thought. We'll define *working* as using your time and effort to produce income; *investing* as giving your money to other people and hoping it grows; and *saving* as putting cash in the bank.

In real estate, there is no gold watch, stock option, or pension at the end of the rainbow. We need to amass wealth with our own blood, sweat, and tears. We must build a nest egg large enough to produce monthly income in the event we don't want to work any longer or our health prohibits us from working. How much is needed—$500K, $1 million, $3 million, $10 million, or $20 million? It will be different for everyone. But we need to begin the building process regardless of the goal and regardless of our current financial status at the moment.

Here is the question. Over a thirty-year time frame, are you better off focusing on your work and saving excess funds or working and investing excess funds? For instance, Vince and Dan are both real estate agents. Vince decides to focus on his business for eight hours per day for thirty years and put excess money in the bank. Dan decides to work eight hours daily for thirty years and invest excess money in stocks, bonds, mutual funds, etc. Which one has more money after thirty years? Dan? Are you sure? Are you really sure? "It is the mark of an educated mind to be able to entertain a thought without accepting it"—*Aristotle*. Dan would certainly be the easy and obvious answer based on common sense and compounding interest. Here are some things to consider, however.

Building a business. So your profit this year is $20,000. Fine, but who's to say that you can't build up your business to produce profits of $2 million in ten years? Should you spend your time monitoring, managing, thinking about, worrying about, dreaming about, and hoping that your investment account grows—or should you spend that time growing your own business? Which one do you have control of?

Study. Study self-made, successful businesspeople. The vast majority did it by building a business. And then, they became rich from the profits of that business, selling all or part of that business, or a combination of those two. How big can you build your real estate business? How big do you want to build it?

Additionally, how many name-brand successful businesspeople became successful by putting $100 or even $10,000 monthly into a mutual fund? Don't get excited—it's just a question. I don't know of any, but you may.

Focus. Dan is focusing at least some of his attention on his investment account. Vince is focused solely on building his business. All things remaining equal, who has a bigger business after ten, twenty, or thirty years? Yes, Vince has a bigger business (more profits). Will Vince's larger business offset the compounding nature of Dan's investment account? Yes or no? And, if the answer is yes, by what margin?

I'm encouraging you to think about this topic because, every once in a while, I have seen colleagues literally waste four hours of an eight-hour day doodling on the Internet with their investment account. It takes tremendous mental discipline to be all in all the time. But is it in our best interest to focus on building our business rather than hoping that our investment account is growing? If you like the former option, remember, you are still saving money; you have a nice, healthy cash account at the bank.

I'm sure you'll make a good decision on how to handle this. Here is what I'll leave you with: nearly every successful businessperson that I know made the lion's share of that fortune by helping to build a business—by working. I literally don't know anyone that built their fortune by investing. What is your craft? What is the skill that you are offering the world? You can build a fortune by simply providing the world your service.

Go get 'em!

72

One-Two Punch

If a man neglects education, he walks
lame to the end of his life.

PLATO

WARNING—THIS TOPIC IS A LITTLE dry but I'll make it colorful. There are a couple of basic financial skills you'll need as you navigate your way through the real estate business. You don't need to be a pro; you do, however, need to have some basic understanding of the *financial calculator and Excel.* The one-two punch.

I was brand new as a real estate agent and competing for a listing with two seasoned veterans. I successfully got the listing. I asked the couple, gently, why they selected me. They said, as paraphrased, "Jim, we work in finance. We know you created all your presentation documents from scratch. We know the difference and were impressed you were able to work that financial calculator on the fly. This is a financial transaction, so we wanted someone that had some financial skills." So, the boring news is that you'll need some level of skill on Excel and the financial calculator. The exciting news is that those skills can help you win in this business.

And by the way, I did the exact same thing as a lender when I was presenting the various loan programs to a prospective client. It's a little time consuming to build the worksheets, but rather easy to update once the original documents are built.

Listen, there is nothing wrong with "hitting the button" on the computer and letting the computer print out all the "stuff"—market history, comparable sales, etc. But every once in a while, aren't you curious? I had a statistics class in my master's program, and it made me think. When the computer spits out stuff, are you ever curious on the logic behind the stuff? Some human being told that computer how to think. I don't know that human being, I've never met him or her, and I don't know his or her qualifications relevant to real estate.

More often than not, I did my own math. And I did it on Excel. Number one, I wanted the math to be authentic and specific to what I was analyzing. Number two, I wanted to control the presentation. Some worksheets look like a scrambled mess, and then there are those that are clean and clear. I wanted to present information in a clean and clear manner. So I did it myself. You can do the same thing if you want. For me, I knew the competition was mostly presenting computer-generated documents, so it was an easy way to stand apart from the group.

At minimum, it would be hard to survive as a lender without some skills on a financial calculator. You might be able to survive as a real estate agent without skills on Excel or the financial calculator. But who wants to just survive? How about be big, strong, and muscular—how about *thrive!* These skills make you strong, versatile, and confident.

Imagine this level of confidence: you can give me any problem in real estate that has numbers involved, give me enough time, and I will produce a clean and clear worksheet (Excel) that will show the problem as summarized and some possible solutions. You can have that same level of confidence. Take it one step at a time, get a little better daily, and you'll get there.

I didn't have those skills coming out of college. I couldn't even turn on the computer at my first job, but out of necessity, within one year, I learned the basics; year two I got a little better; and by year three I was on the move—and frankly enjoying it. Today, whenever I have a challenge in business, or sometimes even personally, I retreat to Excel and whip out my financial calculator. I can think and doodle at the same time. It starts with a blank worksheet, then grows as I add numbers, then clarifies as I make it look pretty, then crystallizes as I polish, and then cures as I review it, over and over and over again. Before you know it, I have taken a seemingly insurmountable, complicated problem out of my head and reduced it to a single sheet of paper. Clean, clear, and void of emotion.

Here is my belief, and the following applies to both lenders and real estate agents: 1) We need some level of skill on Excel and the financial calculator to adequately serve the customer. 2) Those skills can be used to help build your business. 3) There is a correlation between those skills and confidence.

Again, don't be intimidated if you are starting from ground zero on this. Everyone starts from somewhere. And remember, it's about balance in marketing, operations, finance, and attitude. You don't need to drop everything and go learn these skills. Spend a little time daily in the four categories above. These skills belong in finance. Chip away at it and before you know it, you'll be a pro.

Go get 'em!

73

Use Your Company

Thrift is great revenue.

CICERO

USE YOUR COMPANY TO HELP you build wealth and manage your finances through *transfer directives*. What is a transfer directive? It is a directive you give your company to "send money."

For example, let's say you earned a $10,000 commission and you are on a 70 percent–30 percent split; your revenue for that deal is therefore $7,000. You may tell your company to take 30 percent of that $7,000 and send it to one of your accounts designated as "taxes." In this case, you would be sending $2,100 to that account. Why would you want to do that? 1) It's one less decision you need to make, and 2) That money is separated from your operating account; therefore, there is very little risk of you spending it by "accident." You can think of this as a cash management tool.

Some companies will offer these *off-the-top* transfer services and some will not. What does *off the top* mean? It means starting from the $7,000 number above. Some people in real estate would consider off the top as starting with the $10,000 number. But as a producer, I have never seen it that way because that $3,000 is not my money. My revenue is based on $7,000, so for me, off the top means starting with the $7,000 number.

Here are some possible transfers the company can help with: tax-deferred income options, medical payments, insurance payments, sending money to a tax account, donating to a charity, and other possibilities; and of course the big one, sending the bulk of it to your operating business account. These can all be set up as transfer directives so you don't even need to think about it. Now, if you decide to take advantage of any of these services, make sure to work with your bookkeeping and tax team to ensure proper accounting thereof.

Do we all need medical insurance? Yes. Do we all need to pay taxes? Yes. Should we all take advantage of tax-deferred income options? Yes. We are doing all these things anyway. Minimize decisions and consider using your company to help you manage your finances.

In addition, think about this: When you set up an auto transfer (to anything), how many steps or decisions did that take? One; that one time that you completed the setup process. How many decisions or steps when you write a check monthly? Twelve per year times the remaining years of your life. That could range possibly from one hundred to eight hundred. Let's take something somewhat in the middle, 450.

Is there risk involved in 450 business transactions/decisions? Look at the process. Step one: I realize it's that time (again) to write the check. Step two: I think to myself, do I have enough money in the account? Step three: I put it off another day. Step four: I think about it again and decide to go ahead and write the check this time. Step five: I forget to mail the check. Step six: I finally remember to mail the check the next day. That process is loaded with risk. Or, I give my company a transfer directive to send it from point A to point B—I don't even think about.

Now don't get carried away and ask me, "Well, what if I don't close a deal in three months? How do I handle that?" You'll need to deal with that on your own or with the assistance of your company and possibly your bookkeeper/tax person.

This whole discussion will be specific to your company and your tax/bookkeeping team. Think about it nonetheless. We have a lot of decisions to make in real estate relevant to marketing, operations, finance, and attitude. Structure is good for us, particularly when it comes to managing our finances. If your company can help, then I'm encouraging you to let them help.

Go get 'em!

74

Financial Strength

———————

The greatest wealth is to live content with little.

PLATO

EVERYONE I KNOW WAS SLIGHTLY wounded (financially) by the great recession in the late 2000s. Some sustained a paper cut, some a black eye, several pulled hamstrings, a broken arm here and there, and some had more serious injuries requiring long-term therapy. It was a broad range, but everyone I know was affected.

Some of the sharpest business personalities in the world learn lessons the hard way. Except, when you are a business person dealing with numbers and money, the hard way usually means *losing money*. I am no different, and all my successful business friends are no different either. This chapter is about financial strength: expenses, cash, and debt. All these areas affect us in real estate, both on a business and personal level.

If my great-great-grandchild asked me, "Great-Great-Grandpa, how do I become financially strong?" my reply would be, "Cash in the bank, expenses under control, and little to no debt. Maintain that posture your whole life and countless opportunities will surface."

Think back to 2008, 2009, and 2010. Imagine if you had some cash in the bank, your expenses were low, and you had no debt. Think about that for a minute. Now—what if you lost your job; or what if the profit of your real estate business went from $400K to $25K? That would have been certainly painful, but not catastrophic. You would likely make it through with just a black eye. That's how the rich mostly get richer. Over a period of years and usually decades, they have worked their way into that position of no/low debt, cash in the bank, and low *fixed* expenses, and they are prepared for the next opportunity.

In real estate, there are four pieces to finance: the financial skills to serve the customer; the financial skills to run our small business; the financial skills to run our personal life; and the financial skills to build wealth and invest. *Cash, debt, and expenses* are (collectively) a core principle of those four areas of finance. Cash in the bank, little to no debt, moderate expenses. That posture creates strength—deep, long-lasting, and mature strength.

Philanthropy. Financial strength also puts you in a position to help others. If you are cruising into an economic slowdown with big debt, big expenses, and little cash, I'm nearly guaranteeing that personal survival will be the primary thing on your mind. On the other hand, if you have cash, no debt, and low expenses, you will be in a position to help someone. You'll have the time, money, or both to reach out.

Try this on for size. Why didn't the commercial market in many name-brand metropolitan areas of America come crashing down to the ground in the recession of the early 2000s or again in the late 2000s? I could drive up and down the freeway and see block after block of new and old commercial buildings sitting empty for months and sometimes years at a time. The answer: A large portion of that product was concentrated in very strong hands. It was mostly owned by people and/or companies that had no or little debt, cash in the bank, and manageable expenses. Their backs were not against the wall; they could breathe, take their time, and make prudent decisions on their own terms. They could do so only by having no debt, cash in the bank, and moderate expenses.

Consider all the above. You never want to be "forced" into a making a business decision. Benjamin Franklin said, "Necessity never made a good bargain." You want to do things on your terms within your own time frame. You want to stay firmly in control of your own financial life so when the next economic hurricane hits town or the next opportunity surfaces, *you are ready!* No debt, cash in the bank, and moderate expenses allow that to happen.

Go get 'em!

75

Financial Pickle

———◆———

A great wind is blowing, and that gives you
either imagination or a headache.
Catherine the Great

IN BASEBALL, WHAT IS A *rundown,* or what's informally referred to as a *pickle*? I'll modify the definition a little: the base runner is working his or her way to safety, and everywhere he or she turns is danger. As hard as we may try in business, there may be times when you find yourself in a financial pickle. I was there once; most businesspeople have been there at least once. A financial pickle is when your cash is low, expenses are high, debt is high, and income has deteriorated—that's a pickle!

As lenders and real estate agents, our personal and financial lives overlap in so many ways, so I will speak to both with one voice. If you find yourself in a financial pickle, here is my recommendation on the game plan:

Step one: Recognize it is temporary. Horace says, "If matters go badly now, they will not always be so."

Step two: Get up early so you are exhausted and can sleep at night. You are going to need your brain to pull yourself out of it. You may (or may not) have a tough time sleeping if you are truly in a financial pickle. So get up superearly, like five in the morning, work like a dog, and work out, so that by the time nine o'clock at night rolls around, you are wiped out and can sleep and can wake up the next day with your brain refreshed and ready to go to work again. "Fatigue is the best pillow"—*Benjamin Franklin*.

Step three: Get control of the money. One of my MBA professors was somewhat of a turn-around business expert. He said the first thing he did when he walked in the door to fix a business was *get control of all the money*. Until further notice, no money leaves the building without his approval.

Step four: Cut all personal and business expenses immediately. Look carefully at all your variable costs first. One of my business-personal friends sold his business for tons of money. He said, "When you are caught in a tight spot, you have to cut everything across the board by 35 percent. Those companies that can do it will be fine; those companies that can't are in trouble." Confucius said, "He who will not economize will have to agonize."

Step five: Cash and debt. If you are truly in a pickle, you have a "structural" problem, so borrowing $20K from Uncle Leroy is not going to help very much. You have to fix things—you can't just put a Band-Aid on a structural problem. Debtwise, you could attempt to contact the bank and see if they will consider a reduction in your payment or a short reprieve on your payment. Note: *Whatever you do, do not let the bank negatively affect your credit score.* You will need a strong credit score down the road. I hate to tell you, but you have limited options on cash and debt in the short term. Don't worry—hope is coming next.

Step six: Hope equals income! You have to unload all your ammunition in this area. You have to flip your profit-and-loss statement upside down. In other words, push expenses down and grow, grow, grow your revenue line. It won't be easy, but go after low-hanging fruit. Where can I spend my time today to generate revenue tomorrow? That should be the question you should ask yourself daily.

Step seven: Over time, you'll get healthy again. This is just my personal opinion, I have no quantitative data to back this up, but *the number of years it took to get into that pickle will exactly equal the number of years to get out of that pickle.* I know that may sound like a long time. Maybe it will be shorter for you.

If you find yourself there, don't panic; breathe, it's fine. You are not alone; nearly all business people get in a pickle at least once. I'll guarantee you this: you will be a 110 percent better business person when you surface from a pickle. There is a reason why old wise men and women are wise! As Benjamin Franklin says, "Life's tragedy is that we get old too soon and wise too late." And to avoid pickles from the start, keep a discerning eye on cash, debt, expenses, income, and the interrelationship thereof.

Go get 'em!

76

Presale Tune-Up Budget

———◆———

Never go to excess. Let moderation be your guide.

CICERO

L ANDSCAPE, PAINT, FLOORING, AND GENERAL cleanup. It's hard to go wrong if the seller contains tune-up dollars to those categories. You list a property that has been a rental for a couple of years. The seller lives out of town, the property is a mess, and the seller wants some advice on improvements that will drive the best possible result. The safe bet is to stay within the scope of landscape, paint, flooring, and cleaning.

The below worksheet is simply a way to organize that project. This was one of my four or five go-to worksheets. You'll have no trouble with it; it is the simplest of all the worksheets I will be presenting.

What is common sense and what is a developer? Common sense is making something sparkle before you sell it. What is a developer? A developer "creates" based on an estimate of a final sales price; he or she guesses a little. When the seller entertains improvements outside of the four categories above, he or she is guessing a little. At times, I would explain this distinction to my client, and sometimes the client would say, "Oh, no. Jim, I don't want to be a developer. Let's do only those bread-and-butter improvements to make it sparkle." Wise choice in most cases.

Are there cases in which you may not want to make any improvements at all? Of course. Those are deal-by-deal decisions. And by the way, you could technically include crown molding, baseboards, and casings within the term *sparkle* if you choose to.

The seller is tiptoeing into developer land when he or she starts considering improvements such as the kitchen, bathrooms, electrical, changing the floor plan, etc. The hard part: there are no guarantees either way. My advice: encourage the seller to exercise common sense and contain the project to high-probability, positive return on investment items such as landscape, paint, flooring, and cleaning.

Are there any other safe improvements? Yes, one more; Section One termite clearance. In 95 percent plus instances, I advised my client to complete Section One termite clearance prior to placing the home for sale. Again, there are exceptions to this rule.

Who is managing this project? The sellers may do this themselves, or they may ask for assistance from the real estate agent. This is strictly a business decision on how to handle this. For me, I loved assisting on these tune-up projects. This was the fun part of the job for me; you can watch something transform before your very eyes. In addition, it's stressful enough just being a seller, I didn't want to add another layer of responsibility for my clients by having them run the project by themselves. I'd rather take on some additional responsibility and have a nice, calm customer as a result thereof.

Go get 'em!

Pre Sale Tune Up Budget

Property Address

Interior painting	$3,100
Exterior painting	$1,900
New baseboard and casing	$2,300
New carpet in master bedroom	$500
Refinish hardwood	$1,700
Termite clearance & inspection	$3,700
Landscape tune-up	$1,750
New toilet in guest bathroom	$150
New exterior lights and mailbox	$200
Repair fence post	$60
Chimney (inspect, clean and sweep)	$250
Cleaning all tile	$250
Cleaning including windows	$500
Total	**$16,360**

77

Everyday Valuation Analysis

———◆———

I conceive that the great part of the miseries of
mankind are brought upon them by false estimates
they have made of the value of things.
BENJAMIN FRANKLIN

THE GO-TO TOOL IN CONSTRUCTION is the hammer; the go-to analytical
tool for me in real estate was the following worksheet. This was my
everyday bread-and-butter working document. A buyer or seller would
call, ask about pricing, and I would retrieve some version of the following
and start doodling.

If you are active in real estate daily, you will likely have a gut feel on
what something is worth. But gut feel is gut feel; no more and no less.
You don't know for sure, I don't, the customer doesn't; the appraiser
doesn't even know for sure. Many factors affect what a buyer is willing
to pay for a piece of real estate and what a property may command
given adequate marketing exposure. The below worksheet was simply
the starting point for me.

Here is the process I follow when working through the worksheet.

Find some comps. The first step is to find some relevant and comparable sales. I say *relevant* because some comparable sales will not

be relevant to what you are doing. Second, tighten up your range. In other words, don't analyze a 2,040-square-foot property against a 3,000-square-foot home or 1,000-square-foot home; that would invalid your final result. Find comps that are similar, so you may want to limit your search to 1,900 to 2,200 square feet. If you can't find enough, widen the search ever so slightly until you find enough to establish a good sampling; five to ten is a good number. And of course, find some that have closed recently; the more recently the better.

Land and building. Frankly, I included this section over the years for my own curiosity. I wanted to see the land value in relation to the building value to see if they were even remotely similar numbers. There will be times when it's completely valid to use the average of the two, and there will be times you don't consider land at all; or, you may not consider the building at times if you are strictly analyzing land.

Remember, let the numbers fall wherever the numbers are going to fall. Your sellers can take it; show them everything. They may not agree, but they can take it. For instance, your clients may not agree with one of the comps that have been included, or they may want to eliminate the land part of the analysis; no problem, it's just a click of a button to make the change and see the new result. Include the customer. We are not God making these amazing discoveries about their money—include them in the process.

Adjustments. So far, the numbers are the numbers, you analyzed some relevant comparable sales on both the land and building, and then you did an average of those methods. No adjustments have been made to this point. This is where gut feel and experience play a role, and your client will have good suggestions here as well. For instance, who is to say that a cul-de-sac location is worth 3 percent or 20 percent? That's an emotional item. It's a safety item. I have seen a cul-de-sac location range from 5 percent to 25 percent. Include your customer in the process. Talk it through. Once you build the worksheet, just hit the button and make the change.

The adjustments will change every time you are studying a piece of property. There could be one adjustment that needs to be made or there could be seven. Here are some possible adjustments: new product, school district, number of garage spaces, cul de sac, traffic, dysfunctional floor plan, condition, and more. Don't make it too complicated, however, because if you add too many variables, you are going to invalid the end result and simply regress to the average. My suggestion: keep it to no more than two to four.

Final analysis. The final estimated analysis shows what it shows.

By the way, I built this spreadsheet when I was a lender working with appraisers; this was back when lenders were allowed to talk with appraisers. However, I used it actively with customers when I starting selling real estate.

Our job is not to prove the sellers wrong and show them how smart we are; our job is to be helpful and execute. It's their money. The worksheet is simply one additional piece of information that can be considered when determining price. I will tell you, however, that seeing it in black and white, as outlined on the following page, tends to facilitate a more thoughtful. cerebral discussion. The numbers are the numbers.

If you are not yet comfortable with Excel or writing "calcs," no problem. Start with something simple; get a little better daily, and before you know it, you'll be a pro. I believe you'll find the following worksheet helpful over time.

Go get 'em!

Estimated Valuation Analysis

Property Address

RELEVANT COMPARABLE SALES

Address	Garage	Schools	Close Date	Building	Land	Sale Price	$/Bldg. Foot	$/Land Foot
xxx	1	xx	xxxxxx	2105	7700	$728,000	$346	$95
xxx	1	xx	xxxxxx	2109	7600	$875,000	$415	$115
xxx	2	xx	xxxxxx	2207	8200	$776,000	$352	$95
xxx	2	xx	xxxxxx	1958	8150	$720,000	$368	$88
xxx	2	xx	xxxxxx	2059	9795	$847,000	$411	$86
xxx	2	xx	xxxxxx	2010	7100	$825,300	$411	$116
xxx	2	xx	xxxxxx	2025	6900	$810,000	$400	$117
xxx	2	xx	xxxxxx	1851	9930	$834,600	$451	$84
xxx	2	xx	xxxxxx	2230	8100	$890,000	$399	$110
Totals				18554	73475	$7,305,900	$394	$99

SUBJECT PROPERTY

	Building	Land		Bldg. Value	Land Value
	2020	8,400		$795,404	$835,244
Average of Two Methods					$815,324

ADJUSTMENTS

New Product			positive	15%	$122,299
School District			negative	12%	-$97,839
One Car			negative	10%	-$81,532
Cul De Sac			positive	13%	$105,992
Net Adjustments					$48,919

FINAL ESTIMATED VALUATION (plus/minus)   **$864,243**

78

Investment Property

———◆———

Buying on trust is the way to pay double.
UNKNOWN

I RECOGNIZE THE MAJORITY OF readers interested in this book will be residential professionals, those dealing with a condo, townhome, or single-family residence. We will refer to that market as the *one-unit residential market*. Anything beyond one unit could and should be defined as investment property. So, if you are dealing with a duplex or a fourplex or a church, those are all investment properties and should be dealt with as such.

If you are active as a real estate agent or a lender, it's going to happen that you will be dealing with an investment property from time to time. Even if you don't want to deal with investment properties, those leads will hit your desk every once in a while.

Do it or refer it. When the call comes in, you can choose to do it yourself or refer it to a specialist in your office that deals with investment properties on a day-to-day basis. As both a lender and real estate agent, I have done them myself, and I have also referred those deals to a colleague on a case-by-case basis. The number one priority is adequate representation for the customer.

Investment property is different. First, you are dealing with rental income and the leases thereof. Second, you are dealing with multiple rental units, in most cases. Third, you are dealing with tenants that have occupancy rights to that property. There are a lot of factors, but just those three alone should be convincing enough that it is a different animal (transaction).

I'll take it one step further. When you are pushing hard and fast in the real estate business, you will be shocked at what lands on your desk—even if you are 100 percent specializing in the one-unit residential market. As a residential real estate agent or lender, we are the "real estate" person. So, we might have helped Joe and Cindy successfully purchase their first home; but we are the first ones they may think of when they want to buy the commercial building down the street. Get it? It happens, and it happens a lot. My clients have contacted me on gas stations, churches, land, warehouses, manufacturing facilities, liquor stores, strip malls, parking lots, skyscrapers, coffee shops, farms, storage facilities, and more.

You have to be smart. I have no idea how to deal with a skyscraper in downtown San Francisco or a gas station in Fresno. There are, however, people that deal with those product lines every day. Find someone that is an expert and make that introduction for your client; *and maybe even collect a referral fee.* It's borderline irresponsible to accept a job too far askew to your wheelhouse. I know commercial brokers that wouldn't dream of listing a residential property. Alternatively, I know one-unit residential real estate agents that wouldn't think of working a duplex. It certainly doesn't have to be that extreme, but responsible representation should be the guiding light here.

Whether I decided to do it or refer it, I *loved* analyzing investment property. Over the years, I needed one single sheet of paper that could analyze anything from a duplex all the way to a complicated mixed-use commercial building—and everything in between. I wanted something that I could simply modify on a case-by-case basis. The below worksheet is the result of that effort.

What are we analyzing? Everyone will approach this differently: what they are analyzing, why they are analyzing it, and how they will be analyzing it. For me, I was primarily analyzing the cap rate and cash-on-cash return.

Cap rate. Everyone will approach financing differently: some will pay all cash, some will put down 20 percent, and some will put down 80 percent. Regardless of the financing, a fair comparison should be made from one property to the next, *property versus property*. That fair comparison is called the cap rate.

Income, expenses, and profit. One change when you are analyzing real property: income, expenses, and net operating income (profit). Net operating income is referred to as NOI, but you can think of it as profit (before taxes). So, when analyzing the cap rate: determine the income, then determine the expenses, and then determine the net operating income. Now that we have the NOI, we are ready to determine the cap rate.

Christy just inherited $3 million. She would like to give up her day job to work full time as a volunteer in her community. She needs income, however, to pay day-to-day expenses. She wants to buy an apartment building to produce that income. She has looked at twenty-plus options. She likes three of them: this one produces $45K of NOI, that one $47K, and another good one $52K NOI. Now, did that apartment building that produced $52K cost $1 million or $2 million? In other words, how much did Christy need to invest to produce that $52K? The asking price on the building producing $52K is $950K; to determine the cap rate, she simply takes $52K divided by $950K. The cap rate, therefore, is 5.5 percent. The higher the cap rate the better.

Cash on cash return. Now, let's say Christy only wants to put down $400K and secure a loan for the remaining $550K; we already know that the NOI is $52K; but now there is an additional expense to consider, *the payment on the loan.* We'll assume it's an interest-only loan at 5 percent. The yearly payment, therefore, is $27.5K (take $52K minus $27.5K, which equals $24.5K); $24.5K is net cash flow before taxes. Christy can now expect $24.5K of income to land on her kitchen table yearly; $24.5K divided by her cash invested of $400K equals 6.1 percent. Therefore, Christy's cash on cash return is 6.1 percent. She invested $400K of cash, and that cash produced $24.5K of income yearly—cash on cash.

Frankly, I modified and simplified the below worksheet for this presentation. You can get fancy here if you want and add possible adjustments for principal reduction, tax considerations, and more. I have literally analyzed everything from churches to mixed-use properties to two-hundred-unit apartment buildings on this single sheet of paper. There have been whole books written on this very topic; so, I will stop here.

As with all things, take what initially appears complicated and simplify it. Christy is buying a building, and she needs a way to compare one against the other. That's it, simple.

Go get 'em!

Investment Property Analysis

Property Address

ESTIMATED YEARLY INCOME

Unit mix	
Five x two bedroom units	$90,000
Two x three bedroom units	$50,400
Laundry machine income	$2,000
Assumed vacancy rate	$14,040
Total yearly operating income	$128,360

ESTIMATED YEARLY EXPENSES

New real estate taxes	$18,000
Insurance	$2,500
xxx	$0
Electrical - owner portion	$1,000
Water - owner portion	$1,000
xxx	$0
Garbage	$1,000
Landscape	$1,500
AC maintenance and repair	$1,800
Other general maintenance	$500
Pool service	$600
Professional management	$10,269
Resident manager	$0
Unexpected misc.	$6,000
Total yearly expenses	$44,169

ESTIMATED NET OPERATING INCOME

Total operating income	$128,360
Total operating expenses	$44,169
xxx	$0
xxx	$0
Net operating income	$84,191

ESTIMATED CASH FLOW

Total operating income	$128,360
Total expenses	$44,169
Total debt service (interest)	$43,200
Total debt service (principal)	$0
xxx	$0
Net cash flow before taxes	$40,991

ASSUMPTIONS & ESTIMATED RESULTS

Building cost	$1,800,000
Immediate improvements needed	$50,000
Closing costs	$20,000
Total commitment	$1,870,000
Monthly rent for a 2-bed unit	$1,500
Monthly rent for a 3-bed unit	$2,100
xxx	na
xxx	na
Ttl monthly income for 2-bed units	$7,500
Ttl monthly income for 3-bed units	$4,200
Interest rate on loan	4.0%
Loan amount (60% LTV)	$1,080,000
Total cash needed for deal	$790,000
Gross rent multiplier (GRM)	14.0
Capitalization rate (CAP)	4.5%

ESTIMATED CASH ON CASH RETURN

Total cash needed for deal	$790,000
Net cash flow before taxes	$40,991
CPI yearly increase	$3,851
Debt reduction	$0
Total cash on cash return	5.7%

79

Small Subdivision

An investment in knowledge pays the best interest.

BENJAMIN FRANKLIN

THIS TOPIC WILL OVERLAP SLIGHTLY with the chapter called *Working Backward*, and I mainly included it so you would have the benefit of the worksheet as a baseline.

In the movie *Seabiscuit*, the car tycoon purportedly disassembled and reassembled a car in an attempt to repair it with little experience, and the education from that struggle launched his career. I lived on a dead-end street up until the fifth grade where we had about twenty boys all roughly the same age within close proximity. Never a dull moment—bikes, bike ramps, skateboards, and forts in every direction. I am certainly not a mechanically minded person, but I disassembled and reassembled my bike well over ten times while we lived there, gaining expertise that I remember to this day.

As producers in real estate, most of us deal almost entirely with the "finished product." We don't assemble, disassemble, and reassemble the product. We don't "build" the product, we don't manufacture it, assemble it, or fabricate it—we deal with the finished version of someone else's creation. For example, we lend money on a three-bedroom, two-car-garage home in average condition. We list a two-thousand-square-foot, brand new home with all the goodies. We represent a buyer on a twenty-seven-hundred-square-foot Victorian with a wrap-around porch. Yes, every once in a while, we may assist in a light tune-up, but that's a process just to ensure the finished product "sparkles." Someone else has already produced the finished product for us. That person is a development company of some kind: a one-man shop, a three-person shop, on up to the big national home builders.

I was active and semicoasting in real estate for roughly 240 months, and not two of those would go by without some form of the following phone call.

"Hey, Jim, this is Danny," said Danny from the one-man development company called Danny's Development Company.

"Hi, Danny," said Jim.

"Jim, I am considering building a small subdivision on the corner of Swollenankle and Bruisedknee Drive. Would you help me analyze it?" said Danny.

When I was lender, I received those calls; the same thing when I was a real estate agent. You could pass on helping out Danny if you wanted, but again, I knew that bike inside and out because I knew the components of the bike and how those components were assembled.

How do we go from dirt to finished? What things have to be considered: cost of the land, zoning, the city master plan, curbside issues, public works issues, traffic considerations, school considerations and fees, topography and civil engineering, sewer capacity, sourcing of electricity, sourcing of water, property lines' setbacks, habitable versus nonhabitable square footage, floor area ratios, basement considerations and impact thereof on floor area ratios, drainage and city requirements, crawl versus slab foundation, cost of the foundation, cost of framing, cost of electrical, cost of all the finish work, such as baseboards, casings, cabinets, granite, and fixtures, cost of the exterior improvement, including hardscape, landscaping, and all those details. When you understand real estate at this level, you are disassembling, reassembling, and disassembling again—all in your head.

"Jim, how does this make me money, improve my business, or both?" I have attempted to write this book in such a way that a person can randomly open it up to any chapter, read it a couple of times, and find something in there that will have a direct positive impact, so try this...

There is a lender named Jim that works for Lumberjack Lending. Jim just completed a bread-and-butter refinance on Barney's primary residence. Barney is a contractor but also does one small subdivision every couple of years.

"Barney, thank you for the business. Is there anything else I can help you with?" said Jim.

"Jim, I appreciate the assistance. Nothing else at this time, however. The only other thing I'm working on is a small development project, but I know that's not really your thing," said Barney.

"Barney, I actually just helped Frank at Frank's Development Company run the math on a similar project," said Jim.

"Really," said Barney.

"Yes, sir, and I am happy to help you run some numbers, no obligation," said Jim. Now Jim is somewhat part of Barney's team, or at the very least Jim is trying to be of assistance to Barney. We go along for a month and talk a little here and there. Another month goes by—and another. Now Barney needs Jim and relies on Jim, just like the head coach relies on his quarterback.

"Hey, Barney, would you like me to have my real estate agent friend, Wilma, look at the project?" said Jim.

"Sure," said Barney. And then Jim introduces Wilma to Barney.

A few weeks later, "Barney, I know a great civil engineer, would you like me to make that intro for you?" said Jim.

"Sure, why not," said Barney. And Jim introduces Stan, the civil engineer, to Barney.

A week later, "Dick at Dick's Painting has done a nice job for many of my clients. Would you like me to make that intro?" said Jim. Jim is helping Barney build a team—maybe not of first stringers, because Barney might already have his first-string team lined up, but Barney knows it's always smart to have your second team ready to go in a pinch. First stringers are never first stringers forever.

Benefits of going through the process. 1) I am helping Barney build his team. Is Barney appreciative of that? Most likely he is. Barney may never buy the lot and do that deal, but do you think Barney might just—maybe—go out of his way to send Jim some leads in the future? 2) And what about Wilma, Stan, and Dick? Do you think Jim might have built up some goodwill with those three? When the topic of "lender" comes up, who do you think they might be thinking about? It's possible that it might be their friend Jim, who just tried to help in a tangible way.

3) And finally, is Jim a little smarter by going through the process and analyzing the deal from the ground up? Maybe the next time Jim is talking with a prospective client and he can be conversational about such topics as floor area ratio, setbacks, drainage considerations, construction costs, neighborhood zoning, building heights, etc., the client may just be thinking, "Wow, this guy really knows what he's talking about." And maybe that little extra is what is needed for Jim to earn the job.

Even if you do not generate a single dollar from this process, you will be light-years ahead from the experience. This is a good example why there is no need to be a robotic-automated-mechanical selling machine in this business. How about just know what the heck you are talking about?

I'm telling you, analyze these deals every chance you can. Think about it like you are going back to school to get yourself tuned up a little. "An investment in knowledge pays the best interest"—*Benjamin Franklin*. When you can disassemble, reassemble, and disassemble again the product we are dealing with (real estate)—all in your head and on the fly and in front of a customer in a very conversational way—you are truly putting yourself in a strong position to win.

Go get 'em!

Small Subdivision Analysis

NOTES AND ASSUMPTIONS

Purchase price of land	$2,000,000	Total garage space	3150
Hard costs per foot to build	$200	Habitable net of garage	19350
Total lot size	50000	Average habitable per house	2764
Floor area ratio of 45%	22500	Final price per habitable foot	$600

INCOME

	SFR #1	SFR #2	SFR #3	SFR #4	SFR #5	SFR #6	BMRH UNIT SFR #7
Sales Price	$1,658,571	$1,658,571	$1,658,571	$1,658,571	$1,658,571	$1,658,571	$500,000

EXPENSES

	SFR #1	SFR #2	SFR #3	SFR #4	SFR#5	SFR #6	SFR #7
Land	$285,714	$285,714	$285,714	$285,714	$285,714	$285,714	$285,714
Hard costs to build	$642,857	$642,857	$642,857	$642,857	$642,857	$642,857	$642,857
Soft costs - permits, etc.	$50,000	$50,000	$50,000	$50,000	$50,000	$50,000	$50,000
Landscape front and back	$35,000	$35,000	$35,000	$35,000	$35,000	$35,000	$35,000
Common areas	$25,000	$25,000	$25,000	$25,000	$25,000	$25,000	$25,000
Carrying costs	$45,000	$45,000	$45,000	$45,000	$45,000	$45,000	$45,000
Commissions	$99,514	$99,514	$99,514	$99,514	$99,514	$99,514	$30,000
Unexpected	$40,000	$40,000	$40,000	$40,000	$40,000	$40,000	$40,000
TOTAL	$1,223,086	$1,223,086	$1,223,086	$1,223,086	$1,223,086	$1,223,086	$1,153,571

PROFIT

	SFR #1	SFR #2	SFR #3	SFR #4	SFR #5	SFR #6	SFR #7
	$435,486	$435,486	$435,486	$435,486	$435,486	$435,486	-$653,571

* The city may require one or more of the units to be Below Market Rate Housing, or BMRH.

80

Working Backward

———◆———

When the mind is thinking, it is talking to itself.

PLATO

R ING, RING. "HI, JIM, IT'S Peter."

"Hey, Peter how are you?"

"Great, Jim. Stacey and I are considering buying a vacant lot. Our plans are to build a home on the lot, but we are having a tough time determining land value. Can you help us?"

"Sure, Peter, let me check it out and get back to you."

The next day, "Hi, Peter. I see what you mean; there are literally no comparable sales anywhere, nothing even close to being relevant. Peter, there is another way to analyze this. Do you know what you want to build in terms of size and scope of the house?"

"Yes, Jim, we want a twenty-seven-hundred-square-foot house with a three-car garage with finish work consistent with the surrounding neighborhood."

"Perfect! I know what *that future house* will be worth when it's done, so we will simply work backward into land value. I'll show you how we do that, Peter." And then I would take Peter through the following worksheet line by line. Simple.

This is a common question on land, but you could also use this worksheet when there is an existing structure on the subject property. That existing structure has no value to a buyer that has intentions of building a new home. So, you would be helping the customer determine land value in that case as well.

Sometimes these phone calls would turn into a deal and sometimes they wouldn't. Either way, I suggest jumping in and going through the process. For me, it kept me sharp because I would need to contact my network and determine up-to-date costs for building, permits, landscaping, etc., and really think through "value" from the ground up.

Go get 'em!

Working Backwards to Determine Land Value

DATA POINTS/ASSUMPTIONS

Finished product value	**$945,000**
Habitable square feet	2700
Three car garage	700
Square feet of finished product including the garage	3400
Lot size	8900
Finished value per habitable foot	$350
Per foot building costs	$100

EXPENSES

Soft costs (permits, architect, reports, etc.)	$70,000
Hard costs to build	$340,000
All exterior work including landscape, hardscape, etc.	$100,000
TOTAL EXPENSES	**$510,000**

OTHER ITEMS A BUYER MAY CONSIDER

Built-in sweat equity estimated at 10%	$94,500
Carrying and opportunity costs of the money - estimate	$50,000
TOTAL	**$144,500**

THE MATH

Finished product	$945,000
Total hard expenses	$510,000
Other items to consider	$144,500

CURRENT LAND VALUE	**$290,500**

Attitude

A Guide to Making It in Real Estate

81

Declaration of *Your* Independence

———◆———

I'll die on my feet before I live on my knees.
PRESIDENT GEORGE WASHINGTON

"[A] ND BY THE AUTHORITY OF the good People of these Colonies, solemnly publish and declare, That these United Colonies are, and of Right ought to be FREE AND INDEPENDENT STATES; that they are Absolved from all Allegiance to the British Crown, and that all political connection between them and the State of Great Britain, is and ought to be totally dissolved, and that as Free and Independent States, they have the full Power to levy War, conclude Peace, contract Alliances, establish Commerce, and to do all other Acts and Things which Independent states may of right do."

If you are new to real estate or a veteran that needs a renewed perspective, you are truly free and independent men and woman of the United States. Declare *that* and your business independence as such.

I declare: *I will be self-reliant. I will take full responsibility for my own success. I will recognize and cherish the freedoms that I have in the United States of America. I will be a responsible member of the real estate community. I will be reliant on no one but be in alliance with everyone. I am a free, independent, and successful businessperson.*

There is a *strong attitude* associated with success in real estate. Think about the amount of courage, dogged determination, and stubborn willpower demonstrated by the Founding Fathers, and the country, to say to the most powerful country in the world at that time, No, we are free. To walk independently as a small-business owner in real estate requires complete self-reliance.

Voltaire said, "Man is free at the moment he wishes to be."

Sometimes the hardest part of anything is simply making a decision. In real estate, make the decision to be independent, recognize that independence, accept that independence, and ultimately celebrate that independence.

Go get 'em!

82

Be Nice

———◆———

Be nicer than necessary to everyone you meet.
Everyone is fighting some kind of battle.
Socrates

I'LL BE THE FIRST ONE to admit that if I think someone is taking a swing at me, I have a tough time turning the other cheek. But aside from that, nice will make you money. Nice is the right thing to do. My wife has an uncle that is a retired colonel and has owned a chain of retail shops, a true American patriot and megamillionaire entrepreneur. He would tell his retail staff to look nice, be nice, smell nice.

Some people confuse nice with weak. A person can be equally nice and strong. Remember the De La Salle football team from Concord, California, that won 151 games in a row? I am guessing those boys were tough as nails but equally loving to one another, and nice kids (I know one of them). I volunteer coach high school football and I tell the boys, "You guys can be tough guys and nice guys at the same time."

Run this down the canal: The lender will go the extra mile for an unstable, irate real estate agent. The listing agent wants to work with a prickly selling agent on a multiple-offer deal. The AAA client wants to refer more clients after you did a "sign-and-disappear job" on the last one. The escrow officer will work like crazy to close your deal on time after you just gave her a tongue lashing. Any of those sound plausible? Nice will make you money. Nice is smart. Nice improves the industry. Anything and everything can happen through other people, them helping you, you helping them.

There is a guy in the San Francisco Bay Area that is crushing it—massive volume, relatively new to the business. He and I have used the same title provider from time to time over the years. One of the employees told me one day, "He is literally one of the nicest and most considerate people that I have ever met and worked with." You think they might just work a little harder on his deals? Go the extra mile? Be slightly nicer to his clients?

I represented a buyer on a condo many years ago, and there were six offers. Sadly, we did not get the deal. I received a call two days later from the listing agent. "Jim, I think I might have an identical unit in the same complex. Does your client want to see it?" Of course we did, but naturally I was curious why he called me over the other four agents. As paraphrased, "Jim, you took the loss like a man. You were nice, polite, and professional about it. Several of our colleagues didn't take it well and gave me a hard time for one reason or another." My client liked it and bought it. Nice works. Nice is profitable.

As a naïve person coming out of college, for some reason I thought that high levels of success were associated with being jerky. Wow, youthful thoughts. As we know, that couldn't be further from the truth; in fact the opposite wins the day almost every time. Think about it: usually high levels of success are associated with either managing or working with large groups of people. How is that humanly possible without good people skills and a nice demeanor? I have read and listened to *Think and Grow Rich* countless times. What was the takeaway for me? Easy! As Napoleon Hill was studying all these successful people around the world, he was trying to determine that all-important link between them. He basically couldn't find it. The only consistent characteristic that most or all these successful people shared was "a harmonious personality." I'll never forget it when I heard that for the first time.

When I was doing VA loans early in my career, I would frequently visit the Federal Building in the Bay Area to get paperwork needed for the deal. There were three ladies and two men that ran the front desk. I would be there at least weekly for a few years. The wait was crazy at times because one to two people would service the line and the rest were at their desks in the back of the office. About the third time I went, I realized this was going to be a long-term relationship, so I needed to get to know some of the workers.

"Hey, Grace, how are things?"

"Hey, George, did your team win this weekend?"

After a couple of months of that, when I got to the front of the line, all five of them would literally jump into action, scurrying around, getting my stuff done as I'm chatting with them all. You think they wanted to work hard and do good for the lady in front me that was yelling at them for one reason or another?

Buddha said, "In a controversy, the instant we feel anger we have already ceased striving for the truth and have begun striving for ourselves." Mother Theresa said, "Kind words can be short and easy to speak, but their echoes are truly endless."

We largely do business with 1) people that are capable, 2) people that we trust, and 3) people that we like. Nice moves the needle and is the right thing to do.

Go get 'em!

83

Get Up

———◆———

The ideal man bears the accidents of life with dignity
and grace, making the best of circumstances.
ARISTOTLE

GET UP! THIS MESSAGE IS one of the greatest lessons anyone has ever
taught me. Coach Reardon would say, somewhat paraphrased,
"Get up, life is not easy, get up." I can literally hear the echo of his voice
from that day to this. "I don't believe in filling you boys full of sunshine
and rainbows. Life can be tough, knock you flat on your back. It's just
part of the process of being a human being. It's not okay with me, however, that you stay down. Get up off the ground and fight."

There was a time in 2008–09 when the world was falling apart and
I hadn't closed a deal in awhile; had negative cash flow on my rentals
of $18K monthly; had my first daughter entering college; had my eq-
uity line frozen; couldn't restructure/refinance debt; and was pouring
through cash reserves at an alarming rate. I felt like a naïve freshman
rolling onto a college field for the first time and getting run over by
the *superstud senior linebacker.* Get up!

I truly believe that whether we're knocked down physically or
mentally, it is actually helpful to be reminded verbally and sometimes
loudly, *get up.* It's habit forming. Stay down, create a habit. Get up

slowly, create a habit. Train yourself to get up and get up quickly; create a habit. No, it's not easy; do it anyway. For me, this trick of saying to myself, *get up!*—that worked. Some people call it mental toughness or resiliency or a number of other possibilities. Whatever works, fine. Just get up, dust yourself off, and get back out there.

I had three buyer clients in the same week pull out of approximately $6 million of real estate—get up. I had the financial markets turn bad and poof, fifteen-plus loans went dead overnight—get up. We can all compete on the severity of the challenges that we face in this industry; the fact remains, however, that if you have been around for more than a minute, you have had your fair share of setbacks. *Get up.* I observed one of my closest friends lose nearly everything close to retirement. That guy is a warrior. After a couple of years, he dusted himself off and is now back in the game and stronger than ever.

The real estate business is not for folks who are short on determination. Be tough, go the distance, and enjoy all those great rewards that only come with staying the course. When you are bruised and your tail is jammed tight in a crack—*get up and keep moving.*

Go get 'em!

84

It's All on You

You have to do your own growing no matter
how tall your grandfather was.
President Abraham Lincoln

YOUR FANS WILL BE CHEERING you on to victory, but it will be all on you to get it done. The good news is that as soon as you truly internalize that fact, you'll unleash a level of creativity that you never knew existed. Your brain will jump with ideas, but it will only do so if you truly and completely accept that *it's all on you*—100 percent of it.

When you have a job, you play a role within that company. When you are a real estate agent or lender, you own a small business and are responsible for everything. Knowing and accepting this creates freedom in your life because you will not depend on anyone for anything within the context of your business life. It creates complete self-reliance, independence, and increased cognitive ability (creativity). That independence and self-reliance translates into a brain that is constantly on the move and jumping with ideas out of necessity. You are training your brain to see only solutions.

It's all on you; accept that as fact. I would love to take thirty new agents that came from a paycheck job and work with them for thirty days on their attitude about this. It's a transition. It's hard to accept, and sometimes we give it lip service, "Yes, I understand that it's all on me." However, deep down inside we are still not taking 100 percent responsibility for our own success. We are waiting for Prince or Princess Charming to come along and show us the magic. It's on us, and by accepting that fact you'll be preparing yourself to fly in this business.

Your manager, vendors, family, and staff will be there for you, and you need this group to support and encourage you. This group should not be underestimated for sure; however, we can't ask them to put on the uniform and score the goal for us. It's on us to get it done.

Why isn't my office doing more for me? It is not the office's job to do more—they do enough. The office provides a brick-and-mortar location to work, some level of training, some administrative support, and some organization infrastructure, as well as synergy, energy, and coaching. Not only that, the office is taking tremendous risk relevant to their fixed costs. The office does plenty. As producers, we can do the rest.

Swim. When Uncle Leroy pushes you in the pool at the barbecue, you have no choice but to swim. When you accept that it's all on you, you have no other choice but to do whatever it takes to *make it!* Accept it and make it or partially accept it and partially make it. Don't accept it and you will not make it.

Let's talk about *creativity* again. This will be slightly philosophical, but stay with me, because it will affect your ability to make it and fly in this business. When you accept that it's all on you, the solution, therefore, is also all on you. What is creativity? Among other definitions, it can be defined as "a possible solution."

There is water under the house and the buyer is scared to death. *Be creative; find a possible solution.* The chimney is coming loose from the house, the buyer won't close without it being fixed, and the seller won't pay for it. *Be creative; find a possible solution.* I know they want to hire me, but for some reason they just won't pull the trigger. *Be creative; find a possible solution.* I need to find four deals before the end of the year. *Be creative; find a possible solution.* How can I possibly manage twenty offers coming in on this home and at the same time be respectful to my colleagues? *Be creative; find a possible solution.*

Listen, when you fully accept that it's all on you, you will unleash a level of creativity that you never knew existed, and your brain will buzz with creative solutions to previously insurmountable problems. This is not hocus-pocus; *it is a commonsense survival instinct* that begins by accepting the fact that it's all on you.

There is no shortcut. If you want to work in real estate and have freedom, unlimited income, and no boss, then you must accept the fact that it's all on you. Do that, and you may find all those things and a whole lot more.

Go get 'em!

85

Make Economic Cycles Your Friend

When things are steep, remember to stay level-headed.

HORACE

E CONOMIC CYCLES NOTWITHSTANDING, KEEP YOUR head down and keep working; you can do business in any market. It's an attitude as well as reality. The world is falling apart; people are still buying and selling real estate and borrowing money. Everyone is apparently getting rich in an upward cycle; people are buying, selling, and borrowing. You can succeed and excel in any market.

When I started in real estate brokerage, inventory was beyond tight. There were fifteen buyers for every house. I was too young and dumb and scared to care; I kept my head down and worked liked crazy. I could hear it all around me, in the bathroom, in the break room, in the hallways, and in the parking lot. "Wow, this is a tough market; if you don't have a listing, you're dead." It was like water off a duck's back. I just put my head down and worked like a dog.

I started in loans in a challenging market as well; the refinance boom was almost over, and rates were on their way back up a few months into my career. Transaction volume dropped so much so that my own office closed about a year into my real estate career. I just kept my head down and worked. What, was I going to go back to my wife and say, "Sorry I couldn't pay the bills, rates went up." Regardless of the current economic cycle, there are going to be a number of transactions that are completed on a monthly basis. Be determined and committed to be part of those deals. "I will be successful this month. I will achieve my goal of completing ten loans." I would say that to myself over and over again. *It's an attitude.* Take a position of stubborn determination and drive hard when the economy goes sideways.

So there are one thousand deals trading this month versus two thousand. Be part of those one thousand. "I will complete ten deals this month." Don't focus on the lack thereof; focus on the abundance of the thousand deals that are going down. Your competition will be focusing on the lack thereof; take advantage of that moment, keep your head down, and thrive.

A boom market. To be honest, I never liked working in a bubble economy or frenzied market. I would take a moderate to slow economy any day of the week. A slow economy for me is akin to a cold winter where everyone is tucked in his or her home, not knowing what to do, but there are a few warriors out there, freezing, working, hunting—but thriving. I loved the downturns because the competition was not working in general; the pros in the industry, however, were working while everyone was sleeping. Your competition will go from working eight hour days to moaning and groaning for six hours and working for two. Keep your head down, work eight-hour days, and thrive.

Bubble markets attract everyone and his or her brother to this industry. So the unit volume will jump (a little), but a large part of that volume will be absorbed by the spike of new people to the industry. New people to the real estate industry is good, but the wrong people are bad. What do I mean? The opportunists are bad for the industry. What is an opportunist? Someone who jumps from this industry to that industry based on how that industry is doing at that moment, spending a few months here and a few months there. There is so much to know and learn in this industry that too many opportunists all at once have a tendency to erode the reputation and quality of service in that industry. This is particularly true in real estate, where any Tom, Dick, or Carol that has a license can jump in and start doing business. The barriers to entry—well, there really are none. The gate is wide open to anyone that wants to come to the party. The opportunists will jump in with both feet in a bubble and will leave as soon as the bubble bursts.

Your business will grow in small, progressive steps. Two steps forward, one back. Every year or two, you'll go through a growing phase. Your business will become a little bigger, a little stronger, a little faster. The foundation will get a little wider and deeper. If you are working hard daily, doing the things that you need to do, it's just the way your business will grow. It's called normal. Economic downturns, however, are the times to make larger-than-normal gains. For instance, let's say you are in year number four of your career, and during that year your business moved from a four to a five on a scale of one to ten. During that same period, however, and given an economic downturn, you can move from four to six. Press on through an economic downturn and you will come out the other side exponentially stronger than your competition. The key is, keep your head down and work like a dog when you see the economy going sideways.

My dad's real estate partner says: "During a down cycle, be prepared to hunker down." He bought over twenty condos in Southern California in the most recent downturn. In a downturn, all those folks that jumped in to make a quick buck in lending or brokerage will leave. The ones that jumped in and are committed to the industry, help them and mentor them. But aside from that new group that is really committed to the industry, everyone will leave. You'll be left with roughly the same team that you started with in the office, in addition to some tough new warriors to the industry that were able to fight their way through.

Socrates said, "Remember, there is nothing stable in human affairs; therefore, avoid undue elation in prosperity or undue depression in adversity." *Pour it on* when the economy goes sideways.

Go get 'em!

86

Take a Long Vacation

———◆———

Diligence is the mother of good luck.
BENJAMIN FRANKLIN

STAY CONSISTENT OVER THE YEARS by taking a looooong vacation as often as necessary.

A consistent product line. As I was writing this book, I called my commercial real estate friend and asked him about topics that should be covered. He said, "Jim, *consistency*, number one. Don't jump from this to that. Don't go from residential to commercial apartments to commercial retail to gas stations. If you look at the guys and girls in real estate that are doing big, big numbers, they picked one product and rode that horse to the end. It's natural to get bored and tired of something. When that happens, take a two-month vacation and get away from it. Then come back to it with renewed energy and focus. Keep doing that as often as necessary. The grass isn't greener. It almost never is. Take a nice, long break, and get back at it." It surprised me how quickly he answered my question and mentioned this topic of consistency.

My uncle in Southern California picked one product to broker, industrial buildings. He became one of the go-to players in that industry and bought a lot of the product that he was brokering. He rides that single pony to this day. In fact, he is technically retired, but people still call him for help with industrial buildings. Sure, at times, customers may have called him to rep a retail center or a gas station or this or that, but then after that deal was done, he went right back to the bread and butter, his target market, industrial buildings.

When I started in real estate doing loans, the broker was a seasoned veteran. He said to me early on, "You have to concentrate to graduate." He kept saying that over and over again with no explanation. He started his career as a retail lending rep for a large bank, calling on new home developments. He did that for roughly fifteen years and became one of the top guys in the country for a period of time in that niche market. I had worked for him for six months when I thought I had finally figured out what he was talking about when he would say "You have to concentrate to graduate." So I went to his office to run it by him. "I think I know what you are talking about. You really mean you have to work day in, day out to become a master at your craft." He was pleased that I was at least within the strike zone.

A consistent work ethic. There was a time when my uncle managed approximately fifty commercial agents. He and I were talking one day about what differentiates the girls and guys in his office that were doing well and the ones that were not. He said, "A consistent work ethic." Coming to work every day; actually working when you get there; putting in an honest eight hours; going home; then, doing the same thing the following day. He said the guys and girls that were doing well were diligent about a consistent schedule and work ethic.

When I started in real estate brokerage, I asked one of the big producers for some advice. He said, "Jim, I work twelve-hour days, day in, day out. Consistency is the key." That guy worked. He was there in the morning. He was there at night. He was available on the phone. He was available in the office. He worked day in, day out, nothing special.

One of my best friends to this day is a guy that I played college football with. He is clearly a gifted athlete, but he *made himself* into one of the quickest linemen on the team. He was one of the hardest and most consistent workers in the program (in my view). He would be first to the gym, the last one to leave, and would run extra, do extra, and be extra. He was an offensive lineman, so speed beyond ten yards or so didn't really matter, but speed within five to ten yards was lethal. I noticed about midway through our sophomore year that his first step was improving. Then, by the beginning of our junior year, he was in the front of the pack on short-distance sprints. As we approached our senior year, he literally had the quickest first few steps of all the lineman. There was nothing magic or special to his workouts. He was there every day, did the work, and then went home. By his senior year he made himself into an All-American player.

Take a long vacation. We started this chapter by talking about a long vacation, so we'll end this chapter the same way.

There is a residential broker in Northern California that does giant volume; we'll call him Mr. Stud. I have never met Mr. Stud personally but have admired his business from afar; he is Steady Eddy, not flashy, just gets it done. I went to college with one of his colleagues and asked him about the dynamics of Mr. Stud's business. He said to me, "Jim, Mr. Stud literally checks out every summer without exception. He packs up the family and we literally don't hear from him for four to six weeks."

I said "Wow, what about his clients?"

"We cover for him, the manager covers for him. Poof, he is gone, not to be seen or heard from for practically the whole summer. Then he comes back refreshed and ready to take on the next ten months."

I was considering selling a business asset several years ago, mainly because I was tired of it. I called a friend to talk it through. He said, "Jim, one the biggest mistakes I ever made was that I shut it down too early, I should have kept my business machine moving well into my seventies. I know how you feel; you just get tired of the day to day. When that happens, take a one- to two-month vacation and come back to it, because when you own a business, once it's gone, it's gone, and it's tough if not impossible to rebuild." During his career, this guy was a very successful small business owner. He retired at fifty-five, which sounds glamorous, but, as he says, "Once you see the world, travel here, travel there, lie on a beach for a year, what in the world are you going to do with yourself?"

We all get tired of it. Even if you love your job, there can be times that we get weary of the day to day. In those instances, don't blow up the ship. Keep the ship moving forward—just slide someone else into the captain's chair for a while, and slide back in when you're ready.

Go get 'em!

87

"Sales" Business

Whatever you are, be a good one.

PRESIDENT ABRAHAM LINCOLN

I HAVE HEARD SOME VERY smart and successful people in real estate say, "Real estate is a sales business first, sales business second, and sales business third." I would encourage you to think about it this way: *we are in a taking-care-of-other-people business.* This is not a black-and-white conversation; there is a happy blend between the Pollyanna thought of helping other people and the sometimes somewhat cold business of "selling."

Let's talk.

How many times has someone "sold you," pressured you, or made you do something that you didn't want to do? Yes, it happens, but how did you feel afterward? Did you feel happy with yourself and the person that pressured you? You probably felt like a bum and had a very low regard for the person that did it to you.

I have seen colleagues over the years that truly believe that "real estate is 100 percent a sales business." Well, sure, go ahead and focus on that. But I have seen those same colleagues ten years into their career still "selling" to get low-quality business when others are generating high-quality business from the infrastructure of their operation. If you concentrate your efforts on "selling" as your primary focus, you will *always* be selling your entire career. If you focus your efforts on taking care of the customer and building your enterprise, as your career progresses, you will spend less time on marketing, advertising, and selling (finding deals) and more time on taking care of those truckloads of great referrals you are receiving (doing deals).

When I made the switch from loans to real estate brokerage, I was sincerely terrified of failing and regretfully found myself focused primarily on *the hunt* (or selling, if you will). And then a couple of years into the process, I turned around to realize that the quality of my business was average at best (I was not generating an acceptable level of quality referrals from past customers). Thank God I recognized what was happening and made that mental shift to taking care of the customer, period (whatever it took and whatever that meant).

Instead of thinking this is a sales business first, second, and third, try this: How about actually knowing what the heck you are talking about? How about knowing that HP12C inside and out? How about knowing what radon gas means? How about knowing what the secondary market means? How about knowing what a cap rate means? How about knowing how to run a spreadsheet? How about knowing the contents of the contract? Yes, you need to have a marketing plan (finding deals) and execute on that plan, but also focus on your own education and skill development. The more you know, the more valuable you become to the community and customer.

On the Pollyanna side of things: How about truly being in the moment? How about trying to help your customer? How about listening to your customer? How about putting your customer first and your ambitions second? How about managing the process? How about being available? How about being approachable? How about being reliable?

Doing that will produce top-quality leads for years to come. And when your tail is in a crack on a rainy day, nothing makes you feel better than a great cash-the-check referral from one of your happy customers.

If you are new to real estate, the more transactions you complete, the more comfortable you'll become around the business. In the meantime, don't become some robotic-drone selling machine. Be you, be sincere, don't fake it. They hired you in spite of your lack of experience; they knew that and hired you anyway. They wanted you, so be honest and be you!

Go get 'em!

88

Muscle

Whatever you do, do it with all your might.

CICERO

AN OFFENSIVE COORDINATOR (IN FOOTBALL) was having a tough time moving the offense out of their own end zone. In other words, the offense would be on their own one-foot line and need just a single yard (maybe two, but that would be a luxury) so that they were not pinned into their own end zone. They needed room to maneuver, and that one extra yard or even a foot made all the difference. It was one of those *must-have* situations. Literally every time (almost without exception), given those circumstances, the team would fumble, throw an interception, get tackled for a safety, have to punt from deep in their own end zone, or have to punt and have the punt blocked. The coaching staff finally designed a play called "Muscle." Brute force, shoulder-to-shoulder football. Muscle right, Muscle left. The lineman lined up foot to foot, the quarterback handed it off to the running back, and he ran straight ahead (no dancing, straight ahead)—all in an attempt to gain that single yard. *That must-have yard.* It was brute force, no slick this or slick that—just a straight-ahead fight. Rough and tumble. Sheer determination football, and it worked.

There are going to be times in your real estate career when your back is against the wall and you are in a *must-have* situation. Your pipeline is dry as a bone, you have no hot leads, no pendings, and haven't closed a deal for a few weeks. And by the way, before you drop your head in shame, that's called normal. It will happen, to me, to you, to everyone. You don't think so? Just wait. It will happen, and it will happen more than once. But that's no time to sit and cry. It's time to call the Muscle play. Brute force was my way of coming back from the bottom of the basement. Nothing slick—just an all-out, straight-ahead effort. What does the Muscle play look like for me in real estate? Glad you asked.

Number one: Work. For seven days I would be working a minimum of fourteen-hour days. Half the time I didn't even know what I was actually going to be doing, I just knew that I would be working fourteen hours that day. It turns out you can actually do a lot in fourteen hours, even if you are only technically working ten of those fourteen. Hey, we all have to eat and go to the bathroom and talk to our friends and goof around a little.

Number two: Cancel nearly all personal stuff for that week. Whatever it is, it can wait for one week; it needs to wait for one week. "Well, I still have to do pickup for my daughter at 3:00 p.m." I understand. I was part of the pickup schedule, I know. But can someone else do it for a few days? At 2:00 p.m., you start tapering down. You don't want to be late, so you leave at 2:30; pick up at 3:00; drive home and drop off daughter at 3:15; go to the bathroom; and have something to eat. Before you know it, you are back at work at 4:00; and then it takes thirty minutes to get warmed up again. You can't afford to lose two and a half hours of prime working time when you are in a *must-have* situation. This is back-against-the-wall time.

Number three: Talk with my wife and let her know that she won't be seeing much of me for a week. She was always good about that; maybe she liked the break! But if your partner or spouse gives you a hard time, it's pretty simple. "The choices are a) see me a little less for a week or b) worry about paying the bills for the next three months." That's how much momentum you can produce in one week by running Muscle.

Number four: No drinking. That was a little hard, but it wasn't an option. It's like giving a racehorse a tranquilizer right before it is about to run the Preakness. Not an option. It's only a week, you'll survive.

Number five: Get up. I hate getting up early. But for Muscle to work, early is better, so 5:00 a.m. was the time, and 5:00 a.m. it was. If you happen to have a problem going to bed or sleeping, you won't the week you run Muscle: 5:00 a.m. wake-up call, fourteen-hour workdays; are you kidding? You won't even remember your head hitting the pillow.

That's it.

I'm not going to tell you to chant for thirty minutes or sing songs to yourself in the mirror; you figure out what to do during those fourteen hours. Ask your manager for help if you get stuck, but don't rely on your manager; it's not his or her job. *You are the producer.* The rainmaker. You are creative, entrepreneurial, and a self-starter. If you are not, you are in the wrong business or in the wrong job within that business. You figure it out. If you want someone telling you what to do, then go get a job. I will tell you, stay in motion and stay focused on marketing. Work for seven days straight; limit personal responsibilities that week; secure buy-in from your family; no drinking; and get up early. That is the framework for Muscle. The foundation of the play.

There are times when you have to force it to get things moving. Trust me: your world will look different after running Muscle for seven days. Muscle will work as long as you do.

Go get 'em!

89

Bambi

———◆———

Be gentle to all and stern with yourself.
Saint Teresa of Avila

YOU COME AROUND A TIGHT corner in your car, and there, standing in front of you, in the middle of the road, with big eyes, is Bambi, fearful, tearful, and scared to death. She doesn't know where to go or what to do, just frozen with fear. I felt that way once in this business and told myself I would *never* forget that feeling (and do what I can when I see people with that "Bambi" look in their eye). Warning—this will be a little gooey; but it's a subject that speaks to running a small business and, more specifically, running a small business in real estate, so I want to deal with it.

It was more than midway through my career, and I was tired of it; I wasn't into it, and my production was showing that attitude. I was short on listings, no pendings, had some weak buyer leads, definitely no hot leads, and hadn't closed a deal in a couple of weeks. I woke in the middle of the night in what I think was a panic. I had never felt that way before and never have again, so I think it was panic. Within seconds of waking, I thought about business. It was an empty, hollow feeling. I guess that's called emotional pain. Whatever it was, I felt like Bambi, fearful and scared to death about business and, more specifically, my production (or lack thereof). It's frankly not my style to be dealing with this topic, but I'm doing it because I don't think I'm the only one; and maybe just knowing that helps people, maybe.

Look, we are out on a limb in this business. You can lose your focus a little when you have a paycheck job (and maybe float for a month or two), but if you lose your focus in real estate, you will get your ass handed to you. You can make $50,000 this month, but if you don't make anything for a couple of months, all of a sudden you are feeling like a bum.

The next day, I was on fire. My way of pulling my tail out of a crack is to get mad. And wow, did I get mad. I think the folks that know me would describe me as a reserved-demeanor kind of person. So when I get mad, you don't see it. But I was mad. For me, when I'm mad, there is no room for self-pity. I use that anger to fuel the machine. And right at the moment I needed to fuel the machine because my tail was *deep* in the crack. In retrospect, I actually felt a little bad for all those leads I called that next day. "Hi, this is Carter, *are you going to buy or sell your home* in the next 24 hours (kidding), yes or no? No? Thank you, good-bye." Not much finesse that day. I think I was able to purge my entire lead file that next day and set three appointments.

Back to Bambi. There were two reasons that I never wanted to forget that feeling: 1) I wanted to remember the pain associated with a temporary bad attitude, and 2) It was SO painful, that I wanted to be able to recognize it and reach out when I see it in others.

This can be an exciting and financially rewarding business. It can also be equally tough at times too. I think we owe it to each other to at least pay attention. At any one time there might be someone in the office that feels like Bambi. Reach out. After that experience, I told myself I would pay more attention to what is going on around me and do something if I can, in my own way.

If you are feeling like Bambi at the moment, know this: it will pass. And if it makes you feel any better, I would bet my left shoe that the prettiest girl at the dance and the most handsome guy on the beach (top producer Jill and top producer Jack) have felt like Bambi from time to time. It's normal. It will be gone before you know it.

P.S.—Anger (healthy anger) is a great kick starter, at least for me. One more note: if you find yourself feeling like Bambi, read "Muscle" in this book for an expanded game plan.

Go get 'em!

90

The Crummy Stuff

Any fool can criticize, condemn, and
complain—and most fools do.

BENJAMIN FRANKLIN

"PLEASE TAKE OUT THE TRASH, Johnny," says Mom. Johnny sits.
"Johnny, take the trash out—please." No movement. "Johnny,
this is the third time I'm asking you—get it done now." Johnny is up
and moving now but heading to his room to play Xbox. "*Johnny!* I'm going to call your dad right now if you don't take that trash out." Johnny
does a U turn and wisely completes the task. Hey, when you are part of
a family, everyone needs to pull his or her weight, even kids (especially
kids), and even on *the crummy stuff.*

Real estate. Are there things that we need to do in real estate that
are not so fun? Are there pieces of the process that you are not so fired
up about? How many steps are there in a real estate transaction, lending, or sales? One hundred, maybe two hundred? I'm guessing you are
just getting warmed up with those numbers. Are there pieces of it that
you like and pieces that you don't? Don't lie. Of course. What is our attitude about the crummy stuff, those crummy-grungy steps along the
way to completing a deal?

Dr. Bob ran a high school district when I was a kid. He would tell me often, "There are pieces of my job that I love and pieces that I don't. The ones that I love are naturally easy to complete. I give the same effort, however, to the tasks that I don't love. It's not fair to the issue I'm dealing with if I don't."

Coach Reardon would tell us, "And when your mom or dad asks you to take out the trash, check your *attitude* and do it immediately. Your parents do enough for you, it's the least you can do." Coaches can be great advocates for parents. There are crummy parts to almost everything in life. On the crummy stuff, the grungy stuff, what is our attitude?

For me in real estate, there were a few things; here is one illustration. Turning in paperwork to the office—I didn't like it; okay, I just simply wouldn't do it. It was hard enough to find the customer; I certainly didn't want to do that part as well. I just wanted to pull the fish (sorry for the bad analogy, Mr. and Mrs. Customer) in the boat and hand it off to someone else to get the internal process moving both in lending and sales. I recognize that this is a task/service that is usually completed by an assistant or the office, but that's not always the case, and I know producers that do this themselves. I hated it—the thought it made my eyes go numb. It's probably only a fifteen-minute task. I just wouldn't do it. I even had times in lending where the processor would fill out all the paperwork and ask me to hand it to the processing manager on my way to the bathroom. I wouldn't say no, but I'd make up some temporary distraction (and "accidently" leave it on his or her desk) and not do it. I mean, come on, all I had to do was take the paper in my hand, walk twenty feet, and hand it to another person. I just had a mental block. In fact, I'm thinking carefully on this, I actually don't think I ever turned in paperwork to the office in over twenty years— not once. It wasn't like I wasn't a team player; I just didn't want to do it.

Who defines crummy? You do for you. I do for me. What is crummy for one person might be chocolate for another. So don't make a judgment. There are going to be things in real estate that you define as the crummy stuff for you. What to do in that instance: 1) delegate it or 2) do it. But if you do it, give it your best effort.

Delegate it. "Jim, I don't have an assistant; who am I going to delegate to?" That's fine; the vast majority of producers do not have an assistant. Your team is more than just an assistant. What about the office staff or your supporting vendors? There are plenty of people around to support you. Trust me, if you are good at finding new business, plenty of people will likely be willing to help you with operations. On my example above, I delegated it because I didn't want to do it. And I also knew that my assistant would be happy to do it and would do it well.

Do it. If you are going to do it yourself, check your *attitude* and give it your best effort. I know we talk *ad nauseam* about real estate being a process. But it is. *Are there negative consequences of having a bad attitude about the crummy stuff?* Do a poor job on step number forty-three, and that could have a negative impact on step number fifty-two. You need to deliver a consistent effort all the way through to produce a good result.

Go get 'em!

(And take out the trash.)

91

Rainmakers

No excellent soul is exempt from a mixture of madness.

ARISTOTLE

MAKE IT RAIN WHERE NO rain exists at the moment. The clouds are brewing, so we know it's possible, but somehow, someway, *someone* needs to reach up into the sky and let it pour. That someone is a rainmaker.

As producers in this business, we have to understand that we are rainmakers and should adopt that attitude. There is a level of intellectual understanding associated with that fact, but it's also an *attitude*. "I am a rainmaker, and it falls on me to get it done—period."

I was talking to my high school friend recently about this topic. His friend, who is a former executive at a big company, went from executive to producer (as a residential real estate agent) and is unfortunately struggling at the moment. This guy was the man! Giant staff, big salary, corner office, the works. He went from employee to independent contractor; employee to small-business owner; employee to rainmaker. It's just different.

Two people: one person has a paycheck job, the other one has no paycheck (he or she eats if he or she produces). Do you think those two people have a slightly different attitude about this or that?

Some of my closest friends are paycheck executives at large firms, so this is not an indictment on paycheck jobs. As a producer in the real estate business, however, you are a rainmaker. What does that mean? *It means you and you alone are 100 percent responsible for the revenue line of your profit-and-loss statement.* No one is going to help you. What? You want me to tell you a fairy tale that someone will be riding up soon to rescue you? You have to lift the weight on your own, 100 percent on your own. Yes, people might be cheering you on.

"Way to go, Jill."

"Attaboy, Jack."

Fans are fans. Doers are doers. Your fans won't have their shoulder under the bar—you will.

Again, we are 100 percent responsible for the revenue line of our profit-and-loss statement; we are rainmakers. You are light-years ahead just knowing that fact.

Once you get used to that fact and accept that fact, you'll be ready to fly as a producer in the real estate industry. The hardest part is accepting that fact. Why? Because it's a white-knuckle feeling knowing that it falls on me, or it falls on you—all of it. Even if you have a partner, do you really want to rely on your partner to make sure your mortgage and food bills are paid next month? *It's an attitude.*

"I am not afraid; I was born to do this"—*Joan of Arc.*

Go get 'em, rainmaker nation!

92

Sixteen Thousand

———◆———

*I never think at all when I write. Nobody can do two
things at the same time and do them both well.*

HORACE

I WAS TALKING WITH A colleague I hadn't seen in a while. He was venting about the number of licensed real estate agents compared to the number of monthly deals. "We have sixteen thousand agents chasing a thousand deals—insanity," he said. I think those numbers were slightly off, but I understood the general concept. "Just the numbers alone work to our disadvantage, even for experienced agents."

There are sixteen thousand agents in my area. Okay. By stating that fact, did I improve my performance today? Did I get better? Was I focused on the other 15,999 or was I focused on doing my job? By *focusing* on the number of sixteen thousand, did I improve my financial standing? Did operations improve? Did marketing improve?

I had an NFL guy come out and talk with my young offensive linemen recently. I was standing there listening to him and a common theme continued to surface as the boys asked questions. He didn't say it in one clean sentence, but here is what he was saying, as paraphrased: "I don't focus on things that don't affect me or my performance." Now, think about that. Could a guy like that be easily distracted with the drama around social media, etc.? Instead, he is focused on "how can I improve my power step?" It's mental discipline. It's staying focused on things that matter.

The number is illogical. There are sixteen thousand licensed agents in my area. Out of those sixteen thousand, how many are "active"? We are going to guess a little, but have some fun with this. Half? I think you are being generous, but that's fine, we'll go with half. Out of that group, how many worked an eight-hour day today? Half again? Okay. Now we are at four thousand. Now, how many *actually* worked a full eight hours (instead of the four-by-four schedule, four hours working and four goofing off). Half again? Okay, two thousand. Feel better? It could be one thousand, two thousand, or nine thousand, but there are certainly not sixteen thousand agents-actively chasing deals.

A line drive. Are there going to be times when a nonactive person stumbles into a deal? Of course there are. The nonactive person might be asleep in center field and the line drive hits him or her square in the chest, with his or her glove open and in the right place. Fine! Can you do anything about that? Of course you can't. So, don't worry about it. Attitude.

Terence says, "You're a wise person if you can easily direct your attention to whatever needs it."

It does you no good to focus on the other 15,999 agents. Focus on your own game; your life, your operations, your marketing, your finances. Show the world who you are. By spending even ten seconds focusing on the 15,999, you are diluting your own authenticity. Your DNA is uniquely your own, as purported. So *show 'em!*

Go get 'em!

93

An Overbearing Opinion

The virtue of justice consists in moderation,
as regulated by wisdom.

ARISTOTLE

"I'D LIKE TO SEE THAT one, Jim."

"No, that one has foundation problems," says Jim.

"I'd like to see it anyway," says Client. We meet at the house. It's a mess, but charming, according to my client. Sure enough, upon visual inspection, the foundation is shot (in my opinion). It doesn't bother her.

I tell her, "Client, I'd suggest we pass on this one; there are others for sale that do not have foundation issues." She brings her dad on the next visit and wants to make an offer. I mentioned the foundation *at least* another five times before finally agreeing to write up the deal. The dad was a contractor and said he could take care of the foundation issues, no problem.

We can only do what we can do.

We can provide an opinion, but ultimately the customer will decide. Can we go too far, be too strong, become overbearing in our opinions at times? For sure! No doubt. Over-the-top strong is no good. All of us naturally want to provide a good service. Would I be doing my job if I continued to pester her about the foundation? I mentioned it once, and then mentioned it a few more times. At what point does it just get old and irritating to the client? And at what point does it turn from me providing honest feedback to me being a pain in the neck (and becoming an obstacle to what she wants to accomplish)? It's a judgment call, on a case-by-case basis. You'll have to make that decision on your own.

"Jim, why are we talking about this?" Number one, it's a customer service topic. And number two, these are those fine-line distinctions that will ultimately have an impact on your revenue line for the year. Take it too far, and it might cost you one to four customers yearly. What does that mean for you? Does that mean $6,000 yearly, $11,000, or $90,000? Let me show you what I mean.

I'm going to change the details, but this is a real-life example. Friends that live in Los Angeles were buying their first house. The price point was roughly $400,000, one side commission of $12,000; married couple with no kids. They found a real estate agent through a friend. They started looking. The agent had an opinion about almost everything, and rightly so; he grew up in the neighborhood they were looking in and naturally knew it well. "Forget that one, this one is a maybe, no way on these, these look okay," says the agent. Some of that is fine; it's our job, right? My friends would say, "Can we see the one over on Greengrove Lane?"

"No way, that one is junk, I'll show you one on Cupcake Lane instead," says the agent. They got tired of it and hired a new agent. A $12,000 hit to the revenue line.

There is a fine line between being responsible and becoming an obstacle to the process.

In lending, it was "Jim, I'd like one of those T-bill programs." This was early in my career, and this guy was fifteen years older than me and was the director of finance at a local firm. "Have you thought about this program, have you thought about that program," says Jim. "Jim, I appreciate what you are saying, but I know what I'm doing, just give me the T-bill program." *He made a decision.* This was the largest loan I had done in my career at that moment. This guy was busy, successful, and knew exactly what he wanted. If I had asked him about other programs one more time, I guarantee he would have just hung up the phone and called the next lender who wasn't so opinionated. I ended up doing several deals with him and his friends.

Can we take it too far? You bet.

People pay us for our opinion (and to run the project). So, for sure, give them an opinion. But remember, it's not our money; it's the customer's money. So our opinion is our opinion, no more, no less. We are simply one of the advisors at the table giving the CEO (the customer) some feedback. Ultimately, the CEO is going to make the decision. "But Jim, I'm the only advisor in this case." Really? You don't think the customer is talking with his or her spouse or friend or mom or dad or work colleague or CPA or attorney or workout friend? They all matter and all have a seat at the table. The customer will make the decision. After the decision has been made, it's our job to execute.

There are people with overbearing personalities; we all know a few. Let's exclude that group for the moment. Here is my opinion on this topic (hopefully it's not an "overbearing" opinion). The more we do something, the better we get. So the longer we do loans or sell property, the better we get. Over time, we acquire lots of knowledge in our craft. Sometimes, we (me too) get too excited about sharing all that knowledge that we have acquired. And it can accidently come across as too strong or "overbearing"; just something to consider for the experienced folks in this business.

Use your instincts and listen to your gut.

Go get 'em!

94

Honor in the Job

———————

I beg you take courage; the brave soul can mend even disaster.

CATHERINE THE GREAT

INEARLY TITLED THIS CHAPTER "Keeping It Real." There are going to be times when the relationship between you and your customer becomes strained—and sometimes an XL-size version of strained. It doesn't happen often, but it happens. To you, to me, to everyone. If anyone says no, wellllllll, it happens. It happens in lending and happens in sales—and it certainly happens in commercial. In those instances, I always check my attitude and think about one thing: *doing the job.* There is honor in focusing in on the task at hand and completing it.

Sometimes, the customer is upset because of something we did or did not do—and sometimes we can't even figure why the customer is upset. The process is taxing on a customer—we have to understand that as a starting point—and many times it's simply the customer reacting to a very demanding process. It's amazing, actually, that any real estate transaction gets completed. What do I mean? I have done a ton of deals and know many of you have done a ton of deals—and I have never had two that are the same. They are all a little different. There are hundreds of moving parts, so anything can go wrong, go bad, go squirrely or sideways. And many of those things are in our control, and many are not. We try to smooth out the bumps, of course, but it's a process nonetheless. When the customer gets mad or upset, there is still a job to be done. There is honor in completing the task. Maybe this is not a popular topic to write about, but it's *real*.

I have to credit one of my lender friends with a lot in this chapter. I asked him, "What topic would be helpful for you to read about in a book?" He said, "When the customer gets mad, what do you do?" I am going edit and paraphrase a little of his notes as outlined in this next paragraph:

"Ultimately you have to have the best intentions for your customer; that will make you successful in the long run. Honesty is truly the best policy in this business. Honesty can get you in trouble, however. I have had deals where the loan is a frickin' *hassle* and borrowers and agents are yelling and pissed. But I was *always* honest about what was happening even if it wasn't good news. They were furious at the end and signed the docs and didn't speak to me. They called me six months later to refinance. They acknowledged how painful the process was, but they trusted me. That is *huge*."

Confucius said, "When anger rises, think of the consequences." Charles Dickens said, "It is a melancholy truth that even great men have their poor relations."

The customers didn't hire us to get emotional or to be reacting to this or to that; they hired us to do a job. They are counting on us. They didn't hire us to duck and run when things get tough. There is honor in doing the job, particularly so in the face of a strained relationship.

Early in my career I had a problem transaction. I had a coach at the time, so I called him. He owned a small brokerage firm, roughly twenty agents. "Jim, welcome to real estate. At any one time, I am dealing with at least five to ten upside-down customers; a couple of lawsuits; and three or four deals that are about to go bad," he says. I really liked and respected this guy. "Jim, what were you hired to do?"

"Well, I was hired to help them sell their home—yeah, that's what I was hired to do."

"Okay, so that is what you need to focus on, no more, no less, to do your job."

"Wait a minute, that's it? I mean this is a mess, Mr. Coach. This is happening, that is happening, this person said this, that person did that. Wait, wait, wait; you don't understand what is happening here," says Jim.

"Jim, do your job, I gotta go." That was it.

Now, just to take it one step further (and this is rare) so that you know you are not alone—are there going to be times when your customer is upside down to the extent that he or she is preventing you from doing your job? It's rare, but it can happen and does happen every once in a while. I suggest you take those to your manager for discussion. I had a deal one time that was driving me up the wall. I do my best to not let this happen, but this guy got under my skin. In my opinion, he did something unethical, and I was not about to back down, and he wasn't either. Like I said several times, I *always* had good managers. My manager said, "Jim, I got this, I want you to completely put it out of your mind." Those are the times that you know you have a good manager. And sure enough, he completely took care of it.

"The customer is always right." Are you sure about that?

How many times has the customer been through this process? Maybe once or twice or four times. How many times have we been through the process? More than that. The customer hired us to navigate through a challenging mountain pass. Remember, a real estate transaction will have a lasting effect on the customer's balance sheet and income statement; this is not short-term business we are dealing with. The customer is making medium to long-range financial commitments. It's our job to lead the way and not be distracted by "the noise."

I have this picture that hangs in my office; I've had for about fifteen years. It's a picture of a lead wolf in a blizzard with two wolves trailing. The two wolves are looking very unsure of where to go or what to do, but they are following the lead wolf nonetheless; the single lead wolf is calm, cool, and steely eyed in the face of chaos and destruction. The picture is called *The Power of a Leader.* I glance at it literally every day.

There is honor in completing the job.

Go get 'em!

95
Can Do Attitude

Work out your own salvation. Do not depend on others.

BUDDHA

THERE IS A LOT TO be said about simply saying, *I can do it, I can do it, I can do it.* It can possibly feel goofy at times, but it works; I've been doing that my whole life. Sometimes, however, it's helpful to have empirical (actual) experiences to reinforce that blind faith. I wrote a paper as a freshman in college about empirical philosophy.

Empirical philosophy. This means establishing an opinion based on actual experiences or actual observations. I'm using the word *philosophy* in conjunction with the word *empirical*, because we all have a filter and interpret experiences and observations differently. An opposing philosophy to empirical philosophy is establishing an opinion based on theory or logic. The theory or logic may not have anything to do with actual reality or actual experiences or actual observations. It's just a theory; sometimes it's a theory based on some fairly credible logic—but it's still a theory nonetheless.

I can do it—I can do it—I can do it. Well, what if you have never done it? What if you have been selling property for ten years and are dealing with a brand new situation? What if you are new to the business and have never closed a loan or have never brokered a piece of real estate?

No one knows it *all* in real estate. We are all constantly learning. So if you are new, you are learning; if you have been doing deals since the beginning of mankind, you are learning. If you are not, you are dying or dead, so we are all learning. Therefore, if you are new or experienced, either way, consider this: 1) Use blind faith (not based on evidence) by saying *I can do it* a thousand times a day, and 2) Use the building blocks of empirical philosophy. Combine number one and number two to produce a rock-solid ***can-do attitude***.

The building blocks. Let's assume you have never closed a loan. That's okay, by the way; we all start somewhere. There are building blocks to closing a loan. Meet some of the wholesale reps; learn what *par* means; study a good faith estimate; learn how to use the financial calculator; learn how to find a client; learn the process within the office. And more.

You start day number one in the business by saying "I can do it, I can do it, I can do it" (blind faith). Day two, you meet a wholesale rep. Day three, you meet four more wholesale reps. Day four, you meet two more wholesale reps. Okay, I understand what a wholesale rep is now. I've met them, I know where they work, I know how to contact them, and I roughly know the service that they will provide for me. Instead of just telling myself I can do it, I can actually do a piece of it now (empirical philosophy). It's a small piece, but it's a piece nonetheless. I just layered some empirical philosophy over my blind faith. No, I haven't closed a loan yet. But I did a piece of it. My confidence is growing. Do that same thing step by step until you close a deal.

When we layer real achievement (actual experiences or empirical philosophy) on top of blind faith (saying "I can do it"), we become *strong as an ox!* That's why people that have never actually done it in any industry really don't fully "get it." They have never had those actual experiences and are therefore only operating with 50 percent of what is needed to develop a strong can-do attitude.

I'll give you a sports analogy; let's assume I am trying to help a four-teen-year-old learn how to play offensive line in football. As a coach, you see potential. You encourage your players to believe in themselves. In some form, you ask them to say to themselves, "I can do it, I can do it." Some will, but most will not just because they are young. You see the end result in your mind as clear as clear gets; this youngster that fires off the ball with perfect technique, speed, and toughness, but he is not doing that at the moment. At the moment, he doesn't even know how to put his helmet on straight. So, we start with that. Then, we go to stance. Then we move on to the *get-off.* Then we work on keeping our eyes up. Then we move to a *pulling technique.* "Wow, coach, I know how to put my helmet on now." Great. "Wow, coach, I know how to get into my stance and get out of my stance." Great. "Wow, coach, I see what you mean about keeping my eyes up." Great.

These are the empirical building blocks to producing a can-do attitude. It's a two-part recipe that includes blind faith and empirical philosophy.

Go get 'em!

96

Coaching

——◆——

To think well and to consent to obey someone
giving good advice are the same thing.

HERODOTUS

ABOUT A YEAR INTO MY active career as a real estate agent, I started hearing about these "coaching" companies. I asked my granddad about it. He said, "Oh, yes, we would caravan to conferences, stay in a nice hotel, eat well, drink, goof off, play golf, and have a good time. I never much actually attended the sessions, but it was a great vacation." I suspect my granddad was there for the party.

As the real estate industry matured, so did the coaching industry that served the real estate industry.

What is coaching? You can think of coaching as education, business consulting, or a combination of the two. The customer is the real estate agent or lender, and the service provider is the coaching company. The customer can also be management; those are more isolated instances, however, so we'll keep it simple and just say that the customer is the real estate agent or lender.

The term *coach*, naturally, comes from athletics; the term has migrated, however, into business over the years. The traditional definition of the word *coach* is "a person who teaches or trains." Additionally, over time, the coaching companies have overlapped business training with personal advice. Personal and business are naturally related, particularly so in real estate, so the overlap made sense.

Here is a list of possible areas the coaching companies cover: personal finances, business finances, marketing, operations, and philosophies. They deliver these services in a group setting or on a one-on-one basis. In summary, the coaching companies teach and train on both a personal and business level; hence, the word *coach*.

Where they fit. In this business of real estate, we find deals, we do deals, we manage some money, and we work to keep our head straight; marketing, operations, finance, and attitude. Coaching fits nicely within attitude. The coaching industry works hard to help us producers keep our heads straight. They overlap into the other three categories, of course; but attitude holds it all together. Therefore, coaching should be considered when you think about attitude.

Where to find them. There are several capable coaching companies in the United States and beyond; it's not my intention to promote a specific company. Do a Google search on "real estate coaching" or "real estate coaching companies" and you'll find them. You'll find companies that are small, medium, and large (and individuals). You'll find some that offer yellow ice cream, some that offer purple, and some that offer the Farrell's bananarama split special. Do your homework, understand the offerings, and then decide what is best for you.

How much do they charge. Many services provided by this industry are free. You can attend a conference for a fee, or you can hire a "personal coach." Personal coaching can run from $100 to $2,000 monthly, depending on the company and level of service.

Time to get away. The coaching industry offers one-day to approximately seven-day business conferences. I have attended many. This is a great time to brainstorm with colleagues, plan, dream, and scheme, and do all this without the demands of day-to-day life. You just pay your fee and go. You don't have to be involved in personal coaching to attend these events. Frankly, I would attend only about 75 percent of the sessions and be planning like crazy (in my room) the other times. I found myself going to a session, becoming energized by an idea, and then wanting to plan while it's fresh in my mind.

Take away from a conference. There is so much information presented at these events that it can be paralyzing at times. I learned early on, for me, that I wanted to walk away with one idea that I could use. By this time, I had organized (in my head) the categories of real estate into marketing, operations, finance, and attitude. So I really didn't care which category the idea fell within, I just wanted one. And frankly, when I found my one idea, I left. Sometimes it took me four days; sometimes I found it within the first day. Right after I found it, however, I was on my way back home. Some of my colleagues would stay for days on end, and that's what they needed, for themselves. Either way is fine. You are running your own small business, so you decide how long you want to stay.

Biggest benefit. One of the biggest benefits of the conferences is the exposure to other people that are working hard to achieve. As it relates to business conferences, it can be worth the price of admission just for this one fact alone. You may meet someone from two thousand miles away that is having the same challenge as you, and he or she may explain a solution in a way that "clicks." It's good talking with people outside your geographical area that are trying to achieve at high levels.

Be careful. There is a chapter in this book called "It's All on You." The chapter talks about the fact that you are 100 percent responsible for everything in this business. By recognizing that and accepting that as fact, *you build mental muscle*, long-lasting muscle that could sustain you for the rest of your life. If you decide to hire a coach, *do not become dependent on the coach.*

Think of the coaching industry similar to the way you think about your manager. The manager will support you, encourage you, mentor you, cheerlead for you, but it's all on you to get it done. The same applies with the coaching company. Don't allow yourself to become weak and reliant on the coach; he or she is there to help, to advise, to encourage, to motivate, to inspire, and, in some cases, to hold accountable. But he or she is not there to actually be doing it. Maintain your muscular independence. Don't lean too hard.

Personally. "Jim, have you ever hired a coaching company?" Yes, I have, several times over the years, and multiple companies.

Does everyone have a coach? No. In my most recent office of about one hundred real estate agents, I am guessing that only two or three had actively hired a coach on a monthly basis. People can produce at high levels with a coach or without a coach. I have colleagues that I dearly respect that have never been to a conference and some that wouldn't miss a conference. That is the beauty of this industry. Be unique to you. Do it the way that you want to do it.

You are a small-business owner. The coach could play a role within your business. But you are still the CEO of your small business. You decide: 1) if you want or need a coach; and 2) what role you want the coach to play. You are in control of your business. That is a blinding flash of the obvious; just keep it mind.

Reinforcing a message. The conferences and other services provided by the coaching industry reinforce messaging from management.

Sometimes, if we hear something from a third party, we get it. We may have heard that same message one hundred times from Susan (the manager), but the second we hear it from Kim (the coach), it sinks in.

On the other hand, by attending some of these conferences, you can also evaluate what your manager is saying as opposed to what the coaching industry is saying. There is nothing wrong with hearing differing opinions: show-up equipped with your critical-thinking cap and take it all in.

Don't be intimidated. When attending a conference, don't allow yourself to be intimidated. You are there for just a window of time. There is an element of "performance" to it, so you are observing things within a controlled environment. Don't allow yourself to be mesmerized by "the stage of it all." You are there for business. You are there to learn. You are there to get one to two ideas that may help to move your life and/or your business forward. That's it. Then, get in your car or on the plane, and go home.

Drunk on the Kool-Aid. I went to a conference one time and allowed myself to get all fired up. I came home and told my wife that our cars were crummy (cars that had no debt). I asked my wife to accompany me to the car dealership, where I proceeded to purchase no less than a $100,000 car. Ridiculous. I was intoxicated on the Kool-Aid from the conference. As I sobered up over the next month, this sinking feeling of *Oh sh&?*t* fell over my body like an anchor. Now I'm dealing with a giant payment for five years. My fault. Be discerning and take small sips of the Kool-Aid.

A global perspective. As producers, we are on the front lines; management is advising from the press box. The coaching industry, however, is looking at the industry from a plane thirty thousand feet in the air. They study the industry as an industry. Their perspective is different because they might be talking with a group in Chicago one day, Seattle the next, and Canada the day after that. Therefore, you can learn things that you may not learn in your home town.

Summary. In a supersensational, simplistic explanation of the real estate business, the business consists of management, producers, and vendors. You can think of the coaching industry as a vendor industry, catering specifically to producers but consulting from time to time with management. The coaching companies play a very important and valuable role within the real estate industry.

Go get 'em!

97

Focus on the Revenue Line

Think for yourself and let others enjoy
the privilege to do so too.
VOLTAIRE

THE REVENUE WE GENERATE IN real estate is largely commission money. We get paid when we close a deal. To run a healthy small business, we need to be focusing some time on marketing, operations, finance, and attitude. I am asking you to consider focusing a disproportionate amount of time on the revenue line.

Why?

Fixed expenses. As producers, our fixed expenses are manageable. Fixed expenses are those expenses that you pay on a monthly basis whether you close a deal or not. Therefore, there is no need to spend too much time focusing on expenses; focus on the revenue line of your profit-and-loss statement and your expenses will take care of themselves.

Giving back. Nearly every successful person I know volunteers, donates money within their community, or both. However, it takes time and money to do that. Human nature is to work like crazy to fix a revenue problem if there is one. Therefore, if you are working to fix your revenue problem, it's unlikely you'll have the time or money to help someone in need. *Focus on your revenue line and you'll have the time and money to help someone in your community.*

Vendors and staff. Our vendors and staff largely rely on us to produce work. This is our team. We need our team to get things done. The team has to be working and earning a living; they need deal flow to support their families. Focus on the revenue line and keep your team employed.

Customer. If you have one customer and are stressed out of your mind because you have no other business, do you think the customer will feel your stress? Do you really think you'll be able to provide a great service if you're worried about money all the time? If you have sufficient deal flow, your business will be hitting on all cylinders; customer service is at a level ten when your business is running smoothly. Focus on the revenue line and your customer will be the benefactor.

Relaxing with family. It's tough to spend quality time with the family when you have no idea how you are going to buy groceries next month. When you have adequate deal flow, there is a natural order to life, and you can relax with the family knowing that your income is solid. Focus on the revenue line and be able to relax with family and friends.

Everything else. By keeping an eye on the revenue line, the rest of your business is likely to fall into place, and your personal life will have the fuel it needs to flourish.

You've probably heard someone say, "Primarily focus on the customer." That would be fine if our job was isolated to the single task of VP of operations. We are running a small business. Never forget or underestimate what that means. We have responsibilities in leadership, marketing, operations, finance, and attitude, and, of course, we are the lead sales representative as well. Six hats. The leader is ultimately responsible for the overall performance and health of the small business. As lender or real estate agent, that's you.

Keep your eyes firmly planted on the revenue line. It's good for your business, your customer, your family, and the world at large.

Go get 'em!

98

Goals

———◆———

When it is obvious that the goals cannot be reached,
don't adjust the goals, adjust the action steps.
CONFUCIUS

I CONSIDERED PLACING THIS CHAPTER on goals within the section called "Getting Started." I decided to put it in "Attitude" because goals affect attitude and attitude affects goals.

What I know about goal setting I largely learned from my dad, Dr. Bob. My friends in high school called my dad Dr. Bob, so that's how the name surfaced. Again, Dr. Bob was superintendent of schools in several school districts in California and Maryland. There were days when I came home from school to find my dad and his staff gathered in the game room conducting complex goal-setting sessions. He traveled around the United States at various times in his career, teaching goal setting. I would be hiding in the back of room at a public board meeting watching my dad and the board discuss goals.

When I was in high school, my dad loved working out with my friends and me. He pushed us. We would walk in the gym, start goofing off, and Dr. Bob would want to know the plan for the day. What are we doing, how many are we doing, how long are we doing it for;

what's the plan and what's the goal? He didn't care what the plan was, he just wanted one.

My mom was a manager as well in the public school system and was involved with goal setting. I played sports as a youngster all the way through college; goal setting becomes part of who you are as an athlete. It was all around me all the time.

When I started having kids of my own, I did what I knew how to do: teach them to think about a goal and have a plan. Starting when they were very young, I would ask the girls, what's your goal? One of them would say, "Daddy, I want to play with Sarah today." Great, good plan. "Daddy, I want to eat ice cream for lunch." Okay, at least you have a plan. One of the girls would say, "Daddy, I want to score a goal this weekend in my soccer game." Great, good plan. As they got older, "I want to earn an outstanding score in math." Great, good plan. Their plan was their plan. I had very little opinion on the plan (well, sometimes I did), I just wanted them to get in the habit of planning and having a goal.

Have one or two. Let's keep it simple for now. How about simply *have a goal.* And then, once you have one, *write it down.* If you do that, you'll be light-years ahead of most people in the world.

Why? Why do you want that goal? I want to bench-press two hundred pounds fifteen times when I turn fifty. "Why do you want that, Jim?" I want to do that because it will make me feel young, strong, and vibrant. I want to finish this book. "Why do you want that, Jim?" Several reasons: 1) I want the sense of accomplishment; 2) I want to extend the knowledge I have gained over the years to help others to be successful; and 3) I want to speak to future generations of my family within a written context. That's my why. What is your why behind your goals? Your why should make sense to you. Maybe it will not make sense to anyone else, but if makes sense to you, then good for you.

"I am one of the people who love the *why* of things"—*Catherine the Great*.

Few is better. Dr. Bob ran districts of upward of four thousand employees at times. The board would decide on some goals. It was the superintendent's job to execute. So the goal may have been to improve average test scores by 10 percent. That was a districtwide goal from the board, very clear and very singular. Now, there were about fifty to one hundred directives that would stem from that single goal. Remember, every goal gives birth to multiple directives. So you might have ten things you have to work on to achieve that one single goal. If you have five goals as a real estate agent or lender, then there might be fifty things that you need to work on. Way too many; completely unrealistic. Few is better.

Holistic approach. Dr. Bob would encourage the staff to have a professional goal and a personal goal. He was drafted by the San Francisco 49ers in 1960 and, based on that athletic background, felt like it was important for people to have a physical goal as well. So he championed three areas: professional, personal, and physical. Many times, progress in one area translates into progress in another area. So three. You can add other areas of your life if you prefer. For me, I limit my goals to those three areas.

Recommit. We can be overmilitant and unrealistic on this topic of recommitting to the goal. I know folks that say: "I look at my goals three times per day, every day without fail." Okay. Whatever that frequency may be for you, make sure you look at your goals often. My dad would review the goals once per month. I reviewed my goals weekly. I did it every Sunday as I was preparing for the upcoming week. I wanted to ensure there was a link between my activities for that week and my goals.

Monitor. Somehow you have to hold yourself accountable. My dad had the benefit of a large organizational structure, so each manager could help his or her subordinates achieve their goals by holding them accountable. There are many ways to accomplish this as a lender or real estate agent. You could ask your manager to hold you accountable, you could hire a coach, you could ask a mentor colleague to do it, or some other option. Find a way nonetheless.

Measure it. There are goals that are difficult to measure. Here is an easy one: "I want to close ten deals this year." That's easy. Here is a hard one: "I want to improve my relationship with my manager." That is a difficult goal to measure. Try nonetheless. For instance, you could say, "I want to have lunch with my manager once per month." You can measure that. And that will likely translate into an improved relationship with your manager.

Idea pad. When you get clear on a goal, your brain will jump with ideas about how to execute it. Again, I took this idea from my dad. Whether my dad was at home or at work, there was always a yellow *idea pad* nearby. To this day, he could likely locate one of his idea pads from thirty years ago. Some ideas are brilliant, but they are also fleeting at times. Write them down.

Lending. When I started in lending, I wanted to be the top-producing lender in my office by the end of my first year. Why? Because I didn't want to work in corporate America, and I wanted the independence of supporting my family on my own without a boss.

Real estate. It wasn't a financial goal at this point. I wanted to get into the top five grouping in the office by the end of the year. Why?

Because I wanted to prove to myself that I could do it; that I could not only produce big in lending, but I could also do it as a real estate agent as well.

Simple, simple, simple. I don't believe in making goal setting mysterious or complicated. 1) Make a goal. 2) Make sure the "why" makes sense to you. 3) Write it down. 4) Look at it as often as possible. 5) Make sure it can be measured. And 6) Find someone to help you with accountability.

Go get 'em!

99

Be You

Be yourself—everyone else is already taken.

OSCAR WILDE

WHEN I WRITE, I WRITE on a schedule. So I had this topic of "Be You" on my schedule for about three weeks. It took every bit of discipline in my bones to not jump directly to this one and go after it. I'm telling you, I am so fired up about this topic of being you!

Who are you? I'm me. Okay, who is me? Me is me. There is only one me. I'll prove it: here is the formula on my DNA: *j (h&g20k*%jks*%!.: hdju&5#klcnu&%khg$048932,&4jch*>*. See, no one else has that formula but me.

There are people in the real estate business that are making millions of dollars yearly. It's true; so what? They are who they are. They did it the way they did it. They have been doing it forever. Sometimes it's easy to become mesmerized, overimpressed, in awe of, enthralled by, or razzle-dazzled by someone else. *Forget about it. Be you!* That is the only way you will make it in this business of real estate and meet your full potential.

The great Horace says, "You may drive out nature with a pitchfork, yet she'll be constantly running back."

If you are twenty-three years old, fresh out of college, and starting in this business as a lender, then be exactly who you are. You are a twenty-three-year-old that is excited, nervous, inexperienced, and eager to make some money. Be exactly that person. Trust me—there will be plenty of people that will want to do business with you exactly the way you are if you are willing to work hard.

If you are new to real estate, fifty-six years old, and haven't been in the workforce for ten years, then for goodness's sakes, be that person. Be that person that is new, maybe a little nervous, but has a truck load of life experiences. There will be plenty of people that will be looking for someone just like you—exactly like you.

If you are reserved, pleasant, successful, have lots of experience, and have been in the business for thirty-three years, then own that person and be that person.

I am telling you right here and right now: be exactly who you are. And if anyone tries to change you—run. We are largely marketing ourselves (personally) in this business of real estate. Change even one atom within your DNA, and you will dilute who you are and therefore will damage your business. I'm not saying be a renegade, although if that's who you are, then fine. I'm saying be true to yourself—and own *you.*

Do I need to be professional? Yes. Do I need to provide a good service? Yes. Do I need to work daily on marketing, operations, finance, and attitude? Yes. Do I need to be true to myself as I do all these things? Yes, yes, yes.

Can we be credible if we are trying to be anyone but ourselves? No way. In fact, the only way you can be 100 percent credible is to be 100 percent you. A giant portion of communication is nonverbal. Don't you think a customer will feel it and pick up on those nonverbal cues if you are trying to be anyone but you? You know the answer. There is a direct link between being you and being credible.

It's not my style to say that God (or whatever you believe in) made you exactly the way you are and that people you met along the way and your environment continued to shape what your Maker produced. It's definitely not my style to say that. Did I say that? What I will say is that your DNA is 100 percent you—and only you.

Show the world who you are, and stay true to you.

Go get 'em!

100

Attitude Makes It All Work

———◆———

I will not be triumphed over.

CLEOPATRA

W<small>E STARTED THIS BOOK BY</small> talking about the four cornerstones of the real estate business; marketing, operations, finance, and attitude. Attitude is the glue that holds the other three pieces together.

Attitude is defined as "how we think or feel about someone or something."

Marketing. Negative attitude: "I am not comfortable asking for referrals. I am not very strategic. I don't know what to do to find business. My spouse is not helpful finding me deals. I can't manage my database. Nobody will send me deals. I always get crushed by my competition. I'm not very creative." *Now reverse it.* "I can always find new business. I ask for referrals in my own way, but I ask nonetheless. I am thoughtful and strategic in all my marketing efforts. I reach out for help when I need it. I maintain my database daily. There are plenty of people that will support me. I compete with integrity."

All those statements above, positive and negative, may or may not have a basis in fact; but they all certainly speak to attitude. Think of yourself as the CEO of your own small business. Marketing has to work for your business to work.

Operations. Negative attitude: "Nobody in my office helps me. My manager doesn't support me. The process is confusing and complicated. My colleagues are mean to me. My customers are so demanding; I really don't think they like me. My assistants never do what I tell them to do. The paperwork is ridiculous. Selecting a price is brain damage. Working through the inspections is a nightmare. People always beat me up on the interest rate." *Now reverse it.* "I am team player in the office. I like my colleagues. My manager is the best. My assistant is world class. The process is easy, step one, step two, and step three. I have great clients. My clients like working with me. I provide a good service and I make it fun. I take responsibility for everything."

Finance. Negative attitude: "I am not a numbers person. I am always behind on my taxes. I never have any money. I don't know how to use the lousy financial calculator. I gloss over the numbers because I really don't have a clue. The customer always gets mad at me when we talk about money. I don't even know what keeping the books means, let alone how to do it. I'm terrible at managing money. Just call me Mr. Broke." *Now reverse it.* "My bookkeeper is the best. We review all financials monthly. My tax team is solid. My financial calculator skills are improving. Excel is a breeze. Talking with the customer about money is easy. I live within my means. I always have money in the bank. I am a prudent spender. I use my money wisely. I run my business like a business."

Attitude will hold it all together. Go get 'em.

To Your Success,

James R. Carter

Author

JAMES R. CARTER WAS BORN and raised in California. He received a football scholarship to San Jose State University where he made Honorable Mention All-American his senior year. After college, he worked at a computer company while earning his MBA. In 1993, he started his career in real estate as a mortgage broker, eventually transitioning to real estate brokerage in 2000.

When he started as a real estate agent, he placed himself in one of the most competitive offices in Silicon Valley, where the extraordinarily large volume of commission revenue he produced led management to ask him to teach a class called "How to Make One Million Dollars Your First Year in Real Estate." His notes from that class were the jumping-off spot for this book.

He and his wife, Jane, live in Northern California and together they have three adult daughters.

———

A Guide to Making It in Real Estate is available on Kindle, Amazon, Createspace, iTunes, Audible and more. The author narrated the audio version of this book.

See *jamesraycarter.com* for more information.